Caviar with Champagne

Leisure, Consumption and Culture

General Editor: Rudy Koshar, *University of Wisconsin at Madison*

Leisure regimes in Europe (and North America) in the last two centuries have brought far-reaching changes in consumption patterns and consumer cultures. The past twenty years have seen the evolution of scholarship on consumption from a wide range of disciplines, but historical research on the subject is unevenly developed for late modern Europe, just as the historiography of leisure practices is limited to certain periods and places. This series encourages scholarship on how leisure and consumer culture evolved with respect to an array of identities. It relates leisure and consumption to the symbolic systems with which tourists, shoppers, fans, spectators, and hobbyists have created meaning, and to the structures of power that have shaped such consumer behaviour. It treats consumption in general and leisure practices in particular as complex processes involving knowledge, negotiation, and the active formation of individual and collective selves.

Caviar with Champagne

Common Luxury and the Ideals of the Good Life in Stalin's Russia

Jukka Gronow

BERG

Oxford • New York

First published in 2003 by

Berg

Editorial offices:

1st Floor, Angel Court, 81 St Clements Street, Oxford, OX4 1AW, UK

838 Broadway, Third Floor, New York, NY 10003-4812, USA

Berg is the imprint of Oxford International Publishers Ltd.

Library of Congress Cataloging-in-Publication Data

Gronow, Jukka.

Caviar with champagne : common luxury and the ideals of the good life
in Stalin's Russia / Jukka Gronow. – 1st ed.

p. cm. – (Leisure, consumption, and culture)

ISBN 1-85973-633-5 (Cloth) – ISBN 1-85973-638-6 (Paper)

1. Soviet Union – Social life and customs–1917-1970. 2. Material
culture – Soviet Union. 3. Consumption (Economics) – Soviet Union. I.
Title. II. Series.

DK268.3.G76 2003

947.084'2—dc21

2003014920

British Library Cataloguing-in-Publication Data

A catalogue record for this book is available from the British Library.

ISBN 1 85973 633 5 (Cloth)

1 85973 638 6 (Paper)

Typeset by JS Typesetting Ltd, Wellingborough, Northamptonshire

Printed in the United Kingdom by Biddles Ltd, Guildford and King's Lynn

www.bergpublishers.com

Contents

List of Figures

Preface and Acknowledgements

Shortly after the collapse of the Soviet Union in the early 1990s I visited Kiev, the capital of the newly independent Ukraine. I dropped in at the small local food store at vulitsa Tshikhorina, which I used to frequent at the beginning of the 1970s when I lived in Kiev for a short period of time. The early 1990s were the worst time for the Ukrainian economy, which had not had any time to recover from the abrupt and almost total end of all trade between the Soviet Republics. The shop at Tshikhorina had not changed at all since my previous visit some twenty odd years earlier except that now its shelves were almost empty. There was no more Estonian canned fish, no canned fruit and vegetables from Moldovia or Bulgaria, no Moscow sausages or cheese. When I turned my head I noticed in one corner of the shop, however, to my great delight a high pile of boxes that looked familiar to me. These were cakes, standardised industrially-produced cakes sold all over the Soviet Union in great quantities during the Soviet times. These were my madeleine cakes. I started to reminisce. I remembered my first visits to the Soviet Union and my first glasses of Soviet champagne with caviar sandwiches. . . .

I visited the Soviet Union in the summer 1968 for the first time as a young student. Living in Finland, I was at that time probably better informed about everyday life in the Soviet Union of the Socialists Republics than most foreigners living in other parts of the world more distant from Russian centres. By the end of the 1960s it was not at all rare for Finns to visit Russia as tourists, and the first Russian tourists had started to visit Finland too. By then I had already heard many stories about the country and its people from firsthand witnesses, relatives included. The Finnish papers and TV news had also covered the main Soviet political, cultural and economic events and developments quite well. Due to the special relations between Finland and the Soviet Union, the Finnish journalists were often relatively careful and ideologically neutral in their reports about their big Eastern neighbour. At the time of my visit, I thought I was rather well informed about contemporary life in the Soviet Union. I thought I knew, more or less, what to expect there. Since my family from my father's side came from St. Petersburg I had from my earliest childhood also heard a lot of stories, often strongly coloured by nostalgia, about life in Old Russia. Despite all this my first visit, followed by numerous others later on, had some surprises in store for me which left many vivid and unforgettable impressions in my memory.

During my three-week-long stay in Moscow I visited all the important sites, from the Red Square and Lenin's mausoleum to Gorky Park and the Exhibition of the Achievements of National Economy, from Tretyakovsky Gallery to the Museum of Revolution. I took a boat trip on the Moscow river and trips to the dachas on the outskirts of the city. August 1968 was hot in Moscow and thunderstorms were regular at nights. The many wide streets and boulevards with amazingly few cars as well as the gorgeous halls of the Moscow Metro with all their thousands of people were certainly something I had never seen before. All this was, however, something I had, in a way, expected and anticipated. I can still remember the smells in the hot streets in particular. The city and its people smelled different, from exhausts of bad gasoline, sweet strong perfumes, cheap soaps and cleaning chemicals.

The long queues in front of many shops did not surprise me either. The shops had very few items on sale and even those that were on sale were often, compared to the standards I had got used to, of a very poor quality. The black market guys who wanted to buy jeans and stockings or exchange foreign currency in front of the hotels were already then an essential part of the ordinary Finnish tourist folklore.

There were, however, other things that really struck me as strange. Champagne was sold and drunk in great qualities not only in the finer tourist restaurants – a habit amazing enough to anyone coming from Finland – but also in ordinary food stores where it could be bought by the glass from early in the morning till late at night. Caviar sandwiches were on offer at almost every café in museums, theatres or concert halls. People ate three course lunches and dinners with all the proper drinks even in modest canteens and local restaurants. In many bigger food stores tens of different chocolate candies and huge piles of cakes were regularly on sale.

These and many similar examples bear ample evidence that it was not only the long queues in front of the shops and the almost chronic shortages of many everyday commodities which characterized the Soviet culture of consumption. This culture was also deeply permeated by the spirit of common or plebeian luxury.

This book grew out of that journey into my own past and the past of the country that once was. It would not have been possible without the help of one person, my good friend Sergey Zhuravlev, Doctor of History and a senior researcher at the Institute of Russian History at the Academy of Russia. Without his excellent knowledge of the Russian historical archives I could not possibly have found what I started to search for, all kinds of traces of evidence of the birth of Soviet luxury during Stalin's time in the 1930s. First, I simply wanted to find out who had invented Soviet champagne, why and when. But, as piles of evidence started to grow, the project expanded almost naturally. Thanks to the centralized Soviet system of administration everything was preserved in the archives, often down to the smallest, apparently trivial details. Soon I realized that what I had found was unique. Nobody had set their eyes on the pages of the numerous collections preserved in the Central archives since they had been carefully catalogued by the archivist sixty or seventy years earlier. While discussing my findings with my Russian friends on many occasions I soon became convinced that this was a story worth telling. They responded quite often with a surprised enthusiasm: yes, that is how it was but we have never thought about it in quite that way. . .

Sergey Zhuravlev did not only help me find my way through the archives. He has also taught me a lot about Soviet history, about the USSR's economic and social problems and developments as well as about the functioning of its system of administration and surveillance. He also introduced me to the work of many interesting modern Russian historians who, as I soon discovered, had conducted excellent research and published new exciting monographs and articles from which I could learn a lot.

Sergey Zhuravlev has read the manuscript and made many valuable suggestions of improvement to it. In addition to Sergey, Professor Natalie Lebina, University of Economy and Finance in St. Petersburg, Markku Lonkila, University of Helsinki, Sofia Tchouikina, The European University in St. Petersburg, and Professor Alan Warde, University of Manchester, have all read the manuscript at various stages and thoroughly commented it. In addition, Sofia Tchouikina helped me transliterate the Russian names and edited the text otherwise too. I'm grateful to them all for their invaluable help. As always, the author alone answers for the final result.

Ms. Kathleen May has read and commented on the manuscript as the senior commissioning editor at Berg Publishers. Her experienced editorial advice has been very welcome. She has also gone to a great deal of trouble, far exceeding what one is used to expecting from a book editor, rewriting my clumsy English into a more fluent and readable style. For this, I'm truly grateful to her.

I would like to thank the editor of the Leisure, Consumption and Culture Series, Rudy Koshar, for admitting my book into the series. He also read and presented many valuable comments on the manuscript.

Last but not least, I'd like to mention Professor Richard Stites, Georgetown University, Washington, D.C. His 'spirited' support at the various stages of my project has been extremely valuable. This encouragement has come from a person whose work in Russian and Soviet cultural history I have learned to appreciate highly and to regard as a model of such history writing which is both innovative, learned and entertaining.

This study started as a part of a larger project, Cultural Inertia and Social Change in Russia, financed by the Academy of Finland in 1995–97. My nomination to the position of a Senior Researcher at the Academy of Finland in 1997 made its successful completion possible. Both the Scandinavian Institute for Administrative Research (SIAR) and my present employer, Helsinki Collegium for Advanced Studies, have financially supported the publication of the book. I'm truly grateful to all these institutions for their generous support of my project.

Introduction: The Birth of the Soviet Consumer

The Look from Abroad: Everything Looks Grey

In the summer of 1936, a Soviet delegation made a much-publicized excursion to the heartland of capitalism, the United States. Anastas Mikoyan, the Minister of Food Industry, headed up the delegation, which also included government assistants and other prominent representatives of Soviet trade and industry. The openly recognized purpose of this visit was to draw on the experience of the most advanced capitalist country in the field of food production and distribution. For Mikoyan, it was his first trip abroad. On their way to the French port where the Atlantic liner would sail to America, the Soviet delegation had to change trains in Berlin. Mikoyan recalled an acutely embarrassing experience that occurred there in an article published years later:

> In Berlin our delegation had a strange experience. In the USSR at that time people dressed very simply. I, for instance, usually dressed myself in a sports shirt, riding breeches, boots and an army coat. Before our journey, a European style suit and shoes were tailored to me. My comrades also had suits made at an atelier in Moscow. When we first stepped down on the railway platform in Berlin we noticed that all the Germans stared at us. I wondered what that was all about. I turned and saw that we were all dressed alike, in similar hats, suits and shoes, all of the same colour and style. We managed to change our look first in the States. I bought myself another suit there and my comrades did the same.[1]

A perception of the Soviet people as indistinguishable lookalikes was common among foreign visitors to the Soviet Union in the 1930s. To a foreigner, Soviet people looked more or less alike because they tended to dress the same in modest clothes of a simple and dull style, usually of greyish or brownish colouring. In the eyes of a Westerner, these people were all similar parts of one homogeneous, grey mass. At about the same time that Mikoyan was discovering the wondrous range of consumer products in America, the famous French author André Gide visited the Soviet Union to attend the funeral of the celebrated Soviet author Maxim Gorky.

1

With well-known pro-communist inclinations, Gide was certainly a sympathetic observer of Soviet society. He made the following notes in his travelogue, published shortly after the trip:

> There is an extraordinary uniformity in people's dress; no doubt it would be equally apparent in their minds, if one could see them. This too is what enables everyone to be able to be and look cheerful. (People have for so long been without almost everything that they are contented with very little. When one's neighbour is no better off than oneself, one puts up with what one has got.) It is only after searching study that differences become visible. At first sight the individual is sunk in the mass and so little particularized that one feels as though in speaking of people here one ought to use a collective singular and say not, 'here are men' but 'here is some man'. (As one says, 'here is some fruit', and not 'here are fruits'.)[2]

Gide's commentary on the standards of Soviet-made consumer goods, which he saw in the shops and department stores of Moscow, and the taste of the people was equally depressing: 'The goods are equally repulsive. You might almost think that the stuffs, objects, etc., were deliberately made as unattractive as possible in order to put people off, so that they shall buy out of extreme necessity and never because they are tempted.'[3]

Ironically, Gide's 1936 visit coincided with a time of Soviet prosperity, at least according to Stalin. The official government line declared that the general scarcity of the post-Revolutionary period had been successfully overcome. Yet this was only a few years after millions of people had died of famine or been deported to distant places during the collectivization of agriculture. Bread rationing, although officially repealed the year before, was still in operation. Despite such hardships, Stalin declared in 1935 that life had become better and more cheerful. The Soviet Union claimed to be the most democratic country in the world. Workers of the socialist experiment enjoyed not only full political rights, but they were also guaranteed the full satisfaction of their material and cultural needs. The theme of abundance played a large part in propagating the new Soviet Constitution of 1936 and in the campaign for the first general elections of the Supreme Soviet in 1937 and 1938. Government officials consistently referred to the emergence and availability of the many new consumer goods as concrete evidence of promises kept. Were such promises just empty propagandistic slogans? Was there any real economic or political action to back them up? The answer to these questions is both yes and no.

As Gide himself also noticed, 'great efforts have been made – efforts towards the improvement of quality; and by looking carefully and devoting the necessary time to it, one can manage to discover here and there some recent articles which are quite pleasing and of some promise to the future.'[4] While Gide was touring the

Soviet Union, the government and the Party were in fact paying a great deal of attention to both the production and quality of consumer goods. The goal was to overfulfill targets. The improvement of quality, *za kachestvo*, was another key production slogan of the time. The twin ambitions to produce more and to improve quality took on a new shape in the middle of the decade. Plans and reports started talking about goals and targets in subtly different ways. The government became increasingly concerned with improving the variety of consumer goods, offering more and more different types of products. These were not merely empty words – real practical measures were implemented.

The extent to which these measures actually effected a change, or to what extent the general public witnessed such a change, is subject to debate. What is clear is that there was a genuine effort on the part of Soviet officials to revolutionize the consumer goods industry in the USSR so that it could rival Western standards. Success would validate the socialist state and demonstrate that the Soviet Union could compete on a world stage. Recent Russian historical scholarship argues that there was a high point of consumer comfort in the mid-1930s but that the situation rapidly deteriorated again at the end of the decade. In 1940, on the eve of USSR involvement in the Second World War, the country seemed to be on the verge of an economic crisis caused by both the increasing militarization of the economy and the years of poor harvest.[5]

In the early 1930s, during the final years of collectivization and the First Five-Year Plan, there was virtually nothing to buy in shops. But by the mid-1930s, consumers were beginning to see foodstuffs, clothes and household items available for sale. New shops were opening. Even if it involved hours of standing in line and purchasing restrictions, Soviet citizens were now able to buy goods such as shoes, suits, hats, kettles, cups, glassware, chocolate, cheese, sausages and even champagne. For the first time, state factories and industrial plants were manufacturing consumer goods and novelties, rather than just heavy industry.

The Soviet Union's new interest in consumer goods, like so many of Stalin's plans, has a patchy history. The USSR boast some impressive achievements, such as the *patéfon*, a hand-operated gramophone, but most goods were of a bad quality and very irregularly available. In one respect the economic policy of Stalin's Party was coherent and unchanging: it did not waste precious foreign currency on the import of food or consumer goods. Almost the only exceptions were raw materials which the domestic agriculture or industry could not possibly cultivate or produce. The production of consumer goods was always subordinate to the needs of heavy industry.

The tremendous leap required to establish a consumer goods manufacturing society cannot be understated. The whole infrastructure for such production had to be created from scratch. With the First Five-Year Plan, the Soviet Union had focused its efforts and resources on the creation of a centralized, state-controlled heavy metallurgical and chemical industry. While the New Economic Policy (NEP) of 1921–22 had allowed for private shops, restaurants and even some small factories, the small-scale private trade sector was essentially destroyed by the early 1930s. Enforced collectivization had destroyed private farming and hampered local agricultural markets. Although the total collectivization of farming and central provisioning of foodstuffs remained the Bolshevist ideal, necessity began to force the government to rethink its policies on local food distribution. With the exception of some very basic necessities, such as black rye bread, potatoes, cabbage, tea and vodka, the Soviet Union at this time was lacking the tools to generate consumer products. It would literally have to invent, or at least rediscover, every item of mass consumption.

The Consolidation of the Stalinist Regime in the USSR

The 1930s saw the final consolidation of Stalin's power in the Soviet Union. By the end of the decade, he had destroyed and annihilated all his major political adversaries and competitors inside the Party. Trotsky and Zinoviev, from the left, had been politically defeated by the end of 1927 (their deaths came later: for Zinoviev in 1936 when he was sentenced to death, and for Trotsky in 1940 when he was murdered in Mexico, after his 1929 expulsion from the USSR). Ten years later, opposition came from the Right, and Bukharin was its most prominent representative. Again, it was quashed, this time without an open contest. By this point, Stalin was sitting firmly in power surrounded by a small group of loyal followers who were entirely dependent on him. No one could seriously entertain the thought of challenging his position as Great Leader. Stalin's fiftieth birthday in 1929 marked the starting point of the cult of personality. From then on, public praise and admiration for Stalin knew no limits.

The end of the 1920s witnessed the beginning of three significant, parallel political campaigns that transformed the country entirely. These campaigns ended the period of the NEP, during which the Bolsheviks had made many concessions to market economy. The First Five-Year Plan started in 1928. Its goal was the industrialization of the country. The emphasis was on the heavy metallurgical industry, electrification, the building of huge hydropower plants and the development of the transport system. The building of the huge Magnetstroi metallurgical plant at the Urals, the completion of the Dneprostroi power plant and the opening of the Turksib railway and Belomorkanal, or the White Sea canal, were all much publicized and celebrated highpoints of the First Five-Year Plan. During the Plan there was a massive demographic shift as over 10 million peasants moved to towns in search of better jobs. The second campaign, enforced collectivization of agri-

4

culture, started in 1928. Millions of victims were deported, others were executed and still others died in the devastating famine that followed.

The Cultural Revolution was the third big campaign of the period. It was directed against former bourgeois specialists and experts in industry and education. Their presence and influence in the factories and educational institutions had previously been tolerated out of necessity, and some had actually been encouraged to stay or even to come back to the country from emigration. The Cultural Revolution put an end to their influence. The Shakhty show trial of 1928, which accused several 'bourgeois' engineers and specialists of sabotage, inaugurated the mass repressions of the former 'bourgeois intelligentsia.' This was the first wave of mass repressions under Stalin. To fill the vacuum left by the educated and skilled workers, a new generation of Soviet specialists of proletarian origin was rapidly schooled during the Cultural Revolution. Formal qualifications were often intentionally neglected.

Despite official proclamations of success, the country was exhausted by 1933. The next few years saw a partial reorientation in the politics of the USSR. Stalin and his Party never retreated from their main political goals: the construction of a state-owned and centrally-controlled economy and the destruction of all the petit bourgeois elements which they feared threatened their goals. However, what distinguished the mid-1930s from the previous period of Soviet history was that now the government used the carrot alongside the stick. For those willing to follow its lead and work hard, personal rewards beckoned. The government promised higher living standards and increased social esteem. The country, according to the government, was celebrating its abundance.

This optimistic mood culminated in the adoption of Stalin's new constitution in 1936, which returned the political rights to 'former people' who had been deprived of their rights after the Revolution. Stalin now declared that there were no more class antagonisms in the Soviet Union. Only three classes – workers, peasants and intelligentsia – existed, and they each had their own necessary and useful roles to play in a successful socialist society. Many of the Soviet Union's major social institutions, industrial and trade organizations and government structures that survived until the end of the USSR were built in the mid-1930s.

In 1937 the Great Repression began. Its millions of victims included both common people and the political elite. The rate of casualties was greatest among the Bolsheviks themselves: of the 1,966 delegates at the seventeenth Party Congress held in 1934, only 858 survived the year 1937. Of the 139 members or candidate members of the Central Committee of the Communist Party, ninety-eight were shot in the same year.[6] This was the same year that witnessed the birth of Soviet champagne.

The Two Stages in the Development of Consumer Goods in the 1930s

In the Soviet Union there was not the drive to invent new products and promote them to consumers as found in capitalist societies. Under socialism, unlike under capitalism, customers were not meant to be manipulated for the sake of profit – to buy all kinds of products they did not really want or need. Nevertheless, in the 1930s the quest for new consumer goods became a preoccupation for the authorities, producers and traders. They were convinced that there was, among the Soviet population, an increasing demand for such things and that it was their urgent task to respond to such a demand. By the early 1930s, the government and the Party no longer felt that their role was simply to satisfy the basic needs of the population, to keep people nourished, warm and clothed. As they saw it, they had succeeded at the basic level, and it was time to raise the standard of living both quantitatively and qualitatively. They wanted to develop the Soviet taste, establish more cultivated manners and enjoy refined goods. Individual taste was also encouraged.

The development of the new material culture took place roughly in two stages closely following one another. The years 1933–35 are preserved in people's memories as the best years before the outbreak of the war. Food rationing was officially abandoned in 1935. The Soviet Union started, for the first time, to produce sausages, canned fish, canned vegetables, cheese, chocolate and other goods industrially and on a mass scale. The history of the rebirth of the Soviet chocolate industry is particularly revealing: within a couple of years its product variety jumped from just a dozen to several hundred. The main slogan for this period was 'for higher quality.' The progress of a factory and the merits of its director were measured by the amount of novelties it could turn out each year.

The second leap in the consumer goods industry was more complicated. In 1936–37 the country was again on the verge of an economic crisis. Many regions were suffering from a serious shortage of food. Yet, at the same time, the Soviet government and the Party started to worry about mass production of champagne. According to the new plan, by 1942 the country was to produce 20 million bottles of champagne per year compared with only a few hundreds of thousands in 1937. Stalin's aim to produce champagne proved to be long-lasting. It is one of the few consumer goods still available in every Russian kiosk and still proudly bearing the title Sovetskoe on its label. Champagne was, however, not the only luxury product 'invented' then. Vintage wines and cognacs were put into production also. The food industry, and in particular confectioneries, increased the production of many seasonal, celebratory products of its own.

Food products were not the only goods to command the special attention of the ministers and the Central Committee of the Party. *Patéfons* (portable hand-operated gramophones) and gramophone records, bicycles, watches, cameras, bracelets, necktie pins, and other products, were now also produced in their hundreds of thousands by Soviet factories. These were to be part of the personal belongings of any cultured Soviet citizen. Perfumes and other items of personal hygiene became extremely important too. Furthermore, now a Soviet citizen could, at least in principle, have a new suit or dress made to order by one of the newly opened fashion ateliers (*Atelier mod*). This was also the time when the more fashionable Gastronom and Bakaleia food stores and the 'exemplary' department stores in the bigger cities opened.

The changes made to the structure and the names of the Soviet ministries or People's Comissariats,[7] as they were called, directly reflected changes in general politics. It was characteristic that during the first half of the 1930s, the Soviet Union did not have a Ministry of Domestic Trade. With no or very limited amounts of retail trade, the Ministry was obviously thought obsolete. The old Ministry of Foreign and Domestic Trade, founded in 1925, had by 1930 been divided into two separate administrative units, the Ministry of Foreign Trade and the Ministry of People's Supply. The Ministry of People's Supply was in turn liquidated in 1934, as if precluding the beginning of the end of food rationing. Two new ministries emerged instead: the Ministry of Domestic Trade (since 1938 simply Ministry of Trade) headed by I.J. Veitser until his repression in 1937 and the Ministry of Food Industry with Anastas Mikoyan at its head until 1938 when he became the Minister of Foreign Trade. Due to an increasing differentiation of administrative functions, the units of central administration (so-called Glavki) that worked under the ministries and were responsible for the activities of different fields of industry or trade increased rapidly at the end of the decade. So, for example, separate Glavkis were responsible for all the state-owned restaurants and canteens, for all departments stores, for the wine and liquor industry and for the perfume and soap industry. These units of administration usually had a total monopoly in their respective fields of operation. In some fields there were alternatives in the form of cooperative shops, canteens or local small-scale industry. Towards the end of the 1930s cooperatives were, however, generally confined to the countryside or in relatively unimportant local fields of production.

The Object of the Present Study

This study follows in detail the development, introduction and establishment of several strategic consumer goods. The Soviet Union of the 1930s was a unique historical case: almost all its material culture was invented and created from nothing. Every decision to start the production of any single item was made at the highest levels of administration. The Minister of Food Industry, Anastas Mikoyan, personally signed, among others, recipes for the production of sausages and perfume. The rapidly increasing assortment of consumer goods was thus created in a highly conscious and reflective manner. Ministers, their deputies, assistants and factory directors took an active part in the planning of even the smallest details of production and distribution. Officials vigorously debated new product ideas and compared the merits of different varieties. The problems of packaging, paper wrapping or, say, new tops to perfume bottles, were all decided at the highest level. This situation offers a unique chance to follow from the very beginning the emergence of a particular culture of consumption.

The story is full of tragic and tragicomic features. It is, however, interesting from a more theoretical viewpoint too. The historical experience accumulated in the Soviet Union offers an interesting opportunity to reflect upon alternative ways of organizing and developing modern mass consumption. In the Soviet Union almost everything was consciously created and taken into production. The authorities had to present the reasons why something was being produced: for whom, what and why did the Soviet food and 'light' industries produce and the Soviet trade organizations sell or distribute? Once the shortage of very basic foodstuffs, such as potatoes, bread, cabbage, and vodka had been overcome, or at least thought to be overcome, bare necessity was not enough to legitimate the choices made.

In the beginning, there was no overall plan. The authorities probed their way forward by trial and error. The planned economy was in fact quite chaotic, subject to the whims of its leaders and vulnerable to popular reactions. For example, the idea of suddenly producing millions and millions of bottles of champagne – a plan that would demand huge investments and new infrastructure, from the opening of new training schools to the printing of new labels – came from Stalin himself. Likewise, Mikoyan brought back from America five huge production units for hamburgers because he personally felt they were a good idea. Who knows whether, if the war had not broken out, we might have witnessed the emergence of a MacMikoyan chain of hamburgers instead of McDonalds?

Such decisions reflect more than just the personal whims of Soviet leaders. They might have chosen different items to focus on, but the symbolic meaning of these goods and the message that they carried to the Soviet people were much more important than the actual products themselves. The Party optimistically promised every Soviet citizen the best that both the old and the new world had to offer, and at a moderate price.

The New Cultural Policy and Stalin's own Big Deal

Following the beginning of the Second Five-Year Plan in 1933 both more individual and more luxurious lifestyles were encouraged. The country was now supposed to be living in a state of overall abundance and wealth. A period of general well-being had arrived, according to Soviet leaders. Stalin's slogan, 'life has become more joyous, comrades' was much repeated. The Soviet citizen was meant to be and look happy, to dress better and to enjoy life – especially in the sphere of material culture.[8]

Historians of the Soviet Union have documented the major break that took place in the cultural politics of the country in the 1930s. The end of the 1920s and the beginning of the 1930s were dominated by the conception of proletarian culture and the ideal of the ascetic self-sacrificing worker. In the mid-1930s, the former ideals of revolutionary asceticism and social egalitarianism gave way to the emergence of a new hierarchy and a new system of social order, one that allowed for a more hedonistic and individualistic way of life. This 'value transformation' was interpreted by many communists, Leon Trotsky among them, as a betrayal of the revolutionary cause. Some even saw it as the beginning of the end of Soviet communism. In his book *The Great Retreat* the Russian-American sociologist Nicolas Timasheff,[9] who was one of the first to emphasize the radical nature of this change, argues (perhaps with some exaggeration) that Stalin and the Communist Party gave up almost all the central ideals of the Bolshevik Revolution at this point. In any case, 1934 was a watershed year in cultural politics.

The political and cultural aspects of this change have been documented in earlier studies, such as those by Richard Stites and Sheila Fitzpatrick. Scholars have also analyzed the economic and political reasons leading up to it. Thus far, however, the field of material culture, which is perhaps one of the most pronounced expressions of the nascent Soviet consumption culture, has been largely neglected (cf. however Fitzpatrick's *Everyday Stalinism*[10] and Julie Hessler's article on the history of Soviet trade[11]). This book looks to correct this omission by offering a detailed description of changes in the material culture of the Soviet Union of the 1930s. This 'value transformation' coincided with the emergence and, in particular, with the final establishment of the cult of Stalin.

By analyzing the emerging culture of consumption and the contradictions inherent in a communist system, one can better understand the workings and social mechanisms of Soviet society at large. Underneath the drive for a society, which, at least to some extent, encouraged individual consumption, there were serious political conflicts, but such conflicts were never allowed to be articulated in public debates. Instead, enemies of the people, presumed wreckers and traitors were found in all branches of industry and trade and used as scapegoats throughout the 1930s. No one could hinder the progress of the Soviet state – whatever that meant at the moment.

In the autumn of 1934, the Party leadership condemned all kinds of asceticism ('self-induced pauperism') and libertarianism (free love). Significantly, the doctrine of egalitarianism, which had dominated party ideology, faced the same fate. Egalitarianism was now strongly condemned as a petit bourgeois deviation from true socialism. Radical school reforms were stopped the same year.

In 1933 the Party Central Committee declared socialist realism to be obligatory in art, thus cancelling the ideals of proletarian culture. Richard Stites has aptly summarized the meaning of this turn in art as follows: 'They canonized classical music, ballet, and architecture, realistic theatre, and didactic painting. At the same time they helped fashion a 'mass culture' of socialist realist fiction, state-sponsored folk lore, mass song, military bands, parades, movies, and radio – accessible to all.'[12] According to Stites, it was a culture bearing 'solemn hallmarks of high culture.' It was as if the history of literature, music and art had stopped sometime in the mid-eighteenth century – all the newer developments were declared to be incomprehensible to common people and condemned as harmful to human values and taste.

Those who remember the 1930s fondly recall that the 'joyous life' was not only allowed but positively encouraged.[13] To learn to dance became obligatory to the officers of the Red Army. The Minister of Defence, Voroshilov, and the Chairman of the Council of the Ministers, Molotov, set a good example by learning to dance the tango. The Soviet citizen was supposed to be happy. Nonetheless, the abruptness and unexpectedness of this change in party politics is well documented in a letter cited by Timasheff[14] which was sent to the editor of a youth journal by some members of the communist youth organization Komsomol living in the countryside. They asked whether it was now allowed to visit friends, play the accordion and have fun. Their leader, obviously still loyal to the old politics, had demanded that they stay at home and listen to instructive programmes on the radio.

Not everyone was enthusiastic about the new material and cultural abundance and the way in which it was adopted by the Soviet workers. Warning voices about the potential dangers of the petit bourgeois mentality inherent in such developments were particularly prominent in the Komsomol press.[15] In 1938, Komsomol'skaia Pravda, for instance, warned its readers that 'the vision of the enemy has changed. The enemy is dressed according to the latest fashion. He is gallant. He dances nicely, speaks beautifully. He knows how to charm women. But if you delve into such a person, you will uncover his bestial, alien interior.'[16]

Social hierarchies and their symbols, such as degrees and honorary titles, which had been abolished after the October Revolution, were also re-established in the mid-1930s. On 13 January 1934 academic degrees and titles were taken into use again. Later in the same year, the new titles of 'The Hero of the Soviet Union' and 'The Distinguished Master of Sport', were introduced. The following year, officers' ranks and insignia were also re-established in the Red Army. In 1936 the title of 'The People's Artist of the USSR' was created. It was also characteristic that at the same time Old Bolsheviks' clubs were closed as if to mark the change in the times: the political experience of the old revolutionaries and participators in the Civil War was of no use in Stalin's new Russia. During the previous year, universities and colleges had started restricting the number of new students, adapting a system of *numerus clausus*. Family values were enforced and abortions forbidden on 22 June 1936.

This 'value transformation', in culture had a direct parallel in the politics of material culture. In the analyses of Stalin's times it has become almost common-place to interpret this 'value transformation' as an indicator or proof of the increasing weight of educated specialists, engineers, teachers, doctors of medicine and so on. As previously mentioned, the intelligentsia was codified as a separate social group in Stalin's new constitution of 1936, together with the working class and *kolkhoz* peasantry.

In his speech in May 1935 at the graduation of the Red Military Academy, Stalin announced that 'cadres will decide everything, not machines.' According to Vera Dunham's famous interpretation, the Soviet political elite made a 'big deal' with the new middle class by yielding to its aspirations in cultural politics and lifestyle and received as a reward its nearly undivided political loyalty.[17] This was Stalin's own 'Big Deal.' In Sheila Fitzpatrick's opinion,[18] this new Soviet middle class or intelligentsia, ideally of proletarian origin and schooled in Soviet educational institutions, became the new reference group of Stalin's politics by 1939, replacing the working class.

What, in fact, made this 'big deal' peculiar was that the government created the Soviet middle class and the cultural policy almost simultaneously. Given the chronology, the Soviet government was not in any straightforward manner responding only to the demands and aspirations of these newly educated, upwardly mobile urban people. Various governmental and Party organs eagerly and vigorously encouraged and cultivated new tastes and manners thus taking an active part in the very process of the Soviet middle class' social upbringing.[19] The Party functionaries were themselves part of this new socialist 'intelligentsia.'

Socialist Careers and Increasing Income Differences

Stalin's programmes of industrialization had, in the late 1920s and 1930s, given rise to a large working class that was young and of rural origin. The urban population increased dramatically: millions of people moved into Moscow and Leningrad from the countryside. A ruralization of the cities and city culture became evident. At the same time, a new group of experts and specialists was schooled by the Soviet system itself. They often originated from among the ranks of poor peasants and workers. The Stalinist terror, enforced collectivization and deportations, which were responsible for the deaths of so many people, offered a possibility of social ascent to millions of others – and education was a central channel of this ascent. It was offered almost cost-free to talented and industrious young people.[20] The possibility of forging an individual career and climbing the social ladder was now opened to thousands of workers and specialists. The emergence of increasing income differences was an essential part of the creation of this new social hierarchy.[21]

In the middle of the food crisis in the summer of 1931, Stalin publicly announced his new six-point programme. In addition to some administrative measures, he vigorously demanded that individual skills and efforts be rewarded with higher wages and other material rewards. In his opinion, it had now become necessary to encourage workers to get personally interested in the results of their own work. With the help of various strategies and after many experiments the system started to reward industriousness, talent and skills that were deemed especially useful in building the socialist society. The wage system was amended in 1931. Previously, pay had been based on time alone, but the new system allowed for piece rate pay. As a result, income differences started to grow. This policy culminated in the official condemnation of the 'equal wages policy' in 1934.

The Stakhanovite movement (1935) was publicized by the Party as the final solution to the problems of productivity and labour discipline. While socialist competition had previously been encouraged, it had been collective. Labour *brigades* had competed with each other and been rewarded accordingly. They could then distribute their rewards among individual members according to some agreed or traditional rules. Now, with the emergence of the Stakhanovite movement, individual competition and individual rewards were encouraged and even idealized.

The system of the high-achieving, heroic shock workers (*udarniki*), introduced in 1931, and the subsequent Stakhanovite movement swept through all fields of production and trade. These systems created thousands of workers who enjoyed both higher wages and other benefits, including access to special canteens, shops and tailors as well as better housing. As many – both eye-witnesses and later analysts – have observed, Soviet society was becoming gradually more hierarchic and stratified in the 1930s. The new system of hierarchies was not restricted to income policy alone, but was also reflected in, for example, the ranking of cities. Moscow was the model socialist city and was officially ranked number one. To emphasize its special standing, it had, unlike other cities an administration of its own which was not subjected to the local government of the region. Leningrad was the number two city and other big cities followed.[22] Throughout the history of the Soviet Union the material living standards and the well-being of the population have been directly linked both to one's place of work and the geographical site of one's workplace.

The Creation of New, Cultured Consumers

In the 1930s something that might, with certain reservations, be called 'the New Soviet Middle Class', was gradually born. It did not consist solely of 'non-Party'

*Figure 1   I.V. Stalin, (from the left) I.A. Likhachov, G.K. Ordzhonikidze, V.M. Molotov
and A.I. Mikoyan at the Moscow Kremlin in 1936 admiring a brand new
automobile ZIS from the Stalin Car Factory. (Source: RGAKFD)*

Bolsheviks, educated professionals, engineers, artists and scientists but also of
Stakhanovite workers. Such workers did not necessarily belong to the Party
hierarchy as the old political elite did, but they could still earn and live well. The
new elite consisted increasingly of industrial specialists and workers rewarded for
higher productivity, in addition to the usual suspects of the *nomenklatura*, higher
administrative or party functionaries and officers. There were people, a small but
increasing minority, who came to enjoy the new everyday small pleasures and even
some bigger privileges.

   As long as it was impossible to buy freely any goods in shops, increasing wages
was meaningless. If there was virtually nothing useful to buy or the distribution
channels were extremely bureaucratic, money was all but irrelevant. Therefore, as
the authorities clearly understood, new and higher quality material goods, along
with the shops to sell them, were crucial to satisfying the demand of the new Soviet
consumer. Scholars, including Fitzpatrick and Dunham, have argued that the new
Soviet elite aspired to gain privileges and visible symbols of their newly acquired
social status. They had the money, but not the goods. According to Fitzpatrick
(1979, 252–4), the upwardly mobile segments of the population wanted a well-

ordered society with stability, traditional channels of mobility and easily recogniz-
able symbols of success, as well as rewards in the form of traditional goods.

While this fills in part of the picture, it is necessary to understand more about the
production, distribution, propagation and advertising of these new consumer goods
to gain a fuller view. These new products served an important function in society.
In a manner reminiscent of the works of socialist realism in art or architecture, they
acted as concrete models or examples of the happy and abundant socialist way of
life. They carried the promise of general abundance – a message which was
explicitly attached to them in the minds of their Soviet designers and decision
makers. These products were not destined just for the luckier members of society,
but they were open to all decent, industrious and politically loyal citizens.

Soviet kitch expressed this message most clearly. It was an important and
peculiar part of the new material culture. In food culture in particular, but also in
many other areas of consumption, industrially mass-produced, relatively cheap
copies of formerly expensive luxury products came to play an important part in the
everyday lives of Soviet citizens. Now, thanks to the Communist Party and its great
leader, Comrade Stalin, every worker could live like an aristocrat. Such products
were also essential to the many official and personal celebrations, which were
typical of Soviet life. Soviet champagne, perhaps the best known and most loved
example, was among them.

Historical Sources

This book draws heavily on archival sources. Due to the centralized nature of the
Soviet economy, all documents, letters and annual reports of ministries (*comissariats*), central administration, factories and shops have been preserved in the
archives. The archives include everything, from documents of the CPSU Central
Committee to letters between the Ministry of Food Industry and its different
administrative units, local factories and shops. This material has remained largely
untapped. There is nothing particularly sensitive contained in the vast majority of
documents – most of them have in principle been available to researchers for a
long time. (Some archives were unfortunately destroyed during the evacuation of
Moscow at the beginning of the Second World War.) Unlike the archives of the
secret police, the NKVD, or the CPSU Central Committee, the records tend not to
be politically sensitive, in the sense that they would be personally incriminating or
reveal new, previously hidden atrocities or serious misdeeds. The reason for their
neglect in previous research probably is, in addition to the practical difficulties of
attaining them, that their potential as an extremely rich source of data has been
underestimated. Generally speaking, the social and economic histories of everyday
life are fairly new fields in the study of the Soviet Union.

In addition to these archival sources, this discussion draws on many journals and newspapers. Almost all the major factories and other economic units published their own papers or journals. For instance, the wine trust (*kombinat*) Abrau-Diurso, which came to play an important role in the development of Soviet champagne, published a paper with a title characteristic of the times, *Izobilie* (Abundance). There were hundreds of others, including *Sovetskii patefon* and *Golos konfetchika* (Soviet *Patéphone* and Voice of a Confectionery Worker). Such local or factory papers, often with short shelf lives, frequently changed their names. They include information about the plans and the goals of production, lists of products and prices, articles on problems and conflicts on the shop floor, political campaigns, the hunt for traitors, and so forth. Once again, these sources have rarely been used in historical research in the past.

Ministries and their central administration units also published their own journals and newsletters. Generally speaking, these sources are more abstract and ideologically coloured, but, like similar journals in other countries, they also include a great deal of technical information, for instance the trade journals *Organizatsiia i tekhnika sovetskoi torgovli* (Organization and Technics of the Soviet Trade), or *Za kulturnyi univermag* (Towards a Cultured Department Store). Finally, I also refer to memoirs, interviews, travel reports and novels in order to illuminate specific points.

There is a lack of reliable overall statistics covering the period. Recent work by Russian and Western economic and social historians, such as Osokina, Zhuravlev and Manning, among others, has made it possible to get a more reliable picture about the general standard of living and provisioning in the Soviet Union of the 1930s. This scholarship offers a helpful context in which to understand the evolving ideal of a material culture society. Reading the following pages, one should not forget that even at its most successful, the production of consumer goods was characterized only by an element – or a promise – of abundance in the midst of general poverty. Alongside the new luxury shops selling Champagne and varieties of chocolate Soviet people were queuing for bread for much of the 1930s.

2

Soviet Champagne: Stalin's Great Invention

'Enemy Hands Rule over our Vineyards'

The Soviet newspaper *Izobilie* (Abundance) published alarming news on 18 November 1937:

> Abrau-Diurso is the fatherland of Soviet champagne. . . The quality of the champagne coming out of the cellars of Abrau-Diurso is among the best on the international market . . . However, the most valuable grapes, such as Pinot Franc, Pinot Gris, Chardonnay and others, have been destroyed. Less than one hundred hectares out of the original more than two hundred have survived this destruction.
>
> The destruction has been legitimated by such claims that, in the opinion of many specialists, these types of grapes give a worse vintage than others . . . as if champagne were a bourgeois luxury. But we all know that the motives behind this destruction are all an expression of a hostile attitude.[1]

What this accuser forgot to mention was that champagne was, only a year earlier, definitely regarded as a 'bourgeois luxury' by those in power. The poor wine growers of the state-owned vineyards at Abrau-Diurso[2] could not possibly have anticipated that Stalin would suddenly in 1936 claim that 'Champagne is an important sign of material well-being, of the good life.' Despite the fact that the wine growers must have known of Stalin's statement in the autumn of 1937, they would have had very little chance of reorganizing the whole production of their state farm (*sovkhoz*) within a single year. They started to plant new vineyards, but, given the fact that it takes years before new vines bear a harvest, it would not have done them much good. The central authorities did not allow such practical 'details' to interfere with their planning. The previous orientation, for which the local wine growers were now publicly reprimanded, was to develop and increase the cultivation of grapes with, presumably, inferior quality. This was in line with earlier Party directives, with a focus on quantity over quality. For example, in his extensive 1936 report on the present and future state of the Soviet food industry, Mikoyan did

Figure 2   *'Soviet champagne. The best sparkling, aromatic and refreshing wine.'*
Ogoniek *19, 10 June 1939.*

not even mention champagne when discussing the production of spirits, liquor, beer and wine.[3] Stalin's famous dictate changed all that in 1936 – champagne had become a central symbol of the Soviet good life. Government directives and many popular articles and books on food and eating referred to Stalin's comment.[4] Soviet champagne was also widely advertised in the Soviet Union, portrayed, for instance, together with a laughing maiden, in big colourful images on the Black Marias, which circulated on the streets of large Soviet cities as they took prisoners on their long way to Gulag.[5]

The spring and summer 1937 were, in fact, an intense period of reorientation in Abrau-Diurso. A report by Vurov, the Director of Abrau-Diurso, indicates that the factory was aware of the new Party directives the purpose of which was the rapid increase of Soviet champagne as early as the spring of 1937. They had already taken many practical steps to change the orientation of the cultivation of their *sovkhoz*. The report, dated 30 April 1937, proposed several measures to increase the raw material base of Soviet champagne at the wine *sovkhoz*, including a considerable increase in the area allocated to Pinot grapes, mentioned in particular that the *kolkhoz* farmers were on permanent guard against potential traitors. Vurov could also convincingly add that: 'The *kolkhoz* and the *kolkhoz* farmers are enthusiastic about the Government's order to increase the raw material basis of Soviet champagne.'[6] Later in the summer of 1937, on 20 June, the head of the political department at Abrau-Diurso, Comrade Kozlov, asked for permission to establish a separate political division at the trust to improve the political and ideological alertness of its workers and wine growers.[7] The practical outcomes of such measures were naturally slow to materialize. But this was unacceptable in the political climate of the time. The political climate was such that Party directives and new plans were expected to be put into action almost simultaneously with their public pronouncement, no matter how impossible this might be to facilitate. Since the Party could not possibly be wrong, scapegoats had to be found and traitors blamed for the lack of results.

The story of the defeats and successes of the wine growers at Abrau-Diurso can, at least partly, be followed in the issues of the *Izobilie* in 1937 and early 1938. Several articles concerning the efforts towards and problems facing the increase in champagne production at the *kombinat*, the agro-industrial trust,[8] preceded the revelation of the traitors and enemies. On 18 May 1937, the paper stated that on Mikoyan's order 'we have to give the country 12 million bottles of champagne.' Unfortunately, as the author points out, this goal had not been mentioned to the workers of the *sovkhoz*. Another article admits that the planting of vines best suited to producing champagne, which was meant to be concluded by 1 May, was delayed. Such reports, however, did not give rise to panic. During the summer of 1937 several articles hailed the transformation of the Soviet vineyards into champagne producers. They proudly declared that the region of Novorossiisk (Azov–Black Sea area) was to become another Champagne! The paper published instructive articles about how to improve the quality of raw materials, and the new industrial production ('reservoir') methods of champagne were published repeatedly during this time.

An open letter written in the autumn of 1938 was critical of the new directives from above. It defended the local wine growers and put the responsibility for possible failures on others. In the letter, a local *agronom*, Gritsum, of the wine *kombinat*, asked for more concrete instructions and claimed that the directives given by the leading Soviet viticulturalist, Professor Frolov-Bagraev, were unclear and did not pay enough attention to the local conditions. Despite such partially recognized problems, the Stakhanovite workers of Abrau-Diurso proudly announced that they had fulfilled their annual plan in a letter addressed to Mikoyan on 10 December 1937, a mere month after the accusations about class enemies had been published. It makes no mention of such accusations.

New, more severe accusations appeared early the following year, shortly after Mikoyan had publicly praised the *kombinat* for fulfilling its plans.[9] On 10 January

1938, an article appeared in *Izobilie* demanding that 'Abrau-Diurso should be cleared of class enemies.' Typical of the times, it directly blamed Vurov, the Director of Abrau-Diurso, for all possible misdeeds and mistakes related to champagne production. The Party believed Vurov to have a highly suspicious background. He had acted as a director in a Russian–German cooperative and had protected many ex-generals, ex-kulaks, ex-gendarmes and other class enemies. According to the anti-Vurov article, the wine trust seemed to be on the verge of class war: 'There are Kolchak's [a famous white general in the Civil War] people in important positions at Abrau-Diurso.'

Numerous issues of *Izobilie* from May 1937 to February 1938 must have made for perplexing reading. Its target audience consisted of the workers, specialists, wine growers and viticulturalists of the trust itself, who must have had at least some idea of what was really going on from the inside. Further complicating the picture is the first issue of 1938, which proudly notes the results of a tasting session, which concluded that the *sovkhozes* of Myshchako and Abrau-Diurso had provided excellent raw material for champagne during the previous harvest. As the article, written by the technical director of the factory Novyi svet, claims:

> These results speak for themselves. It is possible now to draw the conclusion that our *sovkhozes* and factories successfully copied the method of producing champagne materials. . . Now one more step remains to be taken. We have to produce high quality champagne. Then our Soviet champagne will not only be made of good raw materials but it will be a high quality product in itself. And we'll do that!

The contradictory picture of the champagne industry, which one gets from reading *Izobilie*, can probably partly be explained by the history of the trust. Originally, the trust was not considered important and mainly produced ordinary table wines and small quantities of 'classical', non-industrial champagne. Suddenly, by order of the Council of Ministers and the Party Central Committee, the trust was pushed into the spotlight. By the stroke of one Minister's pen, it had become one of the model trusts and sites of major importance, enjoying high priority in all matters of planning, financing and production. This was all taking place amidst the background of the turbulent years of the Great Terror in 1937–38 when traitors and people's enemies were rooted out from all sectors of the Soviet economy.

It is still striking, however, that the same paper alternated between praising the exemplary work of the *sovkhozes* and making accusations about traitors within the champagne industry, often within the same issue. This would indicate that the paper was not given an official line or directive in dealing with such issues. The authorities, or different factions thereof, competed with one another to gain control of champagne production. This led to a situation where guidelines were unclear or rapidly changing, resources were insufficient and mutual accusations were rampant.

The contradictory path of the champagne industry is emblematic of the larger Soviet picture of the time. Throughout 1937 and 1938, people's enemies were uncovered not only in wine growing but in other fields of the Soviet economy. This wave of terror was fostered by the high expectations and the following resentment associated with early Stakhanovism. Directors, engineers and technicians were identified as scapegoats both by the regime and the workers themselves for failing to raise productivity, wages and living standards. These tensions were built into the Stakhanovite movement.[10] The expectations could not possibly be realized, partly because the directors had no means by which to guarantee them. The spectacular achievements and the following material rewards were soon inflated as the number of Stakhanovite workers rapidly increased in all fields of industry and trade. The normal standards of work and remuneration were gradually raised. If a majority of the workers in a factory joined the Stakhanovite movement, they could not possibly all enjoy higher wages.[11]

It was also typical that all the new Party directives and Stalin's orders were put into action with the help of huge public campaigns and equally public denunciations. The case of Abrau-Diurso is, however, more symptomatic than many others, since it felt the impact of a very dramatic and sudden shift in the politics of the country. This shift found its specific expressions in the development of material culture too.

The Invention of Soviet Champagne

The invention of Soviet champagne is sometimes dated back to the seventeenth Party Congress in February 1934. In a 1939 article in *Vinodelenie i vinogradarstvo*, one Comrade Karpatsenko from the central administration of the wine industry notes that:

> For the first time in the history of the congress of the Communist Party a special resolution was made about the growth of Soviet wine production. . . . According to the speech by Comrade Molotov, the XVII congress declared, 'In the food industry, we will witness a remarkable increase in the variety of products, and in higher and top quality goods. [The goal is] to increase the production of grape wine and champagne.'

According to Karpatsenko,[12] wine and champagne had become ordinary objects of consumption among the working masses in the homeland of socialism.

In reality, there is no evidence that the seventeenth Party Congress of 1934 specifically mentioned champagne and wine in its resolutions. Both Molotov, then Minister of Light Industry, and Mikoyan, then Minister of Food Industry, paid special attention to the food industry, but they did not discuss champagne. Both emphasized the importance, not only of rapidly increasing the quantity of food production, but also of improving the quality and variety of food products available to the Soviet workers and peasants: 'It is necessary for the whole food industry to re-evaluate its product variety, to stop the worsening of the standards of production.' The quality of meat and fish worried Molotov in particular. Mikoyan meanwhile was concerned with the problems of the chocolate and candy industry (*konditerskaia promyshlennost*).[13]

It appears that the birth of Soviet champagne really occurred in 1936 thanks to Stalin's personal initiative and intervention.[14] This coincides with the time when Professor Frolov-Bagraev entered the public scene. He started enthusiastically propagating a new industrial method of champagne production, which was well suited to the purpose of mass production. In September 1937, the first, and rather low-key report of the future plans and the increasing production figures of the champagne industry appeared in *Izvestiia*.[15]

In the mid-1930s, Frolov-Bagraev advocated the introduction of the new industrial 'reservoir' method of mass production. In his memorandum[16] to Mikoyan and in numerous articles in the trade press, he discussed how the reservoir[17] method had a bad reputation in France and other bourgeois countries. Such champagne was rumoured to have poor quality. But, in Frolov-Bagraev's opinion, the method could be adopted with greater success under the conditions of a socialist economy. The new production units in Rostov were already utilizing this method with success in 1937 and its rapid introduction in other sites would guarantee that the planned huge increase in production could be realized within a few years.

The new director of Abrau-Diurso was duly rewarded for his efforts. Professor Frolov-Bagraev, who had been named director of the model *sovkhoz* in champagne production at Abrau-Diurso, commanded the impressive monthly salary of 2,000 roubles – well over ten times that of an ordinary industrial worker.[18] In November 1937, Abrau-Diurso bought a house in Novorossiisk, the city nearest to Abrau-Diurso, for Frolov-Bagraev for 25,000 roubles.[19]

The summer of 1936 was a busy time in the central and local governmental organs responsible for wine production in the Soviet Union. The Ministry of Food Industry was largely responsible for the measures taken during this time, but as usual the Council of Ministers and the Central Committee of the Party made the vital decisions. On 28 July 1936, Resolution no. 1366, concerning the production of Soviet champagne, dessert and table wines, was adopted and signed by the Deputy Chairman of the Council of Ministers, Chubar, and by Stalin himself. This resolution ordered the Ministry of Food Industry to organize three wine trusts under its direct command (thus emphasizing the importance and the privileged position of wine production in state planning). Abrau-Diurso would combine all the production units in the Azov–Black Sea region, a Georgian trust would take care of all Georgian wines, and the trust Massandra would operate in the Crimea.

ТИРАЖ ШАМПАНСКОГО В ТЫС.ЧАХ БУТЫЛОК.

год	Бутылочный способ			Резервуарный способ				:Общее :количество
	Абрау-Дюр-со	Грузия	Ростов	Ростов	Ростов	Грузия	др.зав.	
1936 год	590	100	—	20	100	—	—	810
1937 "	600	400	—	100	300	—	—	1400
1938 "	600	500	20	100	1750	—	—	2850
1939 "	1000	560	150	100	4800	640	—	7120
1940 "	1200	560	110	200	6800	840	—	9750
1941 "	1200	560	150	200	8800	1040	—	11940
1942 "	1200	560	150	200	8800	1440	1000	13350
1943 "	1200	560	150	200	9900	1940	2700	16650
1944 "	1200	560	200	200	9050	2440	7400	21050
1945 "	1200	560	200	200	8500	3440	10800	24900

ЭКСПЕДИЦИЯ ШАМПАНСКОГО В ТЫС.БУТЫЛ.

год	Бутылочный способ			Резервуарный способ				:Общее :количество
	Абрау-Дюр-со	Грузия	Ростов	Ростов	Ростов	Грузия	др.зав.	
1936 год	200	20	—	17	100	—	—	337
1937 "	200	30	—	100	300	—	—	630
1938 "	200	50	—	100	1750	—	—	2100
1939 "	400	200	—	100	4800	640	—	6140
1940 "	400	250	—	200	6800	840	—	8490
1941 "	400	500	17	200	8800	1040	—	10940
1942 "	1000	500	127	200	8800	1440	1000	13000
1943 "	1000	500	120	200	9900	1940	2700	16367
1944 "	1000	500	127	200	9050	2440	7400	20710
1945 "	1000	500	127	200	8500	3440	10800	24647

Figure 3 The First Five-Year Plan of Soviet champagne production. A.I. Mikoyan, Minister of Food Industry, confirmed the plan on 29 July 1936 by his signature on the left upper hand corner. The ten upper rows give the production figures, the ten lower ones the figures of bottles to be distributed in each year. The figures in the columns refer to the production and distribution figures for the different production units. Abrau-Diurso's is the first column from the left. (Source: RGAE F. 8543, Op. 1, D. 415, L. 25)

This resolution also listed all the economic units and factories concerned with wine production that were to be turned over to the Ministry in the near future. Previously, many vineyards had operated under the Ministry of Local Industry or Ministry of Agriculture. It set the production target of champagne for 1936 at 300,000 bottles, for 1937 at half a million, for 1938 at 800,000, for 1939 at 4 million and for 1942 at 12 million. The resolution also included other practical measures for reorganizing vine growing and production in the USSR. Vineyards which could not be used in the production of champagne were left to the Ministry of Local Industry or the Ministry of Agriculture. The State bank was ordered to open a special account to finance the preservation of wines for a longer period of time. In addition, the newly recruited viticulturalists were each given a loan worth 2,000 roubles for three years to build their private homes.[20]

These same bodies also authorized another resolution concerning the growth of vineyards in Georgia. The areas of cultivation were to be increased substantially by 1940. Special attention was paid to the cultivation of grapes that could be used in producing champagne, like Rkatsiteli, Saperavi, Mtsvane, Pinot, Aligote and others. Attention was also paid to the improvement of 'European type' table wines.[21]

This bustling activity did not stop after the summer of 1936 but continued throughout the following year. Champagne remained a top priority for the Central Committee, the Council of Ministers and the Ministry of Food Industry in particular. At the beginning of 1937, the Council of Ministers and the Party Central Committee adopted another resolution about the growth of the raw material resources of champagne and desert wines in the *kolkhozes* of the Russian federation, including the now famous Abrau-Diurso. It included both a detailed geographical plan for the increase of the area with champagne producing vineyards and a plan for training and recruiting thousands of newly skilled workers.[22] It was this last order that the viticulturalists at Abrau-Diurso were accused not to have followed eagerly enough.

The resolution of the Central Committee and the Council of Ministers was immediately, again in a manner typical of the Soviet system of administration, followed by more detailed instructions from the Ministry of Food Industry. Order no. 1876 issued by the Ministry of Food Industry on 29 July 1936 details preliminary plans to build champagne factories in Georgia.[23] This order was immediately followed by Resolution no. 1889 on 31 July 1936 to build a new factory at Rostov-on-Don utilizing the new reservoir method.[24] The same factory was rebuilt and its capacity increased on several later occasions.[25]

At the great exhibition of Soviet agriculture in Moscow, a special pavilion on wines and viticulture opened in 1937.[26] In 1937 and 1938, production sites were increased on several occasions and new factories, vineyards and warehouses opened to satisfy the plans of the Party and the central government.[27] As one of its main initiators, Mikoyan was personally supervising the development of the Soviet champagne. He joined Frolov-Bagraev on a business trip to Champagne, France in the summer of 1936, thus emphasizing the importance of the matter.[28] When the director of the Crimean Massandra and Magartha wanted an opinion on his product, he sent it to Mikoyan. Mikoyan admitted that the result was not yet perfect, but, in any case, these examples of Crimean champagne marked a new era for the Soviet Union.[29]

The drive to mass-produce champagne was not forgotten or neglected even during the hard years of the Second World War. The always industrious Frolov-Bagraev reported in 1943 on the important task of organizing champagne production in Central Asia – an area with no tradition of wine cultivation at all – since the old vineyards at Abrau-Diurso, in the Crimea and in Georgia had fallen under enemy occupation.[30] And shortly after the war, at the end of 1945, an expert in viticulture Comrade Pronin was encouraging his readers towards further successes in increasing champagne production. In the Fourth Five-Year Plan, the new target for the year 1950 was – again optimistically – 16 million bottles![31]

As previously noted, the Soviet government and its economic planning units were fond of making large predictions on production. Given that the starting figures of the 1930s were virtually zero in most fields of consumer goods, most targets appeared to mark huge leaps. 25 million bottles of champagne in a country with well over 150 million inhabitants was not after all all that much proportionally. However, champagne was, at least at times, on sale in considerably large quantities before the war. For instance, before the October celebrations of 1940, *Leningradskaia Pravda* announced that 25,000 bottles of champagne were to be sold in Leningrad.[32]

These figures and plans are, however, important in another respect. Just a few years after a famine in which millions of people had died of malnutrition and in the midst of a time marked by a serious shortage of basic supplies, the government and the Party suddenly started to worry about the production of champagne. The authorities did not just dream up a beautiful picture of the coming happiness of humankind but undertook massive and expensive measures in order to realize the dream. Whether or not it could feasibly be put into practice is another question. Ultimately the war years made the realization of this dream impossible.

By the end of the 1930s, Soviet champagne had become a very popular item of consumption. It was widely distributed and was available, at least in the bigger cities, before public holidays. Champagne, however, is just one example of a new ideal of the 'good life' that came into being in the Soviet Union in the 1930s. This new ideal was also realized, at least partially, in other fields of material culture and in food culture in general and survived long after the Second World War. Indeed some signs of it are still discernible in the – now once again – rapidly changing region of the former USSR.

The Refinement of Soviet Taste: Cognac, Liquor and Vintage wines

Champagne was not the only higher quality alcohol on the minds of the Party. During discussions on the Second Five-Year Plan, wine was included in a Ministry of Agriculture decree on 3 May 1934. All the wine producing economic units were obliged to preserve no less than 25 decalitres of bottled high quality wines of every type cultivated in their warehouses. Until that point, there had been no system of storing or preserving vintage wines in the Soviet Union. Regular wine tastings were also organized with the adjoining system of quality control.[33] In 1937 the plan of the Moscow Wine and Cognac Plant was adjusted to include more expensive wines.[34]

As Mikoyan later wrote in his memoirs, he had several wine tasting experiences in the first class diner on board the Atlantic liner going to the United States. The price of his dinner included two bottles of wine. Mikoyan decided to make use of the opportunity to get acquainted with good wines. Therefore, he asked the waiter to serve him different wines of good quality. After a while he noticed that he was not served the most expensive wines on the list. When asked why, the waiter explained that those wines were only on the list to satisfy rich Americans. He had not served them to Mikoyan because they were not actually among the best ones at all.[35]

In addition to changes in the production lines and tastes of table wines and champagne, similar transformations were taking place in the whole alcohol producing industry. Vodka had been available even during the hard years of the First Five-Year Plan and forced collectivization – selling and producing vodka were declared a monopoly of the state in 1925. During the Second Five-Year Plan, even those factories that produced strong spirits were encouraged to develop their output of more processed drinks. The Moscow Vodka Factory, for instance, changed its production line from a very strong vodka (56-proof) to 'milder' (less alcoholic) vodkas and other 'finer' alcoholic drinks in 1933 and 1934. The year 1934 saw the widening of product variety in this factory from fifteen to fifty-two, the new products generally being of a higher quality, and as a rule milder. In 1936, for instance, Soviet-made Dutch gin was advertised in *Pravda,* the central Party newspaper.[36] Liqueur, generally regarded in the Soviet Union of the 1930s as a finer drink even suitable for ladies, appeared in the Moscow factory's product list for the first time. The factory also developed new specially designed bottles.[37] So-called export and special orders appeared in its plans for 1934. Export wines, like other export products, were at least partly sold on the home market (first at Torgsin and later at Gastronom shops). As with other industries, 1934 was a watershed moment in the policy of producing better and more refined alcoholic drinks.[38]

In 1935 another ten new products were introduced at the Moscow factory.[39] In 1936 a whole new plant specializing in the production of liqueur was developed.[40]

In 1934, the factory had produced only 10,000 hectolitres of liqueurs, but in 1936 the amount was five times greater. At the same time, the share of strong vodkas with very high proofs diminished, with the approval of the higher planning authorities.[41] In 1938 the first 'vintage' liqueurs, liqueurs that had been kept in store for several years, appeared in the factory's product lists. This category had not even been included in the original plan. In 1939, 27,300 hectolitres of vintage liqueurs were delivered.[42]

Cognac produced by the Armenian wine trust and also known under its own trademark Ararat experienced a similar, rapid rise in status a couple of years later. The 'invention' or rediscovery of the importance of cognac coincided with that of champagne; it took place mainly between 1936–37.[43] In a memorandum about the state and future of wine growing and the wine industry in the Armenian Republic delivered to Mikoyan, the head of the Ararat trust, Comrade Balaian, detailed the tasks of cognac production. It is not clear whether the initiative had come from above or whether the director of Ararat was simply promoting his own cause.[44] The document is not precisely dated, but it probably goes back to July 1937.[45] While the recent Third Five-Year Plan had included directives for Armenian wine production, Balaian claimed that both the conditions of wine growing and the further refinement of wine lagged far behind adequate standards. The older preserves of vintage wines and cognacs had been totally destroyed and only young and low quality wines had been released on the market. The problem with cadres was even more alarming:

> The department of viticulture in our agricultural college is almost empty, there is not even a department specializing in cognac. The commanding posts in this trade are not paid at all satisfactorily and there is even escape from the trade because of low pay: the education of young cadres is underestimated and satisfying conditions for their work are not created. The present cadres are in need of further education and instruction, and even more importantly, there is a big need for the transfer of experience and the management of new wine technology from the advanced regions of USSR and from abroad.'[46]

The author of the memorandum recommended many technical measures to improve the quality of the Armenian wine products. A quantitative growth was promised not only in cognac but also in strong sweet wines, another speciality of the Armenian wine trust, as well as in table wines. This quantitative growth was, however, greatly limited by other priorities, in particular the large increase in the amount of wines and cognacs of longer preservation times. Whereas the amount of stored cognacs in 1937 was 400,000 litres and of strong sweet wines 230,000, the figures forecast for the year 1942 looked quite different: 2,150,000 and 1,360,000 litres respectively.[47] In the case of the Ararat trust the emphasis on higher quality in terms of longer preservation was thus quite explicit. In 1943, according to this

Figure 4   The sales' exhibition at the Ararat cognac factory, Yerevan, Armenia 1947.
(Source: RGAKFD)

plan, the trust should not release any cognac which had not been stored for a minimum of three to four years. Balaian also suggested the adoption of an international (French) quality classification of different wines (Port, Madeira, Malaga, Muskat and others) and cognacs based on the period of their maturation before release.[48]

This programme demanded huge investment (the estimated minimum was 41 million roubles), opening of new vineyards, the construction of new factories and storehouses and the reconstruction of old ones. Mikoyan once again supervised the whole operation down to the smallest detail. This is evident in his communications with the directors of Ararat in the summer 1937. For example, on 16 July Balaian reported to Mikoyan that he had with the latter's permission made a deal with Comrade Temkin, the head of the department of building materials, about the release of cement, iron, copper pipes and copper sheets. He reported that what was further needed, among other things, were electric machines and pieces of equipment as well as motorcars. In particular, Balaian mentioned that the factory needed 1.5 million velvet bottle tops to be put on high quality cognac and wine bottles.[49] Because the deal with Temkin had not so far produced satisfactory results, Sarkisov, the director of the Moscow branch of Ararat, wrote a letter to Mikoyan complaining that Temkin had not kept his promise of delivering the appropriate raw materials: instead of the promised 200 tons of cement and 60 tons of iron, Ararat had only received 100 tons of cement and 20 tons of iron. In conclusion Sarkisov wrote, almost threateningly, that 'such a state of affairs puts our trust in a very difficult position because without the termination of the building of new cellars and the re-mechanisation of our cognac factory, the proper handling of this year's harvest will be impossible.'[50]

Against the background of such news and demands from different factories, it is understandable that Krasnogorskii, who was the head of the whole Wine Administration at the Ministry of Food Industry, wrote the following letter to Mikoyan asking for urgent advice and more practical directives:

> In the Five-Year Plan all wine producing organizations under the command of the Republics have been provided with the task of building wine factories and cellars in all the main industrial sites of the Union. . . In particular, in Moscow and Leningrad during the years of the Third Five-Year Plan the building of ten new wine factories is planned. . . It is necessary to make a list of priorities and therefore I ask for your orders concerning this decided building.[51]

It is interesting to compare the development of the wine and cognac industry with that of beer production. Even though some initiatives were taken in beer production and new larger breweries were planned, the attention paid to beer was by no means comparable with that paid to the 'finer' drinks. Beer was clearly an everyday concern as opposed to a special treat or a sign of the good life. Its propagandistic effect was also evaluated as being of lesser value.

However, what initiatives were taken in the beer industry also began in 1936. In May 1936, the Ministry of Food Industry decided to create a new beer plant in Kiev. On 29 October 1936, the Ministry accepted a technical project of constructing a beer factory in the city of Gorky, and later the same year the construction of other big beer factories in Moscow (one named after Babaiev among others) and Leningrad (Krasnaia Bavariia). In May 1937, a decision was made about the reconstruction of the Vena (Vienna) factory.[52] None of these great plans were realized before the war. In 1935, the country produced less beer than it had done in 1926.[53] The target for beer production was set at 85 million decalitres in 1937 (according to another source only 40 million), and at 98 million in 1938.[54] In 1938 slightly more beer was produced than in the years prior to the First World War but only 12 per cent of it was bottled and of better quality.[55] Altogether eight different types of beers were produced under the Central Administration of Breweries, Glavpivo, in the late 1930s including, in addition to the well-known labels such as Moskva, Zhiguli and Leningrad, such specialities as Porter and Karamel. In view of the efforts invested in champagne, beer was clearly a lesser priority. In the minds of the Soviet leaders it did not enjoy the same aura of luxury and belonged, together with vodka, rather to the ordinary necessities of daily life.[56]

3

Soviet Kitsch and Organized Carnivals

Soviet Caviar

In 1935, the newly founded Gastronom food stores boasted a supply of 100 tons of black caviar as well as significant quantities of red (salmon) caviar. In addition, the shops sold other highly valued fish, such as different types of sturgeon, both fresh and smoked.[1] A memorandum from the period called for regulations to improve not just the quality of caviar, but also its packaging and selling. The Ministry of Food Industry insisted that portions of caviar sold in Gastronom shops be packaged in small cans (of 100, 250 and 500 grams), better suited for retail sale. Furthermore, the cans were to be provided with hermetic caps with rubber rings, which could be opened and closed without any damage to whole caviar grains.[2] A 1935 inspections report criticized the Moscow Gastronom food shops for failing to stock black caviar, which should have been regularly available. The report also noted that canned fish should be labelled in Russian and that shop assistants should be able to distinguish between different types of sturgeon.[3]

Caviar was regarded as a necessity, at least for major public holidays or formal banquets. When there was no caviar available in Moscow before the celebration of 1 May 1935, it caused a scandal among local Party officials. Their anxiety was, however, alleviated by the fact that a large shipment was on its way to the capital.[4] When publicly on sale, black caviar was certainly an expensive delicacy in the Soviet Union, which makes one wonder why it was so important to guarantee its wide availability. In 1934 in Leningrad, for example, the price of the most expensive caviar per kilo was 60 roubles, or approximately one third of the monthly wages of a young industrial worker.[5] In 1936 the trade journal *Sovetskaia torgovlia* proudly reported that the price of caviar had decreased from 50 to 36 roubles per kilogram. Caviar was still, however, twice the price of high quality ham or butter.[6] While mostly limited to more privileged members of society, caviar was available to the average citizen in urban areas. A surgical nurse recounted living in 1930s Leningrad in her twenties and being able to purchase, along with her colleagues, a sandwich of black caviar at the Soloviev food store.[7]

Figure 5   A view of the caviar department at the Northern Caspian Red Fish Factory, Astrakhan 1947. (Source: RGAKFD)

Although caviar became a highly valued Soviet delicacy, often associated with the more memorable moments in life, in official policy it never attained the elevated status of champagne. As a result, it has left fewer traces in Soviet archives. It is unlikely that the production of caviar was suited to the ideal of highly central-ized units of mass production. Caviar was after all a natural resource whose value was, at least to some extent even within the socialism of the Soviet Union, deter-mined by its scarcity. Its cultivation could certainly be intensified but only to a certain limit. This was one of the reasons why the Soviet Union exported only a minor share of its annual production of caviar despite the fact that it could have been sold for a high price on the international market to get badly needed foreign currency.[8] Nevertheless in many other respects caviar shared with champagne and cognac a common characteristic. They could all be called ideal examples of Soviet kitsch.

Soviet Kitsch and the Birth of the Soviet Material Culture

Soviet *kitsch*, as I am using the term, can be defined as mass-produced, cheaper copies of finer, expensive goods which had the aura of luxury because they had been consumed – or the Bolsheviks believed they had been consumed – by the former Russian nobility.[9] The message that these goods carried was clear: now the ordinary Soviet worker had access to a standard of living that was earlier restricted to members of the nobility or rich bourgeoisie. The new luxuries were symbolic of a lifestyle lived by the Russian elite of the nineteenth century, or rather a life which the Bolsheviks had read about in Tolstoy, Chekhov and Gogol. Some modifications were necessary of course. Instead of horse carriages, for instance, big cars with chauffeurs were available to the new Soviet elite. Common luxuries – or one might even speak of plebeian luxuries – were meant to be an essential part of the everyday life of the Soviet people. Such luxuries played a part in numerous public and personal feasts and celebrations, including the carnivals later described in this chapter, that were typical of Soviet life.

Champagne, cognac, caviar, chocolate and perfume were all part of this new luxury culture. All these goods have a certain sensual pleasure, meant to be enjoyed by drinking, eating or smelling. They were also feminine goods in the sense that they were mainly targeted towards female consumers, towards the new Soviet women, and were considered to be suitable gifts for women of all ages. In the mid-1930s such products were produced in great quantities. Later, other goods such as crystal glasses and vases, amber necklaces, scarves and fur hats were also found in special state shops in urban areas. This limited group of products preserved its extraordinary status throughout the history of the Soviet Union. These – in many ways rather modest – luxury goods were by no means all that was regarded as luxuries in the sense of transcending basic needs or exceeding the regular shared standard of life. Almost anything – other than very basic goods such as plain bread, cabbage, potatoes, or vodka – was a luxury in the eyes of Soviet citizens and the authorities.

Foreign products also held a special cachet in the luxury goods economy of the Soviet Union. In the late 1920s many special hard currency shops called Torgsin opened to serve a privileged Soviet clientele – first foreign workers and specialists who had foreign currency, later even Soviet citizens who had valuables, antiques, art, gold or silver to sell. These shops sold many products of foreign origin. In a country which imported few consumer goods almost any foreign goods became a rare luxury, difficult to obtain and prestigious to own. For instance, in 1939 only 1 per cent of the total sales of the Central Department Store (TsUM) in Moscow consisted of foreign, imported goods.[10] If practically everything that this flagship of Soviet trade sold before the war was domestic, one can easily imagine what the situation was in other more provincial department stores, not to mention ordinary shops. This was a consequence of socialism, which called for a strong reliance on one's own resources and raw materials. Hard-to-earn foreign currency was used to buy machines and raw materials for heavy industry. This is one of the reasons why black markets have flourished throughout Soviet history even during relatively prosperous times. The black market trade in jeans and nylon stockings or Abba records in the post-war decades is probably the best-known example of this phenomenon, while, in the 1930s, Parker pens and imported cigarettes were typical black market commodities.

Other perks and privileges were also developing in the 1930s. Directors of factories and leaders of various organizations had cars with chauffeurs, private homes, large flats in city centers, summer villas, free vacations in health spas on the Crimea, and so on. The truly privileged could even take trips abroad and have access to foreign currency, which could buy almost anything. Alexei German, whose father, the famous Soviet writer Yurii German, received a prestigious state award in the early 1930s while in his twenties, recounted such privileges in his memoirs.[11] He recalled that his family of three lived in a three-roomed flat in the centre of Leningrad, enjoyed a private car with chauffeur, had a cook and a nanny. In remembering his childhood, the son of Lavrentii Beriia, the Minister of Affairs and the head of the secret police, was more modest. His father had, of course, a big *dacha* outside Moscow and a car with a chauffeur, but they belonged to the office and the family lost everything as soon as his father fell from grace.[12] Historian Sheila Fitzpatrick describes a private car as an example of utmost Soviet luxury in the 1930s since it is unlikely that private individuals could buy cars.[13] On rare occasions they could be received as presents from the state.

From the mid-1930s some of the genuine luxury goods and services gradually became accessible not only to the rather narrow political elite, but also to a rapidly growing group of privileged people. This group consisted of educated specialists, or Stalin's intelligentsia (the name given to this group by Stalin in 1936); and top workers, *udarniki* and Stakhanovites. Real luxuries such as cars, large apartments or *dachas* mostly belonged to one's 'office' or were presented as rewards for exceptional work. In principle, they could not be bought with money but were regarded as rewards to be earned through hard work or exceptional talent.

A culture of material goods unique to the Soviet Union was created in the 1930s. What defined the 'good life' is often illuminating. A standard Soviet history of economy published in 1978, for example, proudly summarizes the achievements of the Second Five-Year Plan in the development of consumption: 'Many food items which in pre-Revolutionary Russia were only available to the representatives of the ruling classes were strongly anchored into the everyday life of Soviet people.'[14] If the above catalogue of luxury goods is representative at all, this characterization by a Soviet historian was indeed true to a degree.

Figure 6   A children's ball around the New Year's tree at the House of the Soviets, Moscow 1937. (Source: RGAKFD)

Naturally, it would have been difficult to combine some elements of the 'good life' with the ideals of socialism. But it was still possible, in principle, for a Soviet worker in the 1930s to dine *à la Parisienne* under a crystal chandelier and enjoy the services of a butler in a tailcoat, say in Metropol', Natsional' or Praga restaurants. Or drink a cocktail on the terrace in the new Soviet showpiece, the Moskva Hotel next to the Kremlin Wall, built at the end of the 1930s. The price of a formal dinner was most likely too expensive for the most common workers, but even they could, at least occasionally, afford a box of chocolates, a bottle of champagne or a trip to an ice cream bar. Many ordinary workers and *kolkhoz* peasants could also enjoy these privileges at the state's expense as invited guests to the capital as members of Party delegations or representatives of labour collectives.

The irony is that many wageworkers living in highly developed capitalist societies of the 1930s could ill afford the treats that their Soviet counterparts could. The price of champagne was likely prohibitively expensive. In addition, the capitalist worker had other modern consumer goods to strive for, rather than luxury knock-offs of the rich. The luxury goods offered by Stalin were a form of *kitsch* in that they imitated models and artifacts that were thought to be valued by or belonging to the world of 'high society.' Their propagandistic message was that every Soviet worker lived like an aristocrat. Yet, at the same time, the country was in a perpetual state of deficit, lacking basic necessities such as bread. Such inconsistencies have been rife throughout Soviet history. To buy a bottle of champagne was certainly beyond the reach of millions of *kolkhoz* peasants. On the other hand there were hundreds of thousands of workers and technical specialists who were more prosperous now.

The new luxury goods were often in evidence at family parties, during birthday celebrations or at public holidays. Most of the goods were available in great quantities just before public holidays for a relatively moderate price. The main Soviet public holidays – New Year's, 1 May and October Revolution Day – were firmly established as an essential part of the life of every Soviet citizen in the 1930s. The New Year, for example, became an official annual feast in the Soviet Union in 1936 (to replace Christmas) and many of the rituals and symbols associated with it are preserved to this day.[15] The Christmas tree, along with its decorations, was banned in 1929 because of its bourgeois reactionary roots. The whole New Year tradition was heavily criticized in particular during the Cultural Revolution in 1931. However, the tradition of New Year's was re-instated by 1935 and the Christmas tree was allowed to be reborn as the New Year's tree, just one of the many twists and turns of the Stalinist regime and another example of the significance of the more relaxed period of the mid-1930s.[16] From that point, the administration in Leningrad ordered that trees and decorations should be on sale throughout the city. By 1938, 210,000 trees were to be sold in Leningrad alone.[17]

The reinstatement of the New Year's holiday meant a boom in chocolate production as well, with factories responding more or less immediately to the new demand. The year 1938 witnessed a rapid increase in the production of New Year's and other celebratory candies. According to the original plan of 1938, the Red October factory should have produced 11 tons of such seasonal candy but, in fact, produced 149 tons.[18] Likewise, in the late 1930s Moscow department stores started organizing special New Year's bazaars specializing in items such as tree decorations, children's toys and special chocolates and sweets. These bazaars were enthusiastically advertised in the local press and on the radio.[19]

Carnivals and Organized Demonstrations: 'Life has Become more Joyous, Comrades'

On 11 June 1936 an article called 'Carnival at night' appeared in the journal of food industry, *Pishchevaia industriia*.[20] It reminded readers about a huge carnival organized for the following evening in Gorky Park in Moscow.[21] The carnival was dedicated to the newly adopted Soviet constitution, much publicized by Stalin, the Party and the Soviet government: 'Today at night at the Central Park of Culture and Rest named after Gorky in Moscow a carnival will be organized dedicated to the Constitution Day.' The paper explained what the purpose of the carnival was to Soviet life, thus indicating indirectly that such occasions were something of a novelty in the Soviet Union at this time: 'Carnival is a bright party of the merry life, a party of abundance, demonstrating the increasing material well being of our homeland.'

The preparations for the carnival were widely reported in other all-union papers as well, but *Pishchevaia industriia* naturally paid particular attention to the role of the food and catering industry in the celebrations:

> In the square named after the Five-Year Plan there is a sugarhead. On its top, white as snow, a red flag is hanging with the text: 'World record in sugar production.' In the middle of a small pond there is a frying pan on a burning primus [portable] stove with a jumping fish – this is the fish industry's corner. The toreador from the meat trust has become good friends with the bull. Comical cows play volleyball with a ball of cheese. TEZHE [the cosmetics trust] provides an alley of beauty and freshness. The fox is staring enviously at a piece of soft cheese produced by a Moscow factory, which is hanging from the beak of a crow.
>
> These are not all the characters present at the carnival representing food industry. It is necessary to provide all the 100,000 participants with cooling drinks, sweets and cakes etc. 100,000 bottles of water, beer and wine, six tons of ice cream, 100,000 pies and cakes have been ordered from the catering organizations of the Moscow food industry. In the park 75 distributors of drinks, ice cream and sweets and cakes, 160 stalls, 35 drink dispensers will be working.'

The carnival had a dual purpose: to celebrate the joyous life announced by Stalin and to demonstrate publicly that the Soviet Union was a country of abundance. Food and drink were important elements of the celebration because they helped demonstrate the advances that the country had made in mass manufacturing a wide variety of quality consumer goods. Although in truth the majority of Soviets were poorly fed, Stalin could show off food and drink products that could compete on the same level as those in the West.

The day after the carnival ended, *Pishchevaia industriia* reported its impressions of the celebration:

> Hello, you sausage! The sausage strolling by on the alley turned its head and laughed revealing a set of white teeth in its open mouth. This was Ivan Tsyrkin, a worker at the meat plant who wanted to celebrate his own product at the carnival.

Ivan Tsyrkin was in the company of a nice white kid. The kid asked the sausage to dance. And an orchestra was playing, flags swayed on their masts, lanterns shined – and everyone joined in a common dance, merry and wild. Chocolate flew around, serpents flew around like arrows, and rockets fell from the sky in a bright rain.[22]

This Constitution Day carnival was not the only one in 1936. In fact, there was a boom of carnivals in Moscow at this time. Rosalinda Sartorti, a historian who has analyzed other similar celebrations in Moscow, discusses in her work a carnival on Manage Square close to the Kremlin in August 1936. In newspaper reports about this carnival, the abundance and, even, excess of food again played an important role. Referencing the newspaper reports, Sartorti describes the carnival as follows:

> In the night of the 4th to the 5th of August, a hundred thousand participants in costumes and masks were dancing waltz and tango, slow and fast fox trot; they were enchanted by the torch fountains which resembled burning asters, by the nightly sky brightened by the play of projectors, by the fireworks and the rockets, and they went down the river Moscow in boats decorated with pennants.[23]

As Sartorti demonstrates, these carefully planned and orchestrated carnivals were entirely new to Soviet society. Their explicit purpose was to transmit an atmosphere 'characterized by a holiday mood which knows nothing of scarcity, tension or necessity, but quite the contrary, a world of overabundance, amusement and forgetting.'[24] During the summer 1936, there appear to have been such carnivals virtually every month in Moscow. The following is a report of the 1936 May Day celebrations published in *Komsomol'skaia Pravda*, 4 May 1936:

> It is hard to describe how Moscow enjoyed itself in these joyous days of the May Day celebrations. . . We have to talk about the garden of plenty behind the Manage building, this garden where sausages and *Wurst* were growing on the trees. Where a mug of foaming beer was accompanied by delicious Poltava sausages, by pink ham, melting Swiss cheese, and marble white bacon.[25]

Dancing was an essential part of these celebrations and was encouraged in other contexts too. In the newly opened fine Moscow restaurants of the late 1930s, such as Natsional', Metropol', Praga or in the architecturally heralded Moskva Hotel on Manage Square, big bands directed by famous conductors and singers played 'Soviet jazz' and other popular music.[26] Dances and carnivals were organized at numerous workers' clubs in the Soviet Union to celebrate, for instance, New Year's Eve[27] when, understandably, no outdoor carnivals could be organized in the north because the temperature could drop well below 30 degrees Celsius. Judging from the press photographs of the period, dances also occurred more or less spontaneously on the fields of the *kolkhoz* farms – often only to the accompaniment of an accordion. These dances celebrated traditional seasonal feasts such as the end of a successful harvesting or sowing. The popularity of dancing coincided with the mass production of gramophones and records in the Soviet Union.

It is no wonder that dancing became popular and was encouraged by the authorities. What could be a better symbol of the many trends combined in the cultural politics of the 1930s: a new etiquette, the new emphasis on orderly relations between men and women, the importance of the family and enjoyment of Soviet music while having fun in a civilized manner. Learning to dance was regarded almost as a duty of every Komsomol girl and boy. Numerous dancing schools were opened in Moscow.[28] The big event of 1936 in Moscow was a dance show by 'American Negro' Henry Scott, a well-known figure in a place where most people had never before seen a black man, and his Russian girlfriend at the *Udarnik* theater. Thousands of people came to watch them dance the 'Lindy Hop' (Lindotchka), which became the fashionable dance of the season among the more trendy youth of the capital.[29]

As Russian historian Natalia Lebina has pointed out, the enthusiasm for dancing – and in particular modern European dances like the one step, tango or foxtrot – was not unanimously shared by Soviet political and cultural activists of the late 1930s. Many regarded such forms of mass enjoyment with suspicion, and demanded that youth should instead dance authentic 'Russian' dances like the *krakoviak, padespan, pol'ka or kadril'* which, in their opinion, were closer to the 'common people' and more 'democratic' in character. According to Lebina, what also differentiated these dances from the modern European or American ones was that they were always accompanied by a dance leader and, as such, were conducted under the guidance of an older, responsible person such as the cultural leader of a local youth club. As Lebina argues, the Soviet culture of the late 1930s was thus characterized by a kind of 'double standard' of morality or etiquette of good behaviour accompanied by a certain tension. The urban elite and young, new 'middle class' favoured Western, 'bourgeois' habits with traditions of balls and festivities with modern dances, whereas the more traditional and more 'orthodox' cultural workers preferred 'genuinely Russian' folk music and dances, undoubtedly often with the enthusiastic support of the huge masses of the *kolkhoz* boys and girls.[30] By the late 1930s, the more conservative mood seemed to have the upper hand in this cultural conflict.

Popular dances of both kinds could also be organized privately and in a more spontaneous manner among a group of friends, but they more typically involved a high level of organization. For example, a New Year's party at a worker's club would be orchestrated by an appropriate organization or club and a limited number of participants would be issued invitations. Such invitations were often earned as rewards for good work and decent conduct.

Figure 7   The field brigade 'The Fighter for Culture' organized a dance, Stalingrad region 1938. (Source: RGAKFD)

There had been a strong tradition of mass celebrations, of the appropriate kind, in the early 1920s. One can also see a direct link between the traditional Russian orthodox processions and the more recent political parades. During the Civil War, demonstrations with mass participation were part of popular culture as well as the cultural policy of the Party. In the 1920s such demonstrations were often spontaneous, participation voluntary and slogans and banners chosen and painted by the participants and local political activists. Mass spectacles with the participation of hundreds, if not thousands, of workers, under the direction of professional artists and actors were used to revitalize the memory of important revolutionary dates and events such as the siege of the Winter Palace in Petrograd.[31]

Towards the end of the 1930s, demonstrations became institutionalized and centrally organized. Central Party committees decided beforehand on all the slogans. Participation was no longer voluntary. People were invited – or ordered – to take part and this was understood to be a special privilege reserved for exemplary workers, peasants and intellectuals. According to sociologists Temkina and Zdravomyslova[32] the people who played a more important role in these demonstrations, like those bearing the banners, were often also rewarded with material goods. Demonstrations thus became more and more official state rituals with a written script of their own which the demonstrators were supposed to follow down to the letter.

As Papernyi has noted, they were also supposed to be held in places dedicated specifically to the purpose of demonstrating. The old practice of organizing demonstrations, say, in theatres was now regarded with suspicion and condemned. Each city or town had a special place dedicated to this purpose.[33] Decorations now had to be approved by the Executive Committees of the Local Council of People's Deputies six months in advance, 'so the authorities had enough time to check the design for political accuracy and to distribute orders for the decorations, banners, etc. with local enterprises.'[34] The increasing rigidity in the preparation and organization of the demonstrations went hand in hand with the increasing rigidity of the political system in general.

The demonstrations of the 1920s had often had a strong carnivalesque atmosphere: 'The decor was designed by avant-garde artists, creators of the concept of proletarian art. Staging the galas was likewise trailblazing and indeed produced a mobilizing effect.'[35] The transformation of such demonstrations from popular carnivalesque events to strictly organized official rituals was rapid. The new style was part of the increasing depoliticization of the masses and centralization of the initiative. The role reserved for the Soviet workers and peasants in these celebrations was that of silent spectator or happy, enjoying consumer. In the Soviet Union, the social division of labour was supposed to be functional. Every citizen was supposed to play a role determined by his or her own position in the productive life of the country. The importance of these roles extended the limits of work life and determined every citizen's position in the society at large. This helps explain the impression one often gets in reading reports like the ones above about such Soviet occasions – a feeling of enforced enjoyment and pleasure, as if a huge invisible sign was hanging over Gorky Park with the command: 'Thou shall have fun!'

This is not to deny that many participants genuinely had fun and fully enjoyed such Soviet rituals, which often then turned into fond memories. Many were certainly proud of their socialist fatherland, its government and leader. The greater availability of consumer goods, which came to mark the major public holidays, also helped make these holidays an integral part of the life of most ordinary Soviet citizens. One could even argue that the consumption of particular foods and drinks, such as champagne and chocolate, and other consumer goods, such as gramophones and musical instruments, at certain political rituals was an effective way of inculcating loyalty among the citizens of the state. Rather than relying on previous methods of straightforward political agitation, this new mode of using consumer goods as incentives helped unify the public around the Soviet state. When political punishments became both more severe and more arbitrary with Stalin's repressions, the system of rewards likewise became more varied. In a sense, Stalin's 'engineering of human souls' was less straightforward and allowed for more individual gratification and variation than the earlier political manipulations.

4

Increasing Variety

Chocolate Boxes and other Small, Sweet Luxuries

The mass production of champagne was not the only luxury goods concern that worried the government and the Communist Party in the 1930s. Food culture in general witnessed a similar shift starting in 1933 when the Second Five-Year Plan was discussed and finally adopted. The Party Congress of February 1934 was a watershed moment in the development of material culture, and food products in particular, in the Soviet Union. The Leningrad Party leader, Kirov, named it the 'Congress of the Victors.' The Central Committee Plenary Meeting in November 1934 adopted the much-repeated slogan 'For better quality.' The year 1935 witnessed another 'great leap forward' when Stalin declared that 'Life has become more joyous.' In his famous and oft-quoted speech from the Party Congress, the Minister of Food Industry, Mikoyan, discussed several options for improving both the quantity and quality of food products, consumer goods and other everyday necessities. He emphasized the importance of chocolate and confectioneries in particular.

The active search for novelties in all fields of consumer goods was, somewhat amazingly, openly motivated by the Soviet buyer's demand for expressing his or her individuality and of cultivating his or her taste. In 1934 the same care for more individual expressions of taste was extended to mass production where it was reformulated as the problem of increasing variety. In this respect the development of product variety in the famous Moscow Krasnyi Oktiabr (Red October) chocolate factory was certainly exemplary. Krasnyi Oktiabr was a model factory working directly under the Minister's orders which as early as 1937 produced well over 500 different types of candies and chocolate. Over a hundred of these were seasonal products released for the New Year celebrations.[1] As will be discussed later, other industries of consumer goods, such as cosmetics, closely followed suit.

The Krasnyi Oktiabr' confectionery set the example of mass-produced consumer goods in many ways. As early as January 1934, it was recognized as the best confectionery in all of Moscow.[2] During the previous year, the factory, which consisted of three main departments producing ordinary caramels, *iris* (soft cream

Figure 8   The instructor of the Red October chocolate factory E.G. Krivoukhova, the brigadier K.G. Kasatkina and a female worker inspecting the product assortment released before the 1 May celebrations, Moscow 1937. (Source: RGAKFD)

candy) and chocolate, exceeded its annual plan with a production level of 116.4 per cent. The only department lagging behind target was the chocolate one. The reasons given in the annual report were the usual ones: lack of raw materials and poor conditions of transport. There had been a greater number of unexpected stops in production than the year before.[3] However, rather surprisingly for the time, there was a remarkable increase in the production of some of the more expensive types of chocolate.

In his report to the Party Congress, Mikoyan told the delegates that he had formulated a plan to encourage the production of better quality food products. According to the standards of quality, all the products were classified in different categories, of which the export category was the highest. As the title of this category revealed, such products were originally meant to be exported abroad. Now a new class was added: *vnutrennii eksport* (inner export, or export to home market). Thus, the producers were seduced into producing more expensive goods of higher quality in the belief that they would be realized on the world market.[4] This trick could not work for very long since the secret was now openly revealed to everyone but, in any case, the new category remained in the system of quality classification of Soviet products for a long time. A further category of 'higher quality' was also introduced at this stage.

When the original plan for 1933 was drafted, there were no target figures for 'inner export' since the class was only invented that same year. Consequently, the plan had to be redrafted, and, according to the annual report, this new, ad hoc plan was realized up to 250 per cent. Nonetheless, well over four of the five thousand tons of quality export products were still sold abroad.[5] Despite the moderate quantities produced, the very fact that these new classes were introduced proves that there was a genuine effort to increase the quality of food products destined for the home market. The better quality chocolate and candy, although produced in the beginning in small quantities, were important for the example that they provided in what the Soviet economy could and should be doing.

The real breakthrough in Krasnyi Oktiabr's history took place in 1934. As would happen with the champagne producer Abrau-Diurso a couple of years later, it was transformed under the direct command of Mikoyan, the Minister of Food Industry. The plan for 1934 was immediately reworked and the targets for higher quality products lowered or made more realistic. Even the new figures were unreachable due to a lack of cocoa beans, coconut oil and other such imported raw materials.[6] However, despite these difficulties and changes, the share of export and other higher quality products increased rapidly: whereas in 1932 the factory had produced 1,952.1 tons of export goods, in 1933 it produced 5,066.8 tons and by 1934 9,151 tons, almost five times as much as two years previously.[7] The product variety increased rapidly too; there were fifty new items in the 1934 product list, forty-six of which were 'totally new'. The production of higher quality and filled chocolates, such as chocolate bombs, cigars, pillows, fruit and others, was encouraged. The general quality grading of these products also improved.[8]

In 1935 the factory's new position as a model for the whole confectionery industry was evident in the results it managed to achieve. Due to its new status, it was in a privileged position with regards to the provisioning of raw materials and financing. The plan for 1935 was over-fulfilled by 123.6 per cent, and the chocolate department did even better: its plan was realized by 215.6 per cent. The plan for higher quality and export products was also fulfilled above the average.[9] In 1936 the factory produced 224 types of products, of which about one half had been taken into production during that year. Among these new types, higher quality products predominated.[10] Product variety, then, had almost doubled during one single year.[11] In particular the quantity of 'paper wrapped chocolate' and the number of chocolates in gift boxes had increased remarkably.[12] And glazed soft chocolate had appeared for the first time on the factory's product list.

These new developments and demands led to some changes in the factory's organization. A new department was founded, and the chocolate department began working in three shifts instead of the standard two. Only chocolate was produced at exceptionally high speed day and night.[13] As mentioned above, from 1934 higher quality chocolate had been put under the special care of the Communist

Party and the Soviet government. The Party thus regarded the production of luxurious chocolate boxes as one of its prime goals, almost as important as the production of tractors, airplanes, electric power plants and other machines. Despite these high aims it should be noted that, in reality, neither food nor any other 'light' industry ever seriously challenged the privileged position of 'heavy industry' in Soviet economic policy.

That chocolate was a high priority in the country's production plans throughout the 1930s is evident in the figures of import statistics of raw materials. Import for the purpose of consumption was very restricted throughout the decade, and most product categories, such as raisins, almonds, coffee, tea, or rice, never exceeded the pre-Revolutionary levels of 1914. Cocoa beans were a clear exception. As early as 1935, their import had reached the level of 1914 and it exceeded it in the following years. In fact, the pre-Revolutionary level had already been reached during the 1920s but the import had all but stopped during the forced collectivization of agriculture.[14]

In 1936 the same line of development at the Krasnyi Oktiabr' was continued: rapid increase of higher quality sweets, chocolate in particular, at times at the cost of lower quality products. Indeed, some lower quality products were taken out of production altogether. The production of chocolate glazed, filled sweets and caramels continued to increase as did the quantity of novelties, discussed in the next chapter.

In 1936 a fifth department was opened to handle the task of weighing and packing the factory's sweets into small portions mainly to be sold in restaurant wagons on the railways. A new design and toy shop, which would come to play a very important role in the future development of the factory, also opened. This new shop started designing stylish paper wrappings, gift boxes and chocolate toys for children. It employed eighty-nine people, mostly artists and designers, two of whom were occupied only with children's toys. The factory cooperated with the Moscow Children's Theatre and its director, Natalia Sats, the wife of Trade Minister Israil Veitser, who suggested several new ideas. Chocolates called Skazki Pushkina (Pushkin's Fairy Tales), for instance, were initiated by Sats and date back to the year 1936 – when the country celebrated the anniversary of Pushkin's death and cemented his role as the greatest Russian poet in official Soviet history.[15]

The chocolate department received new imported machines in the same year. This equipment allowed for totally new types of chocolate to be produced, such as Ekstra, Standart, Tri Porosenka (Three Piglets) and so on.[16] As the annual report proudly mentions, these new products were superior in terms of quality to anything produced before. At the same time, a lot of effort was directed into developing higher quality recipes to match international standards. New brands were introduced such as Prima, Turist (Tourist), Krasnyi Oktiabr', Dvorets Sovetov (Palace of Soviets), the latter commemorating Stalin's plan to build a huge palace in

Moscow on the site of the demolished cathedral of Christ the Redeemer, rebuilt again in the 1990s.[17]

Following Order no. 286 of 15 February 1937 from the Minister of Food Industry, the factory had full responsibility for the realization and selling of its own products. This was a further sign of the high status it enjoyed in the economic planning system. Accordingly, a separate sales department was organized. If earlier the state was bound to buy everything that the factory produced at stable prices, now the factory had to take care of selling itself. Consequently, it needed to pay more attention to the demand for its products and, at least to some extent, start 'orienting towards the market', as the common saying went.[18]

In 1937 the first reports started to come in of lower quality products that could not find buyers. Consumers were exercising their newly found ability to choose. This led to new problems within the factory. Continually plagued by an irregular supply of raw materials, the factory was unable to meet its targets in many departments.[19] Thus, it shared the destiny of many other Soviet factories in the mid-1930s: after a short burst of energetic activity caused by the Stakhanovite movement and the availability of better financial resources and raw materials, it was faced with shortages in raw materials, a lack of qualified workers, transport problems and organizational failures. Despite these difficulties, in 1937 the relative growth of the chocolate department was bigger than that of other departments (soft cream and other caramels). In particular, chocolate glazed sweets enjoyed greater popularity among the customers than other types of lower quality sweets. Almost the entire production of the chocolate department consisted of producing them.[20]

The workings of the plant in 1938 continued in a well-established pattern. Production targets were met for most products with the exclusion of chocolate; there were problems it would seem with truffles in particular. The general quality ratings of 1937 and 1938 remained stable. Some of the so-called export products were sold in the home market satisfying more demanding needs. They distinguished themselves from lower quality products both by their improved taste and by their new 'artistic' packaging.[21] Thus, Soviet shops receiving provisions from the Krasnyi Oktiabr' were now selling both normal sweets of a higher quality and some new higher quality products originally aimed for export.

The story of Krasnyi Oktiabr' is exceptional. As previously mentioned, it became Minister Mikoyan's special 'pet-factory' enjoying all kinds of special privileges, ranging from material supplies to employment policy. Just like the champagne producer Abrau-Diurso it was a model factory. Its task was to set an example to others in two senses. First, by its exemplary success it was meant to inspire production units working under less favourable conditions. Second, its high-quality products provided a concrete example for common people of what was to be expected in all fields of production in the future. Even those who could not buy its products – either because of poverty or lack of supply – saw advertisements or heard descriptions from their luckier friends and relatives who had visited the capital. At least in principle, it was now in the middle of 1930s possible to buy a nicely decorated box of chocolates as a birthday present or decorate one's New Year's tree with chocolate toys from the provisions of Krasnyi Oktiabr' or some other Soviet chocolate factory.

Although Krasnyi Oktiabr' was a huge industrial enterprise growing at a rate that would make any director proud and enjoying nationwide fame, it was still unable to meet potential demand, given the size of the Soviet population. In 1937, 10 million kilograms of chocolate were produced. In a country of 160 million this amounts to one chocolate bar of some 70 grams per capita. In practice, Krasnyi Oktiabr distributed and sold a large proportion of its annual output to Moscow and some other privileged places.

There were other big confectioneries in Moscow, Leningrad, Kiev and other big cities which grew and developed nearly as rapidly in the mid-1930s. However, the reports and plans of other factories have not, unfortunately, been preserved as completely and therefore information about them is often more scattered. Nonetheless, another famous Moscow factory Rot Front reported developments similar to those of Krasnyi Oktiabr.' The reconstruction of its chocolate department had started in September 1933 with the main aim of increasing both the diversity and quality of its products.[22] The annual reports of 1937 and 1938 have not been preserved but in 1939 the Rot Front was facing problems with ingredients.[23] The difficulties that the more 'normal' Karl Marx chocolate factory in Leningrad faced in trying to cope with the new task of answering ambitious expectations were probably typical. As usual the inability to meet targets was blamed on failures with deliveries of raw materials or lack of packaging or paper wrappings. The joint organ of the Party unit and the factory commission wrote in 1934 about difficulties with packaging: `They had ordered boxes to pack 200 and 100 grams of *Theater City monpensie*. But in actual fact 100 gram boxes only took 75 grams and the bigger ones only 150–175 grams.' As the author concluded, 'it would be interesting to know who ordered these boxes, who is responsible for the lack of order.'[24] In the same year in a report asking why the variety had not increased in spite of new targets, the lack of adequate raw materials was mentioned. At the same time, however, some products were being produced in excess. Demand and supply did not correspond:

'At the factory there is an excess of some labels like Forest. On the other hand, the factory has not been able to produce Coffee or Honey or Essence at all because of the total lack of raw materials. 19,221 kg of Forest had been produced by the 25th instead of the planned 3,796 kg, i.e. 1,130 per cent, and its further production has been stopped because trade organizations have not been willing to take it any more from the factory.'[25]

In 1936 both the Mikoyan factory in Leningrad and the Bolshevik factory in Moscow reported the realization of their plans. Following the example of Krasnyi Oktiabr' and Rot Front, Bolshevik proudly reported to Mikoyan about the improved quality and increased range of its products. It planned to introduce a number of national specialties to honour the Eighth Congress of Soviets.[26] The Leningrad Mikoyan factory produced 124 different products in 1936 compared with only twenty-five in 1933.[27] Meanwhile, the biscuit and chocolate factory Samoilova in Leningrad produced increased numbers of sweets of the highest quality during the first nine months of 1936: 8,470 tons compared with only 2,912 during the whole of 1932.[28] The Babaiev chocolate factory seems to have specialized, at least to some extent, in the production of *monpensie* of different kinds with medicinal properties, such as Pektoral, Enka-Menthol and Aisberg. The factory also produced such 'high-tech' sweets as caramels with liquor fillings.[29]

The improvement of the general quality of Soviet candies and chocolate was, as in the case of champagne, closely followed and strictly directed by the Minister himself. In a message to Mikoyan, the Chief State Confectioner, Glavkonditer reported: 'Following your instruction the confectionery industry has changed the selection of its caramel output. Starting from 1936 we have totally stopped the production of the caramels Podushechka (Little Pillow) and Oreshek (Nutty) with fruit filling powdered with sugar of the old type.'[30] The main engineer of the Babaiev factory reported at the All-Union conference of the confectionery industry that, in 1936, they had stopped producing the Little Pillow, which had been the factory's main product the year before.[31] On 13 June 1936, Mikoyan personally signed the new recipe for *monpensie* Aisberg (Iceberg) with the detailed instruction that they should be delivered and sold only in solid plate boxes.[32] An order dated 4 February 1936, with the proper recipe included, was signed by the Vice Minister of Food Industry, Levitin and sent to all confectioneries. They were told to start producing a new type of a caramel named Nonparel.'[33] This is one more piece of evidence that the production of such goods took place under the special care of the highest authorities.

From 1933 until the outbreak of the Second World War – or rather its preliminaries of the Finnish War and the occupation of Western Ukraine and Eastern Poland by Soviet troops – there is a great deal of evidence showing that the Communist Party was deeply involved in creating a luxury goods society. They were especially keen to develop items for everyday consumption and family and public celebrations, items that would better satisfy the evolving tastes of Soviet citizens. While reliable overall statistics are lacking, one can glean the changes in consumer culture through the problems that factories reported. Often the drive to increase productivity and refine quality came at a cost – usually meaning that production of other goods was slowed down.

In the case of chocolate production some indicators show that the overall quantitative increase in the production must have been quite remarkable. The published statistics on the import of cocoa beans, the main ingredient of chocolate which could not be cultivated anywhere in the Soviet Union, show an abrupt increase in the year 1935. From a negligible amount of 1,400 tons in 1934 it rose up to 4,600 tons in 1935 almost reaching its pre-Revolutionary standard. The import of cocoa beans continued to soar in the following two years (7,100 tons in 1936; 11,100 tons in 1937). There was a simultaneous abrupt and sharp increase in the import of coconut oil in 1935 but unlike the import of cocoa beans it declined slightly again during the following year. It remained, however, on a higher level than in the early 1930s.[34] These figures support the conclusion that until 1935 many essential raw materials of the chocolate industry were diverted to 'elite' factories, like the Red October, but that later the materials were more readily available to chocolate factories throughout the country.

By the late 1930s, then, it was quite possible for a young man to court a woman by presenting her with a box of chocolates and a bottle of champagne on her birthday. At least, it was conceivable if they lived in Moscow or another big city, such as Leningrad or Kiev, and if the man was a shock worker making a lot of money. It was another matter if the young couple lived in a non-urban area since the availability of luxury products was limited due to the supply chain. Many of the novelties in food industry were designed to be consumed collectively during official celebrations and holidays. Such seasonal products were, however, meant to be freely sold to any individual consumer, more or less regularly, in standard commercial shops, restaurants, cafés and kiosks.

Increasing Variety and the Demand for Novelties

One of the main pressures on production was the demand for increasing variety. The success of a factory in the food industry was no longer merely judged by the quantity of products manufactured, nor even by their quality. The number of different types of products a factory could invent and produce became equally important. The rapidly growing varieties of chocolate, meat, and perfume where all examples of these new trends in the Soviet economy.

From 1934, nearly all annual reports from chocolate factories included detailed lists of novelties. The figures were often quite impressive. In this 'novelty fever' no one seemed to pay much attention to the fact that often the actual quantities produced were all but negligible. Variety was king. The novelties produced at Red October are summarized in Table 1. In 1934, the first year from which such information is available, Red October produced fifty novelties of which forty-six were 'totally new.'[35] At the end of the following year the total product variety was

Table 1 The total amount of novelties and products produced at the Red October 1934–37.

	Novelties	All products
1934	50	(not known)
1935	101	224
1936	89	479*
1937	61	510

* The total figure for 1936 included 172 'totally new seasonal specialties.' These, and presumably some other seasonal products, must also have been included in the total for the following year.

reported to have grown to 224, of which 101 were new that year.[36] In 1936 the factory introduced eighty-nine novelties plus 172 seasonal novelties meant to be consumed by children or on particular occasions such as New Year's Eve or 1 May. Altogether, the total amount of products had now increased to almost 479.[37] In 1937, sixty-one more novelties were added to the total number of products raising it to 510. Among them were many 'celebratory' or seasonal products.[38]

The Babaiev chocolate factory could proudly declare that it had increased its variety from a mere eleven to forty between the beginning of 1935 and the first quarter of 1936.[39] For the later pre-war years such data is not available but one can presume that this 'novelty fever' was somewhat lower, particularly as a result of overly ambitious targets. In the mid-1930s, the Rot Front also reported a remarkable increase in novelties (see Table 2).

A detailed list from the period shows what all Soviet confectioneries produced in 1934 and 1935 (see Table 3). In 1935 alone almost 2,000 novelties were taken into production. Even if we take into account that these novelties included many versions of the same candy in different form, the amount is still impressive and demonstrates the importance of increasing variety.

Table 2 Novelties produced by the different departments of the Rot Front confectionery in 1935 and 1936 according to the annual reports.[40]

	1935	1936
Caramel department	50	75
Chocolate department	52	63
Biscuit department	18	26
TOTAL	120	164

Table 3   Novelties produced by all the confectioneries in the Soviet Union in 1934 and 1935.[43]

	1934	1935
Candies, wrapped	184	270
Monpensie, drops	22	45
" open type	138	306
TOTAL	344	621
Biscuits packaged and in boxes	92	111
" with 30 per cent flour	61	72
" with 75 per cent flour	42	53
TOTAL	195	236
Gingerbread	30	46
Viennese biscuits	170	251
Soft chocolate glazed sweets	200	254
of which in boxes	38	108
Other soft chocolates	107	146
TOTAL	307	400
Iris	44	50
Chocolate bars	78	98
Chocolate products	58	62
Marmalade and lozenges	48	50
Halvah	10	11
Drops	88	107
GRAND TOTAL	1 372	1 932

Published by the Leningrad authorities of trade, a 1935 list is also impressive in detail. It shows the prices of hundreds of different sweets and chocolates, which were, at least in principle, supposed to be on sale in the city and the surrounding county. It includes products from seventeen factories located throughout the Soviet Union, in Moscow and Leningrad, Kiev, Kharkov, Voronezh, Odessa and Vinnitsa.[41] In 1936 the six Leningrad factories alone produced sixty-seven brands. The price of the most expensive one – black plumes in chocolate – was as high as 67 roubles per kilogram, that is higher than the price of caviar.[42]

Figure 9   *'A great variety of decorations for the New Year's tree.' An advertisement for the Central Department Store at Moscow.* Ogoniek *32, 20 November 1940.*

Seasonal Delights

After 1936 a big share of the novelties of chocolate factories consisted of seasonal products. The production of New Year tree decorations was started in 1936 at Red October and some other factories – shortly after the introduction of the New Year's tree (formerly the Christmas tree) in the USSR. A December 1936 memorandum addressed to Mikoyan mentioned that, in the whole Soviet Union, the seasonal candy toy selection comprised 3,500 different kinds of products of which 2,915 were from factories and 442 from various craftsmen and *artels* (association of craftsmen). A factory in Leningrad, named after Mikoyan himself, submitted on 19 November 1936 a long list of its New Year's tree decorations with the names of their famous artists.[44] This lively correspondence between the production units and the Ministry about seasonal specialties again demonstrates the importance of novelties. Their production had not at all been foreseen in the Second Five-Year Plan. Similar lists of seasonal novelties from Bolshevik, Marat, Babaiev confectioneries have been preserved.[45] Just like Krasnyi Oktiabr', the Rot Front was proud of its wide selection of special, seasonal sweets: in the year 1939 it produced 873.3 tons of these special party goods.[46]

In 1936 the only seasonal specialties produced were New Year's decorations but there were plans to produce similar items for the two other main Soviet public holidays, the May Day and the October Revolution celebrations. In the following pre-war years huge numbers of special products were dedicated to each holiday. They were often sold on special bazaars organized by the department stores in big cities. The December 1936 memorandum also included a rare reminder that one should develop these toys in such a way that would bear a political message.[47] This reminder is a noteworthy one because of its rarity – usually such reports and memoranda were concerned with technical and business matters, not political ones.

How German *Wurst* Changed its Citizenship

Novelties were not restricted to the chocolate and confectionary industries. The newly established meat industry showed its concern for novelties in the 1935 report of the Central Meat Administration of the Ministry of Food Industry. The chairman of the meeting, Comrade Konnikov, informed the audience that the selection of Soviet sausages had greatly increased during the past three years: in 1933 the industry turned out only seventeen types, but in 1934 there were forty-seven and the target for 1936 was 116. While the majority of production in the past had consisted almost exclusively of second- or third-rate sausages, now first-grade sausages dominated production.[48] As Konnikov could proudly declare 'Comrade Mikoyan was right in saying that German sausages had become Soviet sausages; they had changed their citizenship.'[49]

The increasing product variety of Soviet meat factories also revolutionized meat and food shops. All Soviet shops were now divided into four classes. Each class had its own minimum product quotient that it was meant to keep in continual supply. Only five shops in the entire country belonged to the first category, two in both Moscow and Leningrad and one in Kiev. According to regulations, their counters should regularly stock at least seventy-nine different types of sausages and *Wurst* including twelve types of smoked meat products like salami, beer *Wurst*, smoked tongue, ham, bacon and so on. The second category consisted of the remaining shops in Moscow and Leningrad and some shops in other bigger cities. The obligatory product minimum in the third category shops was still as high as fifteen.[50] The requirements of the fourth class were more modest. The shops belonging to this class were expected to have only a couple of varieties of sausage on sale.

The quest for higher quality was one of the constant issues recorded in the reports of the meat industry. As everyone admitted, this goal was by no means easily achievable. The reports are filled with complaints about unqualified workers who did not follow instructions and caused disturbances on the production lines. Comrade Saksoganskii, a representative of the Moscow meat factory, complained in a 1936 report that because of the lack of a disciplined work force 'we cannot for the time being prevent unwelcome items from falling into sausage. In our department every day something falls: a piece of glass, iron, a bolt, a nail. They [the workers] seem to think that we do not have enough meat and therefore add iron, no matter how hard we try to convince them that iron is expensive, and there is a lot of meat – nothing seems to help.'[51]

In light of this and similar complaints it is safe to presume that practically all the factories and shops fell well behind their targets concerning quality and variety.

The construction of the modern meat industry started in the Soviet Union in the early 1930s.[52] Again, the years 1933–36 witnessed a rapid growth. On 16 July 1931 the Council of Ministers adopted new targets for the growth of the meat and canned food industry. It was followed by a similar order by the Central Committee of the Communist Party shortly afterwards.[53] Trusts in Leningrad and Moscow were the first to be opened. The Leningrad trust officially started in November 1931. When its sausage plant opened in December 1934 it was proudly declared to be the biggest in Europe. Its machinery was bought from the United States and, as the authorities also proudly declared, it made use of the latest American technology.[54] The giant meat trust in Moscow was opened at about the same time.

The 1935 report on the Moscow meat trust recorded that its sausage department had opened and was fully functional. What was then the world's biggest sausage plant was turning out the impressive amount of 166 tons of sausages per day. In October, a pie department was opened and later one producing *pelmeny* (similar to Italian ravioli).[55] The 1936 report showed an increase in the novelties produced by the sausage department: in December 1935 – forty-three novelties, January 1936 – fifty-three, February 1936 – fifty-five, March – sixty-four, April – ninety-four, May – 100, and September – 114 novelties. Minister Mikoyan personally controlled the recipes for all these sausages and observed closely that they were actually followed.[56] For instance, he supervised the production of special dietetic (or medicinal) sausages such as sausages consisting mainly of animal brains, which were recommended to neurasthenics, and blood sausages, recommended to people suffering shortages of blood.[57]

At the same time, other novelties, like canned smoked tongue, were introduced with plans for a huge output of 1,800,000 cans in 1935.[58] The shops of the central meat administration, Glavmiaso, organized the sale of hot pork chops and shashlik in Moscow in early 1937.[59] In 1936 Mikoyan had given an order to organize the selling of ready-made meat dishes and semi-finished products (*polufabrikaty*), in the bigger cities.[60]

The plan for the quantitative growth of the whole centrally organized meat industry was also impressive. The sausage and smoked meat target for the year

1937 was 300,000 tons, and in 1938, 30,000 tons more.[61] On the other hand, if one keeps in mind the size of the population to be catered for, and the very low previous levels of production, such achievements, even though impressive in themselves, could not have guaranteed a regular supply of sausages and *Wurst* to all the millions of consumers in the Soviet Union.

According to statistics published later by the Soviet historian Dikhtiar, the meat industry in 1934 produced only forty-one different types of sausage and ham, 110 in 1935 and 150 in 1937. It is interesting to compare these figures with those for dairy products, another important field of the food industry. In comparison, the increase in the selection of cheese was rather modest: it went up from ten in 1934 to twenty-nine in 1937. For some reason, the authorities did not seem to care as much about dairy products as they did about meat. Before 1936 there hardly existed any large-scale industrial production of cheese at all in the Soviet Union. In July 1936, however, the Ministry of Food Industry ordered that foreign experience should be actively imported into Soviet dairies. After that several new and previously unfamiliar cheese types were taken into production.[62] Nonetheless, compared with the chocolate industry, both the sausage and cheese industries achieved modest success in terms of variety.[63]

Perfumes: Stalin's Gift to the Ladies

In his novel about the 1930s, the author Anatolii Rybakov tells a story about a female relative of Stalin's wife Nadezhda Alliluieva whom Stalin despised because she smelled of expensive French perfume.[64] By 1935 Stalin obviously had changed his mind about the way a proper Soviet lady should smell. Now strong perfumes were allowed – at least if they were of Soviet make. Stalin's earlier suspicions concerning cosmetics appear to have been shared by many respectable Soviet women. In a 1936 interview in the Soviet women's journal *Rabotnitsa* (Female Worker), Beta G., a young Viennese woman recently employed at the new TEZHE cosmetics department in the Moskva Hotel, complained that many Soviet women still thought it was not proper, indeed bordering on indecent, to pay attention to one's face or body.[65] Such ideals of female decency typical of Russian peasant culture were more commonly heard in public in the late 1920s[66] but clearly they were still prevalent among Soviet citizens in the 1930s.

The total number of cosmetics, different kinds of soaps included, produced in the country in 1938 was reported as having reached 500 different types of products. The Central Administration of perfume production commanded seventy-eight wholesale bases, 108 shops and sixty-two stalls. Moscow had twelve shops and thirteen stalls, Leningrad eighteen shops and six stalls.[67] The Institute of Cosmetics and Hygiene in Moscow, with five branches in the 'provinces', com-

Figure 10   Workers at the no. 1 perfume shop at Tiflis, Georgia inspecting perfumes on sale on 1 May 1938. (Source: RGAKFD)

pleted the picture. According to the 1938 annual report, the industry was characterized by a huge demand for cosmetics. The authors of the report interpreted this demand for cosmetics as evidence of the increasing material well-being of people and increasing cultural standards.

The development of the cosmetics industry can be understood through an examination of one single trust, TEZHE, which operated a near total monopoly in the field. It was the main Soviet manufacturer of soap, perfume and other products of personal hygiene. This state trust, which consisted of several production units, had been founded in 1921 and reorganized in October 1934 after which it functioned under the Ministry of Food Industry. Molotov's wife, Zhemchuzhina, the director of one of TEZHE's perfume and soap factories and later Deputy Minister of Food Industry, became its first director in 1934. In addition to soap and perfume, TEZHE produced toothpaste, candles, washing powder and other products.[68] It became a well-known trademark widely advertised in the press. There was even a slightly ironic popular rhyme (*chastushka*) attached to it:

On the eyes – TEZHE
On the cheeks – TEZHE
On the lips – TEZHE
But to kiss – nowhere

The 1934 TEZHE annual reports reference the seventeenth Party Congress that gave impetus to the development of perfumes and other cosmetics. Much attention was paid to the development of higher quality toilet (face) soaps.[69] As we have seen in relation to other goods, the emphasis on higher quality for soaps and personal hygiene products was initially dramatic. According to its 1933 annual report, the Moscow cosmetics factory Svoboda had been ordered to produce exclusively cheaper, lower quality soaps which included clay as an ingredient. The push for quantity at the expense of quality, which was in line with other products such as wine, contributed to official campaigns to improve the hygienic conditions of work and home, one of the main issues in the early 1930s. The industry shifted in 1934 when Svoboda was ordered to produce only higher quality soaps and to increase drastically its product variety. A hectic search for new products and a re-adaptation of old ones started immediately. Naturally this was accompanied by huge technical challenges.[70]

Some major improvements were, however, already noticeable by the end of the year. Quality soaps increased from about a quarter to over half of the total of soap production. By the end of the year, the factory was already producing 100 different types of products compared with only four or six in 1933. Among these novelties were brands such as Otvet gruzinskomu komsomolu (Answer to the Georgian Komsomol), Geroi Severa (The hero of the North), Stratostat, Pobeda kolkhoza (The victory of the kolkhoz) and Belomorkanal (White Sea Canal).

Perfume manufacturing underwent a similar process. Novelties, including such popular and well-known brands as Magnolia, Karmen, Kamelia, Novaia zaria, and the famous Krasnaia Moskva (Red Moscow) were first produced in 1934, and many remained available until the end of the Soviet Union. At the end of the 1934, TEZHE had seventy-six perfume shops throughout the country. In addition to TEZHE shops new special exemplary shops opened in Moscow, Leningrad and Rostov.[71]

The annual reports for Novaia zaria, another Moscow-based cosmetics factory, show that production was doubled from 1932 to 1935. Once again, the main emphasis was on quality and diversity. The declared goal was to reach international standards on high quality goods.[72] The factory introduced fifteen new perfumes, ten new eau de colognes, eleven new powders and nine new surprise (gift) collections in 1935. Among the new perfumes were brands like Krasnaia zvezda (Red Star), V Vozduhe (In the air), Lavanda, Krasnaia roza (Red Rose), Krymskaia fialka (Crimean Violet) and the firm brand TEZHE.[73] The names were thus a clever combination of classical romantic ones, like Crimean Violet or Red Rose, with new ones, either referring to contemporary issues or extraordinary accomplishments. Perfume names might mark the achievement of Soviet heroes, such as the flight pilots who had broken new records.

By 1939, however, the factory was already facing serious problems and could not fulfil its production targets in many product lines, including perfume and cosmetics. Among the reasons mentioned in the annual report were the usual ones – a lack of imported raw materials and adequate bottles.[74] Even under these conditions, the factory undertook to introduce ten new products. This time focused almost exclusively on expensive gift collections with such names as Exhibitional, 22nd anniversary of the Great October, VSHB (The All-Union Exhibition of Agriculture), and The 8th of March (to commemorate International Women's Day).[75]

To combat the lack of raw materials, the government attempted to increase domestic cultivation of the main epheric plants essential to the industry. In an attempt to surpass international standards, there was a newly found focus on creating domestic raw materials and honing crafstmanship.[76] All raw materials could not, however, be cultivated in the USSR, at least not in large enough quantities. Therefore, the import of etheric oils rapidly increased from year to year during the second half of the 1930s. It increased in four years from 6,100 tons (in 1934) to 121,000 tons (in 1937).[77] The fact that the government spent its limited and highly valued reserves of foreign currency to buy raw materials to bolster the cosmetics industry is highly illuminating. This expenditure clearly indicates the value that the leaders of the USSR placed on perfume and cosmetics.

In addition to valuable raw materials, adequate boxes, packaging and bottles were another major problem of production. In the case of the cosmetics industry, such supplies were even more crucial than in the case of chocolate and candies. Following traditional standards, perfume would typically be sold in small, delicate bottles, usually specially designed and often made of crystal glass. The Moscow Crystal Factory was the only supplier in the country of such containers. During the 1930s this factory was occupied solely with the production of perfume bottles for TEZHE factories, Svoboda and Novaia zaria, among others. Quality, naturally, was an issue. In 1934, TEZHE suggested that the factory start producing fourteen new, more beautiful crystal bottles, as well as bottles with crystal stoppers, an innovation taken from foreign examples. By the following year, these new items were mass produced to satisfy the demand of TEZHE although they slowed down the quantitative rise of production to some extent because of the higher labour input required.[78] Further innovations followed, including technically challenging screw tops or finely grinded stoppers. Until 1939, which brought about the introduction of new imported machines, the crystal was made by hand. As a result of mechanization production nearly doubled in 1939 alone.[79]

The evolution of the cosmetics industry can be explained in part by the greater emphasis on both personal and workplace hygiene during this period. In many fields of industry and service, the food industry and catering in particular, inexperienced workers from the countryside needed to learn the importance of personal hygiene. Urban living also demanded a greater attention to personal cleanliness. Soviet men and women were encouraged to pay more attention to, and spend more money on, their personal appearance. The dozens of new cosmetics and rise of cosmetic shops appealed largely to the female population. As the authorities now acknowledged, altering the look of one's face or one's scent was an endeavour that women relished. At the same time, they recognized a woman's right to a more individualist expression of her personality.

Patéfons and Bicycles to the Industrial and *Kolkhoz* Workers

One of the most oft-mentioned items of technical consumption in the pre-war years, of which the Soviet authorities were evidently very proud, was the portable Soviet-made and hand-operated gramophone, the *patéfon*. It is difficult to imagine a better symbol of the new 'joyous' life. Such gramophones and the records that could be played on them were widely dispersed and available in the Soviet Union of the 1930s, witnessed both by production figures and reminiscences of common people. Old inhabitants of Leningrad remember gramophones belonging to many households in the late 1930s; if they or their own families did not have one they could, at least, listen to gramophone records at some friends', relatives' or neighbours.'[80]

Together with such 'durables' as radios, bicycles and all kinds of musical instruments the *patéfon* was available in both cities and the countryside. An inventory of 'commodities of culture' (*Kulttovary*) conducted among 7,138 young industrial workers in nine big cities (Moscow, Leningrad, Kharkov, Dnepropetrovsk, Donbas, Ivanov, Orekhov and Sverdlovsk) in 1936 revealed that such consumer goods could already be found, but that most of them were still relatively rare even among this avant-garde of industrial youth (see Table 4). All these types of commodities were more common among men than women.

Skis and skates belonged to the list of the items (*Kulttovary*) that a cultured Soviet worker should own and they were, together with radios and musical instruments, the most common and popular goods. Even though comparable data of their ownership is not available from later years of the 1930s one can, from their rapidly increasing production and sales figures (see Table 5), safely draw the conclusion that they remained popular.

These figures convincingly show that most of these items, with the possible exception of watches and sewing machines, were readily available after the mid-

Table 4 The ownership of cultural goods among young industrial workers (per cent) in the big cities of the Soviet Union in 1936.[81]

	Men	Women
Radio receivers	20.2	17.0
Patéfons and gramophones	5.3	4.6
Guitars, mandolines and *Balalaikas*	23.9	17.8
Accordions	4.6	1.7
Other musical instruments	3.0	1.2
Cameras	4.8	1.5
Bicycles	8.0	2.0
Skis	21.5	13.6
Skates	29.5	19.8
Chessboards	14.3	5.4

Table 5 The purchases of some main items of mass consumption in the Soviet Union in 1932 and 1937.[82]

	1932	1937
Watches and clocks	3 100 000	3 400 000
(sold in rural shops)	1 950 000	2 150 000
Sewing machines	319 000	510 000
(in rural shops)	0	80 000
Radios	29 000	195 000
(in rural shops)	0	75 000
Cameras	30 000	353 000
(in rural shops)	2 000	21 000
Patéfons	58 000	675 000
(in rural shops)	4 000	202 000
Bicycles	112 000	500 000
(in rural shops)	0	247 000

1930s. The selling of radios was not promoted as eagerly as, say, that of *patéfons*. At the end of the 1930s private radios which could be tuned to any radio station had to be registered, and once the war broke out they were all confiscated by the state. Shortly before the war, at least some of these goods, such as *patéfons*, bicycles and cameras were produced in such great quantities that they could, in

Figure 11   Customers buying patéfons *and gramophone records at Kishinev, Moldavia, March 1941. (Source: RGAKFD)*

principle, have been gradually transformed from rare luxuries of privileged consumption into items of everyday consumption.

The authorities were equally, and almost as naively, enthusiastic about the ever-increasing production figures of these items as they were about various kinds of luxurious food products. There was, however, one main difference in the expectations and demands put on such light industry. There was no similar expectation of variety. Reports speak only of gramophones and bicycles in general; no makes, models or designs are mentioned. Different models of bicycles were, for instance, available to children and women but otherwise the Soviet consumer did not have any choice. There was just one Soviet bicycle, one *patéfon*, one guitar. A natural explanation would be that whereas it was technically and economically easy to produce tens or even hundreds of different types of candies, it would have been considerably more expensive and time-consuming to construct separate production lines for different types of bicycle. It is interesting, however, to notice that the plans and reports do not record any such desire for variety or express any demand either. Any Soviet consumer who was lucky enough to buy a bicycle or a *patéfon* appeared to be satisfied. In the mid-1930s he or she did not have to show his or her individuality, or cultured taste, in any other more complicated way. The lucky owner of a gramophone could, anyhow, freely choose from among a great variety of recordings of all kinds of music.

Gramophones, radios, musical instruments, guitars, *balalaikas* and accordions were in many ways ideal Soviet products of the time. By the late 1930s it became almost obligatory for a good Soviet citizen to enjoy music. Gramophones in particular were highly appreciated *kulttovary*. If life had become merrier, as promised by Stalin, what better proof could there be than the sight of a gramophone on the table of a *kolkhoz* hut or in the summer garden of a *dacha,* with old and young gathered around it in a joyous mood. They could listen and dance to the accompaniment of the latest Soviet *schlagers*, popular songs like 'Katiusha', the big hit of 1939, or to the celebrated Liuba Orlova singing her extremely popular melodies from the film musicals *Merry Boys* or *Volga, Volga*. In addition, gramophones and gramophone records were technical innovations that had only recently, in the late 1920s before the onset of the Great Depression, made their victorious entrance into the lives of the people living in the 'advanced capitalist countries.'[83] By producing and providing Soviet citizens with gramophones and records, the Soviet government could boast of – if not being ahead of the times – at least closely following the latest achievements of technically more developed nations. In 1939 the impressive number of 60 million records was sold in the country.[84]

The gramophone industry boomed almost as spectacularly as many other consumer goods industries discussed previously. This rapid development started in 1933 and 1934, but, as we have seen before, plans had to be adjusted more realistically by 1936–37. On 17 September 1937, the Ministry of Machine Building Industry issued an order, signed by the Minister himself, Comrade Mezhlauk, concerning the production figures of gramophones and records.[85] The Ministry was deeply worried since the previous plans had not been fulfilled. In addition to detailed technical instructions and plans for the construction of new production units and the delivery of raw materials, the order included the following product targets for the last quarter of 1937: 230,000 *patéfons*, 22 million records, and 400 million needles. The figure for needles is interesting because it indicates, if we think that a needle could be used to play a record only a few times, that each Soviet citizen could have, on average, played a couple of records during the last three months of 1937. The new, adjusted plan for 1938 looked even more impressive as can be seen in Table 6.

In 1933, the first step in the gramophone industry was taken. In a resolution by the Council of Ministers, a special gramophone trust was founded – until then the production had taken place under the Ministry of Heavy (sic!) Industry. The production figure for 1933 was announced to be 155 thousand gramophones. In this first plan the target for the year 1937 was 1.5 million, that is almost half a million more than according to the new adjusted plan of 1937. The original 1933 plan for records, however, was much more modest. Both the need for and the capacity of the production of records had been seriously underestimated in 1933, in particular in relation to the number of gramophones with which these records were supposed to be played.

Table 6 The planned production of gramophones, gramophone records and needles in 1938.

Vladimir gramophone factory	300 000 *patéfons* and 2.5 billion needles
Kolomenskii gramophone factory	300 000 *patéfons*
Leningrad gramophone factory	360 000 *patéfons*
Noginsk gramophone record factory	70 million records
Andreevskii gramophone record factory	20 million records

Table 7 The production plan for gramophone records 1933–37.[87]

1933	3	million records
1934	7	" "
1935	15	" "
1936	25	" "
1937	40	" "

The same resolution paid special attention to the artistic quality of these records: it was deemed necessary to promote only eminent artists and to prioritize the music of the Soviet Union. A special artistic council was created to control and promote the realization of such goals in future gramophone recordings.[88] This was a step typical of the cultural politics of the time: all cultural enterprises were becoming more tightly regulated from the center.

As usual in the planned economy of the Soviet Union, these impressive production figures tell only half the story. As many reports and letters of complaint prove, even though *patéfons* were widely available in the late 1930s, their quality was poor and spare parts often impossible to get. The following letter addressed to *Sovetskii patefon*, the newsletter of the Leningrad Gramophone Factory, expressed typical worries. It was written by an agronomist Tugashev working in the autonomous Soviet Tartar Republic. The letter began with an explanation of why he had bought a *patéfon*. He explained that he spent a lot of time alone in the village after work: 'In order to spend my time a bit merrier during my dinner or in the evening I bought a *patéfon*. After a week's play its spring broke. I had it repaired, and it broke again. During one month it was repaired eight times. After the tenth time I threw it away; spare parts are nowhere to be had.'[89]

Another problem was, paradoxically, caused by the new quality regulations introduced in 1934. As Comrade Likhov wrote in *Sovetskaia torgovlia* 'we do not have gramophone needles [they were badly needed] in our department store while other shops have them.' The reason for this situation was simple and in many ways typical: the central department store was allowed to sell only 'high quality products' but the needles which would have qualified were not produced in the country.[90]

Confiscated Soviet Watches and Jewelry

The history of Soviet watches, clocks and jewelry has been different from that of many other consumer goods. They were produced in extremely restricted quantities before the late 1930s, yet they were available in significant quantities even before the beginning of their actual industrial production in the Soviet Union. Before their official production, many retail and repair shops bought or otherwise received old watches, repaired them and resold them; in the 1930s a major proportion of all the watches sold in the country were second-hand. The same was true of jewelry and other gold and silver valuables. Members of the former upper classes, as well as people who were labelled 'collaborators', had their property confiscated and political and economic rights denied. Their only means of survival was selling off family valuables they had managed to preserve. In practice, this meant that goods such as watches and jewelry were redistributed into the hands of the new Soviet elite or well-to-do 'non-party Bolsheviks'.

The trade and production of jewelry and watches was reorganized in 1936 through the creation of a new centralized unit of trade. In 1937–38, there were approximately 100 jewelry shops in the Soviet Union (in eighty-one cities). In the Urals and Siberia they were, however, said to be relatively rare. The biggest part of the annual turnover of the unit consisted of restored second-hand goods, watches in particular. In addition to jewelry, clocks and watches, it bought and sold typewriters. As late as 1937, a quarter of its sales consisted of second-hand watches and clocks, and about one tenth of gold and silver each. Most of the restored clocks and watches had originally been imported from abroad.[91] However, for the first time in 1938 the share of Soviet-made, new watches exceeded second-hand sales.[92] A big exhibition of jewelry was planned in Moscow for 1939. Active advertising to promote the sale of jewelry was also planned during the final years before the outbreak of the war.

In a conversation with the *kolkhozniks* from the Odessa region in 1935, Stalin had promised that the production of 'light' industry would triple during the Second Five-Year Plan or until 1937. As the above discussion has shown, this was not a totally empty promise. Serious efforts were made. Most of the targets were, however, totally unrealistic. They could not have been reached even under the most favourable conditions. To admit this would have opened the doors to a fundamental self-critique inside the Party, which was not allowed. Many were convinced that the only hindrance to such plans was the threat from traitors and class enemies, perceived to be active throughout the country. For instance, as early as 1933 the polygraphic industry should have turned out 700 million exercise books but during the first nine months of the year it had only produced 335 million. 'How could this be explained in any other way than by criminal negligence of the directives of the Party', Minister Lebedev stated in his annual report of the achievements of 'light' industry.[93]

5

Soviet Novelties and their Advertising

The Problem of Authentic Soviet Novelties

Before the Revolution and during the NEP period of the mid-1920s, luxury goods such as perfume and chocolate were often manufactured in small private factories and workshops. These private factories and workshops were all closed down by the end of the 1920s. In the mid-1930s, such goods were actively reinvented, after a period of absence, with the help of old masters and skilled workers who were now suddenly in great demand. Government planning organizations were well aware of this skills shortage. Many factories proudly announced that they had now mobilized their senior workers to recall and memorize what they had produced in the earlier period in order to rediscover the old quality products. As the Leningrad journal *Golos konfetchika* (The Voice of the Confectionery Worker) reported 'the old workers', *caramelshchiki*, have responded enthusiastically to the call of the governing board of the factory and have produced examples of over 30 new specialties with all types of consistency and form. . . The most interesting examples are caramels with liqueur, lozenges (*monpansie*) with special fillings and a medicinal *monpansie*.'[1]

Not everyone, however, was as enthusiastic about these newly discovered old consumer goods. Many complained that rediscovering old products was not the proper way to develop the new luxury economy. What was needed was the creation of genuine 'Soviet novelties', preferably of a higher technical standard that would demonstrate the advancement of Soviet engineering. Such home-grown novelties would answer the new demands of Soviet buyers better than the many cheap copies of the old luxury. Skeptics thought that the production of Soviet kitsch was only motivated by necessity and a sign of backwardness. It was not what the Soviet consumer really needed and deserved. Such opinions were common among many Soviet trade specialists. For instance, in an article by Perepeletskii from the Central administration of trade published in 1936 in the journal *Organizatsiia i tekhnika sovetskoi torgovli*[2] the author paid attention to the fact that 'it is forgotten that we should create new Soviet goods which should satisfy the taste of different categories of new buyers.' After this declaration he presented a long list of examples:

The chocolate industry is producing many types of chocolate but, in most cases, they are only new by name. Bakeries only copy the old pre-war variety. Dairies have succeeded only in producing some new types of sweet cream cheese. Sausage factories have not so far produced any new products at all and they also continue to produce products with old names that are not understandable to the buyer: Langerskie, Mortadella, Bologne. The Bolshevik chocolate factory recently announced the release of new cakes with pompous names such as Othello, Windsor, Festival and Manon. Specialists have already expressed doubts that, in fact, these novelties only repeat what has already existed. Breweries have chosen an even easier way: they have just replaced foreign names with Russian ones: Pilzen has become Moscow, Munich – Ukraine. The renaming is welcome but it has nothing to do with the widening of variety as such.

The only truly new products the author felt worthy of mention were related to the development of freezers in the food industry: frozen *pelmeni,* Eskimo and Paipsiki ice creams. Despite their admirable uniqueness, even these ice creams were not entirely satisfactory to the author because of their strange foreign names. In conclusion, Perepeletskii strongly recommended – not surprisingly for a representative of trade – that one should turn for advice to the trade specialists.

It was typical of the situation in the 1930s that the shopkeepers or specialists working in the new big department stores were often highly critical of the products they received and were supposed to sell. This was not simply an issue of poor quality. Given their close connection to the consumer, they felt that they were better informed of the needs of the population and could therefore better judge the merchandise. As a typical representative of Soviet trade, Perepeletskii claimed that 'trade workers can give much valuable advice about new varieties since they know the taste and demands of their buyer. This would be much more useful than reminiscing about old product names.'[3]

In the same trade journal, *Organizatsiia i tekhnika sovetskoi torgovli*, a report[4] was published on a Moscow fashion show in the Central Department Store, which opened on 12 December 1936. Its author, Mikulina, was even more critical than Perepeletskii and did not spare words in criticizing the goods exhibited. After admitting that artistically the display itself was at the level of Western European standards, she listed all the essential goods and items that were missing from the exhibition:

In every European shop a pair of boots is sold accompanied with a shoe horn to put on the shoes and a hook to fasten the buttons. You could buy the whole department of the central *univermag* [department store] and could not find a single shoe horn. Our industry does not produce them at all. The exhibition has a special corner for 'small things.' There are rotating displays for *patéfons*, pillows for divans, some lampshades, and artificial flowers. But buttons, hooks and pushpins have all been forgotten. Equally forgotten are important details of costume like gloves. Only the Kharkov factory demonstrated two models of gloves, and, I must say, both were rather poor. Little attention has been paid in the workshops to ladies' collars, breast frills, scarves, and three-cornered scarves.'[5]

In the author's opinion, other department stores had paid even less attention to such small, but important, details of dress. As the author suggests in the above list, the main problem for Soviet trade and industry was not the lack of any genuine novelties but the lack of the most basic and conventional items of dress, all of which would have been commonplace in any Western department store for many years. The only real 'Soviet innovation' – a folded pocket umbrella – was praiseworthy, but taken alone did not change the overall depressing picture: 'The head of the [Leningrad] workshop of umbrellas, Comrade Perl, has developed a folded pocket umbrella, which has been patented at the commission of inventions at STO with the number 5993. This very delicate, carefully finished umbrella can be folded to fit into an ordinary ladies' bag. But this is all that there is!'[6]

At a 1935 meeting of directors representing Soviet department stores from throughout the country, one of the directors reported that his department store had received sixty men's suits of imported wool and they had been taken by surprise by the crowd that they had drawn: They were sold at the huge price of 1,000 roubles each and still everyone said, 'give it to me.' This was in stark contrast to the experience of the department store director who exclaimed that no one was willing to buy common suits of domestic make.[7]

At the same meeting, many technical, administrative and economic problems of trade were discussed quite openly. The Trade Minister, Veitser, admitted that no one had tackled many important areas of consumption, which were necessary in any individual household:

> No one bothers about small items of consumption like haberdasher's goods, buttons, manchette buttons, clothes hangers, etc. In any case this is quite unavoidable because no one is producing them. They must be made well and be cheap. There is no place to buy manicure (nail) scissors. Small booklets, all things from perfume [sic!] to small notebooks – all this must be introduced. Our *univermag* has a character of luxury.

One of the participants added the following items to Veitser's list of everyday household utensils: brushes, brooms and bowls or vessels – 'all Moscow will queue for them.'[8] Paradoxically and characteristically, these eminent Soviet directors of department stores considered such items, many of which would have been regarded by Western consumers as the most basic necessities to be luxury goods.

The Party and government were acutely concerned with the production and promotion of Soviet novelties. The results were welcomed with varying degrees of enthusiasm by the customers and specialists alike. Many felt that this obsession with novelties was a red herring – it was not truly developing the Soviet culture of consumption when the goods that people really needed were being ignored. Some eagerly looked to the most advanced capitalist countries for inspiration on consumer goods. In the popular weekly journal *Ogoniek* (the Soviet version of *Life* magazine) one could, for instance, in a 1937 issue, find a full-page advertisement dedicated to ketchup. Ketchup was proclaimed to be a great delicacy that one could find on every kitchen table in America.[9] Alongside the cheap imitations of previous luxury one could thus also see examples of the new capitalist mass culture. The new American way of life – with jazz music, the foxtrot, the tango and film musicals, as well as ketchup, hamburgers and cornflakes – was making its first cautious steps into the lives of Soviet citizens. Before the Cold War the 'American way of life' could still be openly discussed and admired. There was nothing wrong with the American culture of consumption as such. If only the capitalist exploitation of the wage earners in the process of its production was abolished, many of its features could easily and with great success be transferred to a socialist society.

The Three Sources of Novelties

In the 1930s, Soviet authorities were obsessed with the quest for novelties. Novelties were felt to be in great demand in every field of production, trade and service. As the French author André Gide observed during his visit to the USSR in 1936, Soviet people were much occupied with and very enthusiastic about any such novelties: 'For that matter people of the USSR seem to be delighted with any novelties that are offered to them, even those which to our Western eyes are frightful.'[10]

In principle, whenever a new consumer good was 'invented' in the Soviet Union it had to be available to everyone almost immediately, at least during the ongoing Five-Year Plan. Production was always planned on a mass scale from the very beginning. Once the production of some item was accepted in the annual plan, possible lack of demand had little effect on production. In this way, there was no 'natural' process of selection in consumption. The Soviet authorities were aware of this problem and they even experimented with some methods of market research, with varying degrees of success.

The Soviet planners and engineers considered three possible sources for the creation of novelties. First, one could reinvent an old product, as we have seen. Old, experienced workers were encouraged to come forward with suggestions about which items should be taken into production again. Many luxuries of the food industry are good examples of this. A wide variety of chocolates, cakes and biscuits, wines and champagne, as well as many fish products, caviar included, are

Figure 12   *'A nourishing, tasty and cheap dish.' An advertisement for canned maize,*
Ogoniek *16/17, 20 June 1937.*

examples of such 'traditional' novelties. Perfumes and other cosmetics could also be mentioned here. They were now produced on a mass scale with new industrial methods, but the products themselves had existed in the past.

The second possibility was to import new models from abroad. One could copy or simply steal foreign models. There was much to be learned from the example of the advanced capitalist countries in the field of consumer goods, as the official slogan went. The import and imitation practice was widespread, whereas the direct import of consumer goods en masse was almost non-existent in the 1930s. Some raw materials of the food industry, which could not possibly be cultivated in the Soviet Union, had to be imported, such as cocoa beans for chocolate and etheric oils for the cosmetics industry. At times small shipments of exotic, southern fruits, oranges and bananas, were also imported but these were such rare occasions that they were reported as major news in All-Union newspapers. In the spring of 1936 *Pravda* reported, for instance, about a shipment of oranges on its way to Murmansk destined for the Leningrad shops.[11]

It was the explicit purpose of the Party and the government to produce as much as possible domestically; the country was supposed to be self-reliant, economically autocratic. But one could learn from experience and follow the example of others, totally free of charge. One had to take lessons from the industrially and economically more advanced countries. Among the specialists there was no doubt that machines and technologies, as well as prototypes and models, could be freely adopted into the socialist economy and industry. All things promoting the advancement of standardized and efficient mass production and consumption were warmly welcomed in the Soviet Union. It was a generally shared belief that they would even better fit into the context of a socialist society than in private capitalism where, as the Marxist-Leninist doctrine argued, the private ownership of the means of production often was a hindrance to the effective use of large-scale technology. And if this was true of modern production technology in general why could not one just as well imitate Western models of consumer goods or foodstuffs?

The third method of creating new novelties was acknowledged to be the most demanding and difficult. One could invent from scratch genuinely new, authentic 'Soviet' products. The invention of such products was actively encouraged. The new Soviet way of life needed its own unique material objects that could adequately express both the objects' and society's novel character. As contemporaries often complained, such novelties were virtually impossible to create anew. To combat this challenge, producers would alter the names, labels or packaging of goods, but inside the wrapping one often found the same old thing, or even worse, an inferior copy of an older product. When pressed, the authorities themselves struggled to find new Soviet inventions. A folded pocket umbrella and thermos plate, are among the few such items mentioned. As the trade specialists admitted, the thermos plate was a 'commercial failure' because it was very difficult to sell. There were some real Soviet inventions, or inventive modifications of foreign models, created to make the life of the Soviet citizens happier and more comfortable, like electric *samovars*, rotating flower stands and drinks dispensers. Meanwhile, for lack of better alternatives, the process of imitation continued rapidly and the adoption of Western models of consumption from the capitalist countries was not considered seriously problematic.

The development of services and trade differed slightly from that of production. Here again, much was copied from abroad or from pre-Revolutionary Russia. Small private shops were, however, still the predominant form of trade and service in other countries. They did not fit well into the Soviet ideal of centralized and highly standardized large-scale merchandising. Nor could one manage to establish a complete net of trade organizations throughout the country overnight. Therefore, new shops, department stores and ateliers were opened only in the largest cities. Their purpose was to act as concrete models and examples to the less fortunate rural or small town shops and stores and also to act as a kind of showcase to the whole Soviet population. The windows said: this is how your life will look in the near future; this is what you will get in a year or two. It goes without saying that such propagandistic gestures had their risks. Why was life in Moscow better than in a rural village? Why could the workers of the local factory not order their dresses from a fashion atelier of their own? What if the promises concerning the future could not be kept after all?

'There is a lot to be Learned from the Advanced Capitalist Countries'

As is well known, the Soviet government made an attempt to learn from the industrial experience of the advanced capitalist countries during the First Five-Year Plan with its huge programmes of industrialization. If necessary – if the building of communism so demanded – industrial espionage, with the willing assistance of European revolutionary workers, was actively promoted.[12] Thousands of foreign industrial experts, engineers and mechanics, as well as experienced workers were encouraged and invited to work in the Soviet Union. Many North Americans with pro-communist and pro-Soviet attitudes, often disappointed with their experiences of the capitalist system during the years of the Great Depression in particular, answered the call from the Soviet Union. According to various estimates in 1932 there were from 20,000 to 40,000 such foreign workers and specialists in the country. The biggest group consisted of Germans, the second biggest of North Americans. Most of them left the country voluntarily after the end of their labour contract, those few who stayed until the years 1937 and 1938 were either repressed or deported from the country.[13]

In the mid-1930s another strategy was adopted and widely practised by the Soviet authorities: delegations of Soviet experts were sent abroad to economically more advanced countries to learn from their methods of work. Mikoyan himself, together with his assistants and many of his directors in the food industry set the example by visiting the United States for two months in the summer of 1936. On his way back from this trip, he visited, together with Frolov-Bagraev of Abrau-Diurso, Champagne in France.

What he and the other comrades most admired in the United States was the high level of organization of work. During their trip through the country they visited hundreds of food factories, trade organizations and restaurants. In addition to ice cream and hamburgers, Mikoyan mentioned milk powder and tomato juice, among other things, as products that he was impressed by. As Mikoyan said, 'we came here to study the most advanced technical achievements to apply them at home. Why invent a bicycle again?'[14]

Probably the most amazing 'present', almost totally forgotten by later generations, that Mikoyan brought home from this trip was the American hamburger. In
the United States, he explained in his report,

> there are machines that make 5,000 steaks an hour. This, of course, makes them cheap. I
> ordered some examples of these machines as well as street roasters. These are constructed
> as follows. A plate of stainless steel is heated either with electricity or gas. All this is fitted
> into a cabin, which is a bit bigger than a guard's stall so that one can stand in it on the
> street. The seller puts the meat on the plate without adding any fat because the hamburger
> steaks have enough fat; no extra oil is needed. The steak is roasted on one side first and
> then turned over – in a couple of minutes it is ready. The same seller has buns. He cuts a
> bun into two, puts the steak in between, adds tomatoes, a slice of salted cucumber or
> mustard, and a hot sandwich is ready. For a busy man it is very convenient. I ordered 22
> such machines, which can make two million steaks a day.

The production of hamburgers started in Moscow and some other places. The
government built kiosks to sell them, but the war stopped further development.[15]
A picture published in *Miasnaia industriia SSSR* in 1941 shows that such kiosks
really were opened, at least in Moscow, shortly before the war. In the photo there
is a man eating a hamburger standing in front of a kiosk with a sign of a hot dog
and a hamburger. Underneath a text announces that by the end of the Third Five-
Year Plan in 1942 the amount of hamburgers produced should have increased by
27 times.[16]

Hamburgers would have been an ideal, 'socialist' solution to mass catering for
the 'busy man' in Soviet cities. Their production fitted in well with the dominant
mode of thinking regarding goods – they were cheap, effective and standardized.
Hamburgers, though, were by no means the only modern industrial food products
imported from the United States in late 1930s. In May 1937 *Pravda* advertised
cornflakes,[17] and, as has already been mentioned, ketchup was also advertised in
Soviet journals.

Mikoyan was not the only one to take advice from the West. This process was
especially active in 1936. According to reports submitted to the Ministry of Trade
after such journeys to the West, the trips often lasted from a few weeks to a couple
of months. The reports show that almost anything, from the smallest and often
rather trivial details to great organizational principles of trade, interested the Soviet
delegates. Many obviously had never before been abroad and never in their lives,
or at least not after the closing of private shops in the late 1920s, seen, for instance,
a real department store, a common restaurant or a commercial food store. The
reports of these trips openly admired all kinds of things that any department store
or food factory manager in Western Europe or the United States would have taken
for granted. This naivety is often quite revealing: it shows, as if looking at an
alternate reflection, what was missing in the USSR.

A director of a jewelry factory, Rakhmalevich reported to Trade Minister, Veitser, about his 'study' trip to Germany and his experiences of German trade.[18] He purchased jewelry to be copied at home and also offered to buy a complete set of machinery to make jewelry from a German firm, which was the main purpose of his trip. He used his time wisely in getting acquainted with German shops and restaurants of various kinds – probably not an altogether unpleasant business trip. In his opinion there were many things to be brought home from Germany. In Germany, for instance, paper cups and plates were widely used; such items were unknown in the Soviet Union at that time. He wrote, 'in Germany ice cream is sold in paper cups. In the same shops it is possible to eat sausages on paper plates. We have to organize immediately within the system of Trade Ministry special shops in which everything is sold on paper plates and in paper cups.'[19] (The Ministry of Domestic Trade was ordered to produce 12 million paper cups by the end of 1936.)[20] Rakhmalevich saw many interesting ways of packaging fruits, haberdashery products and linen products in Germany. Well-designed labels and price tags also made a big impression on him. But window decorations made the greatest impression of all:

> All shop windows are decorated with flowers. In spring, for instance, firms selling clothes, without exception hang in their windows small green trees. In the windows of food stores it is often difficult to say whether there are more products than flowers. I ask for permission, with the help of some pictures I brought with me, to organize a couple of windows like that in Moscow, preferably in the Gastronom no. 1 [former Eliseevskii] and in an exemplary *univermag*.[21]

The sight of numerous colourful street restaurants was also alive in his memory: 'In street restaurants all the chairs are painted in yellow and all tables in red to draw attention.'[22]

These international excursions were not limited to Western Europe or the United States. Comrade Erman, an employee at the Trade Ministry, was sent to Japan at the beginning of 1936. His task was mainly to negotiate new orders of textiles and clothes and to redirect old ones. These clothes were to be sold to the Soviet population through the new system of exemplary department stores. One of the main results of this trip was 'concerning silk or demi-silk products as well as products made out of artificial silk definitely to change orders in the direction of better quality and, in particular, better designs.'[23]

The business trip of the comrades Gumnitskii and Breidov, two prominent representatives of Soviet trade, to the United States, and New York in particular, had a broader range. Gumnitskii was to study American department stores, and Breidov was to study food stores. The largest part of their report to the Trade Minister on 21 November 1936 consisted of a detailed description of the organization and functioning of one of the best-known and biggest department stores in New York, Macy's.[24] Reading the report reveals what was missing in Soviet department stores.

In general, no critical, ideological or political comments can be found in this report. Indeed they are very rarely to be found in any such reports. Occasionally some reports reminded the government of the fact that in the United States or Germany everything was done for profit, while in the USSR this clearly did not factor in the equation. In the USSR, everything was meant to be done in the best interests of the workers and 'toiling masses.' Such considerations, however, did not appear to have any bearing on the practical applicability of any inventions of the capitalist world, whether they concerned work organization, special forms of services or individual products. Neither was America met as a totally alien place. This is evident in Gumnitskii's report from Macy's:

> When we came to America we thought that there were conveyer belts everywhere in the shops. This is not true. Today there is nothing in trade there that we could not adopt quickly here. There is but one thing – thought through, strict organization. . . There, before introducing anything new, they approach the question carefully, experimenting first, calculating, and only then they take it into practice . . . As far as the organization is concerned it fits into any shop.[25]

The main problem with the Soviet system was also quite obvious to these two travellers – probably they had realized it long before their trip even started. It was its excessive centralization:

> There are thousands of people sitting in Glavunivermag [The Central All-union Administration of All the Soviet Department Stores]. Can one really sit in Moscow and direct the whole corporation and know all the needs and peculiarities of all the regions and correctly direct every commodity in relation to the needs and reasons why they are bought? . . . Glavunivermag should be changed into a small department consisting of 5–6–8 people who should have the responsibility of analyzing the work of all *univermags*. Then the system would be properly construed.[26]

The very size of the stores and the seemingly endless variety of products in the United States had understandably made a great impression on Gumnitskii, who was coming from a department store where many of the most elementary items of consumption were still totally unknown. Most of all Gumnitskii was impressed and made detailed notes about the organization of work at Macy's, the effectiveness with which the sales personnel dealt with commodities both on their way in and out of the store. Many of the remarks made by Gumnitskii could obviously still be made concerning any big modern department store. But the detailed report proves that most things were new to him and his colleagues. For instance, at Macy's all male shirts were displayed on open shelves, each size on a separate shelf. The observers paid special attention to the self-service. The shop assistant came to the customer's aid only after a while if he or she seemed to be in need of help, or was not able to make up his or her mind. Where more valuable commodities were concerned the assistant came to help the customer much sooner. Each counter had a cash machine and the salesperson took the money unless the price exceeded five dollars in which case the head of the department took care of the money and returned with the change.[27]

In the opinion of the Soviet specialists, Macy's was not only effective; it tried, above all, to make the customer feel comfortable. It offered all kinds of services: telephones, rest rooms, clubs, barbers, lockers, cloak rooms, a post office, and so forth.[28] The widely practised systems of home deliveries, phone orders and mail order firms were also of great interest to Gumnitskii.

There was much to be learned from Macy's about 'breaking down' new items of purchase too. Each department of the store had a specialist who first inspected the item and gave instructions about it. Then a small portion was put on sale so that the reactions of customers could be studied. Methods of – in this case rather elementary – market research were also applied: for instance youngsters were sent out to Broadway to look at how many people were wearing a certain kind of a cap or a scarf. The main difference compared with the Soviet system was, however, that in the United States the head of each single department at the store bore full responsibility for buying things in. Once accepted, all products entered their career at Macy's ready to be sold, appropriately sorted out or packed, with a price tag and a product declaration giving its size, material and so on. The date of arrival and the duration of stay of every single commodity was also known and well documented.[29]

Gumnitskii drew concrete conclusions from what he had seen at Macy's concerning individual products and product categories – completely in line with the remarks made by the Trade Minister, Veitser, earlier at the meeting of the directors of department stores. He also commented the high standards of housework and individual hygiene he had seen in America:

What is needed in our shops? In the first place we should have kitchen equipment – all that makes the work of a housewife easier, equipment for bathrooms and toilets. In this respect we are very dirty. Why do we not accomplish anything in this respect? Small wooden bowls, which were very common before have disappeared totally from use during recent times. Such things like brushes and brooms. They are all necessities of everyday life and do not demand many raw materials. Referring to objective conditions is no excuse. Things that are needed in wardrobes and closets – we have nothing. Wooden things, like drying constructions or hangers to hang sanitary bandages to dry after washing, kitchen furniture, etc. Equipment for ironing linen and mangling, small electric equipment and so on. All this is sold ordinarily in any shop, in any drug store. Bread toaster, (the speaker shows it!), equipment for cooking and frying, electric heaters, etc. Furniture for summer cottages and camps – once you enter Macy's you find adjustable tables, sunshades you can open and stick into the earth in any place and this way you can find shelter from the sun. . . Then things of personal hygiene, things belonging to ladies' toilet. We bought a few such things.[30]

As if answering Gumnitskii's appeal, in 1937 the Central Department Store in Moscow advertised its special May Day display of outdoor furniture and other equipment for the coming summer in *Pravda*: 'Everything for the summer cottage.'[31]

The other traveller, Breidov, had much less to report about ordinary food stores in America. These were mostly small, family-run general stores that sold practically everything and were not specialized in selling only foodstuffs. They were less impressive and not as attractive for imitation purposes. The Soviet specialists always thought that 'big is beautiful.' As the historian Julie Hessler has pointed out in her study of Soviet trade, the Soviets were obsessed with gigantomanie.[32] Everything that was done on a mass scale and in standardized form also gained their unanimous approval. They liked all methods that helped to rationalize work, housework included. Even Breidov paid attention to the system of home deliveries and to refrigerators which could be found in every shop in America. An interesting form of instructive food advertising with an experimental kitchen located in a food store had also caught his attention: `There were four girls working under the guidance of a well-known chef. They prepared a menu of a three-person meal, for a family of four, etc. The price is from $12 to $18 a week. These menus are printed and delivered to customers. . . Fruits and vegetables are important items in these menus.'[33]

Again in his typical straightforward manner, Breidov suggested that a collection of these exemplary menus covering a whole year, which he had brought back from the United States, could be translated and published as a special cookbook in the Soviet Union. In fact, at the end of 1936 *Pravda* published such menus of model dinners for a family utilizing new industrial, semi-prepared food products.[34] The Soviet officials and directors appear to have had not the slightest idea that such, in this case rather harmless, imitations might be considered infringements of copyright or even commercial espionage in the West!

The popularity of the idea of copying Western models in all fields of industry and trade becomes ideologically understandable from the premise that was commonly accepted by the Soviet politicians and experts. In accord with the Marxist-Leninist doctrine, the time for a socialist revolution was ripe once the productive forces had developed far enough and, in a way, outgrown the capitalist relations of production under which they had developed in the first place. Once the productive forces and relations came in conflict with each other the old relations had to give way to the new socialist ones. In the Soviet Union, on the contrary, the new socialist social relations of production were more advanced than the state of productive forces. In this sense, the authorities, in fact, admitted that the October Revolution had been untimely. But this also meant that one could with great success, as the specialists believed, copy the most advanced technology from the capitalist countries into the more 'socialized' relations of production of Soviet industry and trade. It would, as a matter of fact, fit much better into the new socialist than the old capitalist relations of production, where private property relations slowed down its development and hindered its efficient exploitation.

Soviet Advertising in the 1930s: 'There are many Stakhanovite Workers who are not at all Familiar with our New Products'

The story is horribly tragic. A woman tells radio listeners that her situation is quite terrible. Today is her birthday, and her husband who has recently got into the habit of coming home late because of some presumably important meetings he has to attend, has not returned. The lady would like to know what the meeting is really for – brunettes or blondes? In other words, she suspects her husband of not being faithful to her anymore. As a verification of this suspicion the telephone rings. She lifts the phone and hears a woman's voice, asking whether Vasilii Andreevich is at home. The wife answers that he is not at home, but could she take a message? The female voice answers that she should tell her husband to come to a certain address, everything is ready and waiting for him. The wife is horrified. Where does her husband plan to go on her birthday? The female voice leaves an address and a phone number.

   The husband arrives home. The wife tells him everything; we witness a scene of jealousy. She begins to blame him: how is it possible, it was a woman's voice and she even asked him to call back. The number is B-1-2461. The husband is astonished. What is this all about; somehow the number rings a bell. In the end it is revealed that this is the number of a newly opened office of home deliveries on Piatnitskii Street.

The moral of this story is rather dubious. Even though proven not guilty of adultery, the husband had almost totally neglected his wife's birthday by forgetting that he had ordered a birthday present through such an office.

   This short story or suggested film manuscript was one of several similar examples discussed at a meeting concerning the development of Soviet advertising at the office of Khlopliankin, the Deputy Minister, with cultural workers and workers of the press on 11 March 1936.[35] As the storyteller emphasized, the main thrust of the advertisement was that the phone number of the office was repeated several times during the episode so that all the listeners were sure to remember it by heart:

The whole scene has a happy ending. The wife assures us that she will no longer show such signs of jealousy, and they both agree that they will always visit this shop which lies on Piatnitskii Street, at such and such a number, which has an office for home orders, the number of which is such and such. Both the address and the phone number are repeated time and time again.[36]

A detailed stenograph of the proceedings of this meeting has been preserved in the archives. It was one of a series of meetings organized in 1936 to discuss the development of Soviet advertising. At this meeting, as Khlopliankin emphasized, many prominent artists, journalists and filmmakers (the famous Soviet painter Deineka among others) were present. The question of film ads was one of the main topics discussed, inspiring those present to invent many fantastic stories to be used in such ads.

It becomes evident from the context that most types of advertising, and movies in particular, were at this time totally unknown in the Soviet Union. Most partici-pators, at least of the younger generation, did not have any personal experiences of advertising at all. Reference is occasionally made to the old pre-Revolutionary times, or the NEP years, or even to what had been seen on travels abroad, in Paris or London 'where every square is lined up with numerous neon ads.' It is therefore hardly surprising that reading the protocol now one gets often a naive but always enthusiastic impression. No one actually doubted the usefulness and even necessity of advertising Soviet trade. Even though many details were hotly debated, no overall critical voices were recorded. Advertising was seen as a necessary means of cultivating the Soviet consumer now supposed to be living under conditions of increasing abundance and choice.

Practically all possible forms of advertising were discussed: from movies to ads in journals and newspapers, from leaflets to live performances on metro wagons, from neon lights to billboards, from radio ads played in between music – or during the pause of a performance of the opera *Evgenii Onegin* – to personal letters sent to the homes of selected customers, from decorated shop windows to ads on buses and trams, and so on. The only forms of advertising, in addition to more direct forms of advertising inside shops, that the participators had at least some personal experience of were advertisements – or announcements, as they were called – published in newspapers and journals. The publication of such advertisements seems to have started in earnest in 1935–36, a further indication of the importance of these years in the development of the 'commercial consumer culture' of the USSR. For instance, *Pravda* and *Izvestiia* started publishing commercial advertise-ments then. Before that many reports had been published on the production and appearance of Soviet novelties but these were not real advertisements, rather short news reports in the daily papers. In 1936 the first regular advertisements of consumer goods started to appear in newspapers and journals all over the country.

These advertised either special shops or restaurants in Moscow or new products, usually from the food or textiles industries.

The following are some typical examples of such ads. The Gastronom no. 1 (former Eliseevskii in the centre of Moscow) announced that it was taking orders by telegram or by mail.[37] The Moscow trust of restaurants was offering its services in organizing parties and evenings. Orders could be made by telephone, no. B 1-64-96. It could offer 'the best cooks, wine, snacks and jazz!'[38] The products advertised in 1936 included Georgian tea, Muscat wine, Dutch gin, toys, fur coats, all kinds of textiles and clothes as well as shoes, small outboard motors, eye glasses and monocles, new, high quality toilet soap, and various vegetarian canned foods. All kinds of dietetic foodstuffs as well as canteens serving them were also regularly informing their potential customers about their services. On 5 May 1937 Soviet-made cornflakes were introduced to the newspaper readers and to their potential customers.

The trade journal of the Soviet food industry started publishing ads in 1936. It is, however, more informative to follow the development of advertising in the most popular monthly journal in the Soviet Union, *Ogoniek*. Its last page or the back cover was in most issues reserved for ads. The earliest advertisements were typically about patent medicines which often had interesting names such as Professor Pelue's Spermin or Spermokrin. Such medicines were recommended as remedies to all kinds of illnesses from blood shortage and lack of energy to arteriosclerosis and neurasthenia. On 5 August 1934 it was announced that contraceptives were on sale in all pharmacies of the country.[39] These early Soviet ads were rather simple in terms of design. They usually presented a drawing of the product in question (say, a bottle of medicine), its name and a lengthy text describing the use, effects as well as availability of the product. By the year 1937 both the products advertised and the style of advertising had already radically changed. These new advertisements, which were published in almost every issue of the journal, tended to be bigger in size, often taking up half a page or a full page. The text was often very short, written in big, clearly visible letters, and pictures dominated. Most of these ads had skilful drawings presenting happily smiling housewives or their children enjoying the new products (marmalade, candies, a bottle of soya Kabul or canned maize) or stylish well-clothed men and women (advertising fur coats, dresses, or new Intourist hotels). In some cases no potential consumers were visible but even then the products were artistically portrayed in the foreground together with other items that emphasized their special qualities, for instance a couple of bottles of the eau de cologne The rose of the Crimean with a picture of a beautiful rose, or a can of crabs from Kamchatka with a plate full of crabs, egg halves, salad leaves and lemon slices. Some advertisements simply made the reader familiar with a trademark, like the very stylish picture of the 'logo' of the cosmetics trust TEZHE.[40]

Figure 13 '*In America a bottle of ketchup stands on every restaurant table and in every housewife's cupboard.*' Ogoniek *20/21, 30 July 1937.*

One of the most impressive advertisements published before the war in *Ogoniek* was a whole page advertisement for tomato ketchup – yet another 'souvenir' from Mikoyan's trip to the United States the previous summer. In addition to a big bottle of ketchup in the forefront, it shows a young woman taking a bottle of tomato sauce from a cupboard. Above her head one can read the following text: 'In America a bottle of ketchup stands on every restaurant table and in every housewife's cupboard'[41]

In following this short period of Soviet advertising in the mid-1930s one can see parallels with the stages of development that commerce in the United States had experienced in well over fifty years preceding the Second World War: from adverts for 'wundermedicines' promising a cure to all the ills of humankind, with a maximum of textual product information, to advertising images of products portraying their smiling consumers asking the readers whether they have already tasted or tried the product.[42] As the ketchup ad demonstrates, the Soviet consumer was, at least occasionally, even reminded that some of his or her global fellow citizens (in the case of ketchup 'everyone in the United States') were already happy owners and consumers of such products.

The government emphasized that Soviet advertisements must be dignified. They should avoid all signs and gestures of vulgarity. As the Deputy Minister said in his introductory speech at the meeting,

> As far as the form of advertising is concerned it is your [the artists' and other specialists'] business. This is a question of influencing the psyche with artistic means, these are questions of designs for advertisements which will give rise to an instant perception that will then be preserved a long time afterwards in the mind of the consumer. This is one of the main tasks, or really the core of designing a skilful advertisement.[43]

In an official published report on the achievements of Soviet trade by the Ministry, the positive development of advertising in 1936 was mentioned in particular. According to this report what made Soviet advertising different from its capitalist counterpart was, not surprisingly, that it was not serving the interests of money making. Instead, as the report continued, 'our advertising should inform the buyer about the meaning of goods, the ways of using them, their price. . .'[44]

Obviously many representatives of the trade saw the task of advertising in a more demanding light. 'One of the tasks is to develop the taste of the customers, in particular in the village' Comrade Kiritsenko wrote in relation to Soviet commercial advertising in the trade journal *Sovetskaia torgovlia* in the same year. It was also deemed important to display the richness of the country: 'The Soviet Union has become a rich country and this richness should shine with all colours on the shelves of the shops, in the city as well as in the village.'[45]

There were obviously many practical and economic problems limiting the free spirit of experimentation among these early Soviet advertisers. For instance, neon lights were in most cases out of the question and had to be supplemented with much cheaper drawings on billboards. The Moscow Light Trust, (Mosgorsvet, later Mosgoroformlenie), which was founded in 1930 as the first enterprise producing artistic 'light' (*svetohudozhestvenny*) designs and advertisements, strived to preserve its monopoly in this modern, expensive type of advertising, even after 1937 when other organizations appeared in the field. It was proud of being alone responsible for the decoration of Moscow, the 'proletarian capital.' Many of the bigger orders to this trust were, however, political not commercial, and paid for by the Communist Party. It constructed, for instance, huge decorations with electric lighting that were shown or carried on October demonstrations in Moscow.

The increasing interest in and importance of advertising led to a reorganization of the Moscow Light factory and the recruitment and schooling of new qualified cadres. A trade school, teaching advertising design and techniques, the first of its kind in the country, was established. In 1937 twenty-nine pupils graduated.[46]

The novelty of the advertising enterprise in the Soviet Union is very clearly revealed in the accounts of firms. The accounting systems of Soviet enterprises did not include any category of such expenses, and neither had the annual plans allocated for their inclusion. Another related question was the responsibility for and the right to advertising. Should advertisements be designed and decided as well as paid for by the ministry, the industry, the central administration of department stores and other shops or by the local shops and stores themselves? Both a central ized and a decentralized system of administration or the division of responsibilities had supporters. One Comrade Senkevich, who represented a Moscow trade organization revealed his own experiences during the March 1936 meeting:

> I was asked to give a couple of announcements. I sent four or five, after that no one talked with me about anything and I knew about them first when they were printed in the newspaper. For some reason they were printed time and time again. I do not know where they came from, and who is going to pay for them. I had to make a phone call and ask where they came from and who is going to pay for them. With hunting guns I had an unpleasant experience. *Pravda* and *Vecherniaia Moskva* etc. had so many announcements about them that I started receiving masses of letters with orders and money for these guns. This is good but not to the degree of numbness. I gave an announcement thinking about Moscow, and orders were sent to me from all over the Union. Therefore I ask to be given the full right to advertise things myself, of course, with all the following responsibility for it.[47]

As the Deputy Minister reminded him, it was not wise or even politically astute to advertise in newspapers like *Pravda* or *Izvestiia* things that could be bought only in select Moscow shops: 'Announcement in *Pravda* or *Izvestiia*, that is for the whole country, and for it the Ministry must take full responsibility.'[48] In addition, only things that were in excess in the shops should be advertised. As admitted by the participants of the meeting, one of the main problems facing good and sensible practice was that the supply of goods into shops was highly irregular. One could never be sure that certain goods would still be available in a couple of days or next week – when the advertisement was eventually published.[49] Sometimes advertising was regarded as a total waste of resources: 'Take for instance a good food store in the Krasnopresnenskii city district. To whom is it necessary that 2 million people read about its existence and that it sells potatoes, herring etc.'[50] On the other hand, newspapers had so far shown a responsible attitude towards advertising, as one of the participants noted: 'Leningrad papers stopped advertising goods of bad quality. They stopped advertising *pelmeni*, saying that no such advertisements will be published as long as the quality of these *pelmeni* is not improved.'[51]

During the meeting the participants were divided into working groups with special themes. One of the groups, which had the task of discussing radio advertising, was faced with a concrete example: how to advertise Georgian tea, one of the novelties launched with big campaigns at the time. They suggested a series of short dialogues between two brothers, Pel and Men (Pelmen when combined). One of them is an optimist, the other a born pessimist:

> One arrives in a very sad mood and starts talking about everyday problems – a tooth is aching or he has flu, a high temperature. The first one then tells him: 'Don't you worry – drink Georgian tea like me.' The same refrain is repeated systematically in all the following advertisements too in which the pessimist always comes up with new kinds of worries. There should be music too to the refrain![52]

That many of the problems discussed at this meeting were still unsolved two years later becomes evident from a newspaper article about the Leningrad-based bureau of advertising Torgreklama. Torgreklama was advertising food products almost exclusively. In the article, workers of the trade organizations were said to be critical of its activities: it was acting almost like a props man in a theatre providing shops with artificial models of food stuffs, like sausages, that could be displayed in windows. Advertising also suffered from the fact that local trade enterprises did not know how much money they could spend on advertising each year since there were no clear rules about that.[53]

Many of the forms of advertising that were discussed at this meeting were, however, practised in the Soviet Union. Given the lack of systematic statistics, it is difficult to say how widely they were practised. The exemplary Central Moscow Department Store was a leading experimenter. It produced its first movie ads in 1938: one on hats (thirty meters long), one on furs (65 meters), and one on toys (115 meters). They were widely circulated and shown at several leading Moscow cinemas such as the Metropol', Pervyi Kinoteatr, Kinoteatr TsPKO im. Gorkogo, Forum, Udarnik and so on. The total show time was impressive too. The film on hats ran for eighty days altogether, furs and toys both forty days.

The lifespan of Soviet movie advertisements was short. In the annual report of 1939, the department store had, with obvious regret, to admit that it had not produced any new movie ads. The State Film Committee had forbidden the production of movies that were shorter than 200 meters long. The estimated price of a film of this length would have been 80,000 roubles, which was regarded as too expensive.[54] The department store therefore had to prioritize other means of advertising. It is not known what the motivation of the Film Committee really was, whether it opposed the idea of such commercial 'misuse' of film art or whether its representative just thought that such 'over short' movies simply did not fit into its production plans. Perhaps the trade union of film workers had its say in the matter too. The Moscow *univermag* turned to other forms of advertisement. Ads were published in the biggest newspapers (*Izvestiia, Trud, Pionerskaia Pravda*) as well as local ones (*Vecherniaia Moskva*) and even in foreign languages in *Moskovskie novosti* (Moscow News; in English and German). Radio advertisements were also used as well as special billboards, shop windows and so on. Radio and local newspaper advertising was mostly about special seasonal events such as the New Year's bazaars.[55]

The mid-1930s witnessed, together with the establishment of commercial shops offering an increasing variety of wares, the emergence of Soviet advertising. The authorities felt that it was their task to cultivate the Soviet consumer, to teach him or her to appreciate the many new novelties. Soviet advertisements are a further example of the emergence of a spirit of Soviet commercialism which was more or less openly expressed and promoted by many specialists and authorities in Soviet trade, particularly during the second half of the 1930s. The initial burst of great expectations and enthusiastic attempts at advertising were followed by a more low-key, anti-commercial period. Contrary to popular belief, however, commercial advertising was practised in one form or another throughout most of the lifespan of the Soviet Union.

6

The Emergence of the Soviet System of Retail Trade

New Department Stores: The Flagships of Soviet Trade

The history of the Russian department store also begins in the middle of the 1930s. Famous trading houses had existed in pre-Revolutionary Russia but no department stores in the modern sense of the word. The famous trading house Gostinnyi Dvor, on Nevsky Prospect in St. Petersburg, and its counterpart on Red Square in Moscow were more reminiscent of a bazaar stall with open, side arches than a modern department store building. Both trading houses continued to function as buildings where shops were located even during the First Five-Year Plan. In December 1933, however, the government founded the Central Department Store in Moscow (TsUM), near the Bolshoi Theater, which operated as a flagship department store until the end of the Soviet Union.[1] According to the Soviet historian Dikhtiar, the Minister of Domestic Trade opened seven such exemplary, flagship stores at the beginning of 1935.[2] In addition to the first one in Moscow, there were department stores in Leningrad, Kharkov, Vladivostok, Irkutsk, Sverdlovsk and Minsk.[3] According to an official report by the Trade Minister, the total number of department stores reached twenty by 1 January 1936. Eight of them had a production unit of their own attached to them.[4]

From the very beginning, the Moscow TsUM became the leading retail trade unit in the country, and it enjoyed a privileged position in many respects. It experimented with many forms of trade, such as home deliveries and telephone orders. It opened several different types of workshop and repair shop, Atelier Mode, (fashion atelier) among them, and it advertised its products extensively in the press or on the radio by the end of the 1930s. Similar, but often more modest, department stores were opened in all the big cities of the Soviet Union. They were supposed to follow the example set by TsUM.

TsUM and the other department stores, as well as many specialized commercial shops, were first created in the mid-1930s to trade mainly in the 'commercial' market. In Soviet terminology, this meant that they traded commodities, which were not in deficit and the amounts of which were not regulated by the state, at least not as completely as some basic items of consumption. Furthermore, they were 'open' shops, which meant that everyone had access to them and could buy anything on sale with his or her own money. In 1939 four departments of TsUM, which traded in deficit goods, were closed down to emphasize TsUM as a commercial store with a more distinct profile than other common city shops. This led to a total reorganization of TsUM. It was not able to fulfill its annual plan. Again an example of the contradictory nature of such controlling measures: there were simply not enough non-deficit products available immediately to fill the gap left by the elimination of deficit products from its counters.[5] In other words, by 1939 at the latest, TsUM was supposed to work – and to set the example – as if there existed no real scarcity in the Soviet Union any longer.

In reviewing the reports and comments on the activities and successes of early commercial stores like TsUM or specialized food shops such as Gastronom, one gets a clear impression of the difficult and contradictory role they were supposed to play in the Soviet economy. The representatives of such shops, as was expressed on many occasions, felt that they knew what their customers needed and wanted. Since the fulfillment of their own plans depended on the rapid and fluent realization of the commodities on sale, they were also eager to make adjustments to answer the changing demand. On the other hand, they were – to a great extent – at the mercy of the highly centralized industry and state planning authorities which provided them with goods to sell. Since their rights to make deals directly with industry suppliers or farmers were extremely limited, they were eager to establish production units of their own to be able to control the supply, at least to a certain extent.

Trade organizations adopted many methods of consumer research to analyze demand. For example, the newly founded Moscow Institute of Trade Research conducted a study using questionnaires with customers. In practice, the administrators of the shops conducted the study, which was declared very useful. The information collected included the fact that men who bought size 48 suits wanted to purchase overcoats that were one size larger.[6] A research booklet produced at the time suggested several different methods of ascertaining the needs of customers: distributing questionnaires about unsatisfied needs as well as about demand in general, observing buyers while in the shops, recording customers' remarks about quality and asking sales persons to keep diaries.[7]

There were many attempts to solve the problems of or at least to improve the situation of trade in the late 1930s. The bigger shops and local trading organizations were eager to make their own deals with local industry or other trading organizations about deliveries that were not part of the regular annual plans and not regulated directly by the state authorities. This practice of decentralized ordering, as it was officially called, was authorized and at times encouraged by the central authorities. It was in practice already by 1936. TsUM, for instance, reported having

Figure 14   A corner of the children's department in the Central Department Store in Moscow 1936. (Source: RGAKFD)

received from the department store at Vladivostok expensive imported (probably Japanese) clothes worth 5 million roubles. Another widely practised solution to gain more independence from government industry was the establishment of workshops within the department stores themselves. At times, such workshops could develop into small production units or independent factories of their own, as was the case with the TsUM fashion atelier. In an article in *Sovetskaia torgovlia* in 1936, the director of the first Kharkov *univermag,* Khaidenov, wrote about the importance of the department store's own production units in creating novelties for its clothes department.[8] The Moscow department store ultimately incorporated a big factory producing all kinds of children's wear and other items.[9] It became famous for its children's departments.

A third strategy was to emphasize the role of and the right to quality control. For example, it was an innovation for stores to demand the right not to accept deliveries of faulty or damaged goods, such as mismatching pairs of rubber boots, or goods that did not meet any demand, such as dull unfashionable clothes made out of poor quality domestic raw materials. The representatives of trade organizations often showed professional pride in knowing best the customers' tastes and the rules of demand. As the Trade Minister, Veitser, commented during the meeting referred to earlier, 'some products are taken into production again (from 1914, 1920, 1925) but taste has developed since. There is need for more comfortable products . . . In line with the reinvention of old commodities we need to start producing new commodities which are more comfortable, more beautiful, and satisfy better the aesthetic taste etc.'[10]

In Veitser's opinion it would be better if, for instance, the Moscow textiles industry served only, or primarily, Moscow department stores and clothes stalls since it was accustomed to producing clothing that suited its own regional market.[11] This was a rare reminder that the prevalent ideal of centralized and standardized production was not entirely without its problems. In official statements the local initiative of the administrators of shops was also encouraged. In 1934, for instance, *Sovetskaia torgovlia* published a story about, in the author's eyes, an exemplary director of a food store in Kiev, who was very active and had made special deals with many local food producers. He had even organized a system of home deliveries. He was, however, said to be at odds with the local bosses who obviously thought him too independent.[12]

The Shopkeeper's Dilemma

Judging from the protocols of a meeting of a special commission of the *politburo* on 21 November 1934, the Trade Minister, Veitser, wanted to increase the role of the Ministry of Trade and, with it, promote regular commercial trade relations between producers and consumers. The special commission, with Andrei Zhdanov, the Party Secretary of Leningrad, at its head, was nominated to discuss the proposal to transfer all non-centrally regulated orders and deliveries, for example deliveries that the *kolkhozes* were entitled to make after fulfilling their centrally planned product quotas and taxes to the state, to the jurisdiction of Veitser's Ministry. This proposal obviously would have promoted the establishment of more regular commercial relations between *kolkhoz* farmers and commercial organizations. It was, however opposed by Zhdanov and other members of the commission. After a lengthy discussion, Zhdanov summarized the crucial point: 'You [meaning Veitser] are going to defend the rights of the village against the city, this will dictate to you the conditions of trade.'[13]

The increasing independence of department stores and other bigger trading organizations – in developing product variety, constructing their own production units and handling *spetszakazy* (special orders) – brought dangers along with it. Given too much freedom to follow the rules of formal economic rationality, the stores were gradually shunning the centrally planned economy, with its goals and targets. This danger was of special concern to the trade and service sector, as well as farming, but it was less of an issue with industrial units, which often did not have independent channels to sell through. But even such industrial units could and did attempt to trade and barter directly with each other, overstepping the 'jurisdiction' of the central planning agencies.

An active, inventive and successful director of a Soviet store always faced the danger of being accused of speculation or 'easy' profit making. Profit making as such was, of course, not denied, since, at least within certain limits, the economic units were expected to be cost-effective. Only a director who focused all, or too much of, his attention on making money and forgot other, more important, goals of the economy, was to be blamed and eventually punished. Ignoring the needs of customers that were not lucrative was one such dangerous mistake. He was especially culpable if he had profited personally from suspect activities. As Ilja Srubar has pointed out, this was one of the most effective systems of social control: an individual economic actor could never know for certain when his actions overstepped the limits of the legally allowed since these limits were in a state of constant flux due to the political situation and were rarely explicitly articulated.[14]

The main pressure on an individual 'shopkeeper' or *univermag* director was, in principle, simple: how to ensure that enough products of sufficient demand were delivered to the store. The reports of the consultation meetings at the Trade Minister's office and the annual reports of the *univermags* are full of details listing examples of 'successful' deals, as well as deficits and shortages. Here are a few examples.

At a Trade Minister meeting held shortly after the founding order for department stores had been issued, the list of shortages was extremely long. In Leningrad, ladies' shoes (in light colors in particular), men's boots and electric goods, such as radio receivers, were found lacking. Consumers meanwhile were asking for high quality and greater variety.[15] In Kharkov radios, gramophones, pianos and good guitars were described as being urgently needed.[16] In Vladivostok radios and various musical instruments were in great shortage.[17] Huge lines formed in front of the departments selling radios, cameras and music in Minsk.[18] Novosibirsk reported that huge demand, outstripping supply, existed concerning all kinds of high quality and higher value products.[19] The longest list came from Moscow. According to the director Bedniakov, ladies shoes were very crude in design and make. Radios and gramophones were in great shortage: the estimated demand of *patéfons* in 1935 was 30,000 and the department store received only 12,000. For radios the respective figures were 7,000 and 2,000. Customer demand for carpets, furniture, wollen clothes and so on simply could not be met.[20] The Moscow department store was clearly more demanding in its desired supply and requested many items that the more provincial organizations did not yet dare to ask for, presuming that the existence of such items was indeed known to them.

In 1935, the variety of all the goods sold in the *univermags* working under the Moscow Trade Trust (Mostorg), consisted of 1,800 different items, 'plus or minus two hundred', according to the report.[21] As this was essentially the first year of the

existence of these department stores, the amount of goods was certainly impressive. Equally impressive were the novelties, which the department stores claimed
to have introduced during these early years. The definition of a 'novelty', however,
was a broad one since virtually no industrially produced commercial goods existed
a year or two earlier. Practically everything that the department stores sold was
domestically produced. For example, in 1939 approximately 1 per cent of the total
sales of the Moscow department store consisted of imported goods.[22]

From the very beginning, it was the explicit task of these new department stores
to establish new consumer practices in the USSR and to encourage actively the
birth of a cultured Soviet citizen. The importance in opening these new venues for
trade was further accentuated by the publication of a special issue of the journal
Nashi dostizhenia (Our Achievements), edited by Maxim Gorky and dedicated to
the department store openings. The articles emphasized the great cultural task that
department stores and their staff were taking on. By their example they were
expected to educate new cultivated Soviet customers.[23]

According to the 1934 accounts of TsUM, the total number of newly invented
consumer goods (including the resurgence of goods that had been in use before the
Revolution or in the 1920s but had been forgotten by the 1930s) reached 600. But,
as has already been emphasized, reinvention and reintroduction were not enough.
TsUM had been negotiating with producers about the introduction of 'totally new
items' such as new fashionable ties and hats.[24] As this example proves, 'totally new
items' did not necessarily refer only to brand new types of products but equally to
new designs or models of old ones.

Table 8   New models and products at the Central Department Store according to their
initiator in 1936.

		Initiator		
	All	industry	commerce	dep. store
Totally new commodities	808	553	16	239
New models of old comm.	321	12	–	309
Newly invented comm.	79	55	–	24
TOTAL	1208	620	16	572

The role of department stores in demanding and retaining high quality goods to
meet consumer demand was expressed in almost aggressive tones by Bolotin, the
Deputy Minister of Domestic Trade, in a lecture delivered in 1935: 'What a fight
we had with Mikoyan. I told him, do not make 'pillows' [a simple hard unwrapped
candy], no one will buy them. The Ministry of Food Industry stubbornly produced

them and now their stores are jammed up with these candies. Twenty tons lie idle and no one takes them. Mikoyan could have convinced me, one man, but to convince 200,000–300,000 people to buy these "pillows", even he is not capable of doing that.' Bolotin's conclusion was familiar: 'We have to study the consumer demand with great care.'[25] At least some prominent representatives of commerce seemed to cherish a belief in consumer sovereignty, even under the conditions prevailing in the Soviet Union of the 1930s.

On the other hand, Bolotin warned his audience of the danger of excessive novelty fever, the tendency to ask for novelties only for novelty's sake. In some fields, he warned, fashions were followed unnecessarily to increase the selection almost endlessly. The First Moscow Food Store had 214 different types of bread on sale. In the Deputy's opinion, no other country had anything like that: it was difficult even to imagine who would want to buy all these different types of bread. These doubts did not prevent *Pravda* from reporting with great pride about the achievement gained in the increasing variety of Soviet bread.[26]

By 1937, the accounts of TsUM demonstrate that there were 1,964 new product brands, of which 818 were totally new, 134 newly created or invented and 545 new designs or models of old items. Among these new or newly produced items the following were mentioned:[27]

- radios and gramophones (*electropatéfons*) in boxes;
- *radiolas* (small radio tuned to one station);
- table fans;
- gramophone record albums (label Grant, twenty pieces);
- jazz flutes (metal no. 2, *pikkolo*);
- tennis strings;
- prams;
- all kinds of toys (telephones, coffee services, surprise boxes with chocolate);
- manicure collections;
- cushion covers with artistic designs;
- liqueur services;
- vases with flower stands; etc.

The list also included curious products such as Briz-bis. The trade in novelties had progressed to become more technical and unique.

By the end of the 1930s, the lists of deficit products had become more detailed and varied, and the products themselves were often more refined or processed. For example, bras in larger sizes and special sizes of corsets appeared on the list of insufficient inventory in a 1938 report of the Moscow Central Department Store.[28] In 1939 and 1940, novelties included many housework utensils of the sort that had not been produced in sufficient quantities only a few years earlier. Only this time greater expectations were placed on them. Typically they were things like electric pancake pans, meat mills of a new kind, DYNAMO electric plates, floor polishers, tie buttons and pins etc. Some novelties or technical innovations, on the other hand, failed to get a response from customers. Despite extensive advertising, the department store struggled to sell items such as thermos plates, mentioned as an example of a genuine Soviet invention in 1939.[29]

Somewhat remarkably, the reports fail to mention the possibility that high prices of commodities were a disincentive to consumers. In the late 1930s, clearly the most overwhelming problem facing the authorities was the absolute quantitative shortage of almost all products. Given the lack of supply, prices were not a primary concern. In several reports, shopkeepers, for example, boasted that many items were almost taken from their hands despite their astronomical price tags. But, by the end of the decade, complaints from the public about high prices grew to a deafening pitch. The authorities and trade officials had to admit that although there were now products on sale, many were too expensive for the average consumer.

The Case of Atel'e Mod

The establishment of fashion ateliers is one of the best indicators of the increasing demand, or at least the authorities' belief in the demand, for better quality and more individual consumer goods. Fashion ateliers were often attached to local department stores and offered privileged customers in bigger cities and industrial centres an opportunity to custom order clothing. They were not small shops of artisan tailors or seamstresses but production units that could develop into small clothes factories. They were opened almost simultaneously with the founding of department stores. In Leningrad, the famous exclusive women's fashion store in the centre of the city on Nevsky Prospect 12 opened in 1934.[30] The Moscow Central Department Store opened its own fashion atelier in 1934 as well. Similar ateliers soon opened in several other department stores across the urban landscape. Some were directly attached to large, important factories or industrial trusts.

On 18 September 1934 *Pravda* published an article on the newly opened fashion atelier at the Moscow Electric Factory, Elektrozavod. It was said to be the first of its kind in Moscow. On the initiative of the Party committee and the Department of Workers' Supply at the Elektrozavod, a former shop on Preobrazhenski Street had been converted into a fashion atelier to serve the workers of the factory: 'How much silk, velvet, carpets, lights and artistic taste was demanded to change this ugly and always empty shop. . .'[31] According to the article, there were also new plans, 'on the request of the workers', to open similar ateliers to make linen and shoes on order. The reporter expressed surprise at the great variety of workers' demands and wishes: 'Recently workers complained about the lack of furs in the

*Figure 15   The ladies' department in the department store on Kuznetskii Bridge,
Moscow 1936. (Source: RGAKFD)*

atelier. They demanded that karakul, rabbit and kangaroo should be brought to the
shop – the best furs of high quality.' It is difficult to say whether the above list of
'high quality furs' ought to be read more as proof of total ignorance on the part of
the reporter or the readers of the paper – or both. Perhaps it was, after all, a hidden
subversive act of irony that had passed the – equally ignorant – censors' look
unnoticed.

According to a typical annual report of the Fashion Atelier of the Moscow
Central Department Store, 'our productive life demanded 100 orders of finished
clothing a day and we were able to take only 12-15 orders a day'. The question
arose as to whether to enlarge the Atelier into a whole production unit inside TsUM
which would answer the great demand among the population for fashionable
clothes on individual order. Altogether the Atelier had turned out 4,500 items of the
product group 'dress' during the year, an essentially negligible figure for a city with
2 million inhabitants. However, at the same time some of the models designed and
worked out in the Atelier were then industrially sewn on a mass scale in local
textile factories.[32] In 1936, the Atelier was elevated into an independent industrial
unit. Thus, TsUM, not satisfied with the ready-made clothes delivered by industrial
factories, started making a small range of clothes sewn on individual order, which
were meant to be in great demand.[33] By 1936, the idea of designer clothes shops
or boutiques with semi-mass fashion had hit the Soviet Union.[34]

Cities such as Leningrad, Kharkov and Minsk closely followed Moscow's lead on fashion ateliers, even if on a more modest scale. As was the case in many fields of production in the 1930s, Soviet specialists made no attempt to cover up the fact that they more or less directly copied models and designs from abroad. It is unlikely though that fashion designers were sent abroad to learn. Another simpler method was used in the case of fashion. Models were copied from French and British fashion magazines quite freely. For instance, a 1938 issue of the Leningrad fashion journal *Modeli plat'ia* included models lifted from several foreign publications, such as *Le Tailleur de Luxe, Costumes-Mateaux* and *Le Grand Tailleur.*[35] According to the historian Natalia Lebina, the 'standard' outfit of the well-to-do Soviet citizen or the ideal of a well-dressed citizen in the late 1930s consisted of a Boston suit, a dress made of *crepe de chine*, a woolen overcoat and shoes of natural leather – all expensive items that only a few could afford to buy, if at all available for general sale.[36]

Foreign fashion magazines and trade publications were rare specimens in Stalin's Soviet Union. Anyone who could control access to them had a valuable asset at hand. In 1936, the workers of the Moscow Fashion Atelier wrote an angry letter published in *Za obraztsovyi univermag* (Towards an Exemplary Department Store). They complained that they had never seen any of the foreign fashion journals that their fashion shop subscribed to:

> What happens with the foreign fashion journals that should be available for our customers to design models. Money is used to subscribe to them. But unfortunately our Atel'e Mod never received any of these journals. One could imagine that our department store never got any of them at all. This is not, however, true. They are regularly delivered. During the first quarter of the year, the director's secretary, Comrade Mikhailovskii, has received 40 exemplars. Just as many were received by Comrade Vulfov, the head of the department of ready-made clothes. Atel'e Mod only received eight. It is time to ask where the remaining 72 journals are.'[37]

This letter was collectively signed by all the workers of the Atelier. What makes this incident even more tragicomic, and at the same time typical of the period, is the simultaneous publication of an advertisement in *Pravda.*[38] In the ad, readers are advised to 'ask for photographs of new models from foreign fashion journals' when ordering their dresses from tailors, thus giving the misleading impression that such fashion publications were readily available throughout the country. The director of the Atelier, thus accused of hiding, if not stealing, such valuable state property, answered the accusation in the next issue of the same journal. In an unsurprising response of outright counter-attack, he accused the workers of a serious lack of discipline rather than addressing the problem of the missing fashion publications.[39]

It was characteristic of the centralized Soviet system of production that in 1939 there was a plan to organize the 'copying' of foreign models in order to make it more effective, more centralized and, presumably, more economical. Previously the leading Soviet 'fashion houses' had been allowed to subscribe to leading foreign fashion magazines. On 3 November 1934, Trade Minister, Veitser, for instance, had given permission for the transfer of 100 gold roubles to the account of the Leningrad Fashion Atelier to be used for subscribing to foreign fashion journals. The Cheliabinsk Fashion Atelier had been given permission to use seventy-five gold roubles for the same purpose in 1934 and fifteen gold roubles a month in the following year.[40] Foreign currency was, however, a scarce and precious resource. Therefore, after a thorough investigation of all options, the authorities decided that the solution was to publish a quality fashion magazine in the Soviet Union. The journal was to reproduce high quality reprints of the models represented in foreign journals. This meant that only one sample of each foreign publication would be needed for the entire Soviet Union, rather than individual subscriptions at ateliers throughout the country. Originally, the journal was to be published in Russian only, but it was later decided that there should be versions in all the other languages of the Soviet Republics.[41] By publishing a 'high-quality' reprint in the Soviet Union, foreign currency spending could be reduced from 20,400 roubles in 1936 to 3,000 roubles in 1939, the planned launch year for the new Soviet fashion journal.[42]

Before the planned publication of this new journal there existed in the Soviet Union domestic fashion magazines of a poor technical quality. These were, however, short-lived. For instance in 1938 the journal *Modeli sezona* (Seasonal Models) was issued. The publisher is not known. It included design drawings, obviously copies from foreign journals, with very short descriptions of the purpose of and the material used for the clothes in question. The new centrally edited journal, was meant to be of a much higher quality than its predecessors, and it was supposed to be distributed to fashion ateliers and shops throughout the Soviet Union. It would also be an effective means of centrally controlling which international models and fashion designs were at the reach of both Soviet designers and ordinary customers. Due to the outbreak of the war these detailed plans were, however, soon totally forgotten.

There were voices of dissent in the fashion industry with reference to the method of merely copying foreign designs. As Comrade Marievskaia, the secretary of the Party organization of the Leningrad clothes' printing factory named after Vera Slutskaia, argued in 1935 'but who has told that we could not produce a better drawing than foreigners. Comrades, we have to produce our own beautiful drawing which could gratify the demands of a young girl, a child and a middle-aged woman alike.'[43]

High Quality Food Stores and other Shops of General Consumption

In 1926–27, before the First Five-Year Plan and at the end of the NEP, the share of private shops in the total retail trade of the USSR was 37 per cent. Cooperative shops were responsible for half of all sales, and state-owned shops had the smallest share of merely 13 per cent.[44] All private shops were closed down at the beginning of the First Five-Year Plan. According to official ideology, state shops were to be preferred above everything else and were to gradually replace cooperatives. Consequently, and obviously prematurely, it was decided as early as 1935 that cooperative shops would operate exclusively in the countryside whereas state shops and the ORS would supply towns. The ORS, or the Organization of Workers' Supply, was founded in 1932. It ran numerous food outlets attached to factories and other workplaces that supplied food for their workers directly from centrally regulated provisions. At the beginning of the 1930s, the whole trade sector was organized under a ministry with a characteristic name, the Ministry of People's Supply. It was divided in 1934 into two ministries – one responsible for domestic trade and the other for the food industry. Throughout the 1930s, many ordinary workers received a much greater part of their food supplies from such outlets and factory canteens than from ordinary commercial shops.

While all private shops were closed in the late 1920s, very few new state-owned or cooperative shops opened to fill their place. According to published statistics, 41,000 private shops were closed between 1928–29, but only approximately 3,700 cooperative and 1,900 state-owned shops opened during the same period. To cope with the rapidly deteriorating supply of food, a strict rationing of all the main foodstuffs was introduced in 1930. The Soviet Union, thus, enjoys the dubious reputation of being the only modern state, which has adopted bread cards during peace time. This rationing was gradually abandoned in 1935. Due to both the lack of goods and the shops in which to sell them, there were hardly any regular shops – meaning ones that sold a variety of goods in exchange for roubles – in existence at the beginning of the Second Five-Year Plan. This was particularly true of specialized shops selling mass consumer goods, such as ironmongers, clothes stores or even food stores. If the existing rare shops had anything to sell at all, it was a few items of only one make. Industry and some of its organizations had, however, their own shops selling non-deficit or non-rationed goods produced by the industry in question, usually at high commercial prices.

The existing state-owned and cooperative general stores sold – or rather gave products away – almost exclusively against strictly rationed coupons. In 1932, the *kolkhoz* market – where peasants could sell under strictly regulated conditions those products that they could produce in excess of state planning – was legalized again. In addition, there were special shops that catered to a strictly limited elite clientele. The chain of Torgsin shops, established originally in late 1920s to satisfy

Figure 16   Customers in a shoe store on Stolishnikov Lane, Moscow 1936. (Source: RGAKFD)

the needs of foreign specialists invited to the country, initially traded only in foreign currency. During the early 1930s, they were transformed into shops which ordinary Soviet citizens could visit in order to buy or trade things but only if they had something highly valuable to sell, such as antiques, art pieces, gold or silver. In addition to second-hand goods, one could buy imported products and foodstuffs which were virtually unavailable anywhere else in the country.[45]

The product variety at Torgsin did not depend as heavily on domestic industry and, consequently, did not offer much of a catalyst to the development of domestic consumer goods. When the heroes of Mikhail Bulgakov's novel *Master and Margarita*, Koroviev and Begemot, visit the famous shop on the Smolensk Square in Moscow, the shelves are filled with obviously imported fine clothes and new shoes. Its food department stocks such luxuries as salted herring, salmon, chocolate and oranges – greedily eaten up with peels on by Begemot to the great amazement of all those standing nearby.

The Moscow Trade Trust (Mostorg or Mosgortorg) was founded in 1932. TsUM, and other special shops selling textiles, shoes, underwear, socks and 'cultural things' in Moscow, belonged to the trust. Before 1934, the Moscow Trade Trust had not a single shop selling watches, photo-optical equipment, radios, furniture or furs. At the beginning of 1934, one of each type of these shops opened up in Moscow, the number of perfumeries increased to five and music shops to two.[46]

If the – as usual over-optimistic – reports of the authorities are to be believed, the years 1933–34 witnessed, a dramatic change, at least in Moscow. Reports indicate that the Soviet Union went from general scarcity to relative abundance, a state in which there even existed an oversupply of particular items on occasion and in which at least some commodities could be regularly bought in shops. In a report on the shops working under Mosgortorg, there are some interesting statistics. In 1932 the realization of any commodity of mass consumption was very easy. They were sold practically as soon as they entered the commercial chain of shops. A commodity stayed in the commercial chain on average a mere 4.1 days. In 1933, a great change was noticed. The average duration increased by 4.4 times to eighteen days. Even seasonal commodities started to build up in shops. This had never happened in 1932. As the report concluded 'people did not any more buy simply anything that was produced.'[47]

As previously noted, the mid-1930s marked the birth of organized Soviet commercial trade, including the establishment of shops. Heavy industry sold items such as watches and clocks to the general public. Light industry focused on clothes and shoes. The authorities centralized production and sales as part of the initiative of state-owned business. The historian Julie Hessler has summarized these new restrictions on trade and craft as follows:

As of December 1935 unincorporated artisans were barred from manufacturing clothes, linen, hats, leather shoes, and notions, as well as leather saddles and harnesses and any goods made out of non-ferrous metals; suppliers were forbidden to sell independent artisans the raw materials for such goods. The Rules of Registration of Manufacturers and Trades, promulgated in March 1936, introduced still further restrictions. Private individuals were no longer permitted to rework food or other agricultural products for resale; to operate inns; or to rent out weights and measures at the bazaars.[48]

The Invention of Gastronom Shops

Gastronom and Bakaleia, the chains of higher quality food shops were founded in 1933. Mikoyan, then the Minister of Food Industry, boasted of having invented the name Gastronom. In November 1934, there were 105 Gastronom shops; by April 1935, there were 139. The increase of Bakaleias was also rapid: from seventy-seven to 105.[49] Gastronom shops could be found in seventy-two cities and forty regions, Bakaleias in twenty-seven cities and thirteen regions. According to one official source, at the beginning of the 1935, 213 Gastronoms operated in the country and that number had increased to 328 by July 1936. At that same time, the number of Bakaleias had reached 259.[50]

The trade inspectors complained as early as 1935 that the growth rates in industry were not keeping up with the demands generated by the new shops. They suggested therefore that virtually all export quality food products should be delivered exclusively to Gastronom and Bakaleia shops. They also recommended putting the opening of new shops on hold for a while.[51] This complaint is understandable if one considers the official statistics (see Table 9) about the minimum level of variety required from any such shop in 1933 and 1934, that is practically from the very moment of their opening.[52]

That the *Gastronoms and Bakaleyas* were really intended to be showcases of Soviet luxury becomes evident if one compares what was expected of them with what was expected of ordinary food stores. In 1939, an order concerning the minimum level of variety required in all of the country's food stores was adopted. All shops were divided according to their size into three classes. The 'first class' shops had to keep at least sixty-seven items on sale, the second class fifty-two and the third only thirty-nine.[53] As one can see from Table 2, the minimum levels of variety for Gastronoms and Bakaleias greatly exceeded those of ordinary shops.

Table 9 The officially required minimum level of variety at Gastronom and Bakaleia shops in 1933 and 1934.

Gastronom	1933	1934	Eliseevskii (The no. 1 Gastronom in Moscow)
Sausage and ham	20	25	40
Meat	–	8	35
Fish	39	72	202
Cheese	10	14	62
Canned fish	22	25	42
Confectionery	62	96	493
Wine and mineral water	144	208	390
Bakaleia			
Cheese hollandaise	1	8	
Canned fish	12	24	
Confectionery	16	51	
Tobacco	15	28	
Flour	–	10	
Macaroni	–	32	
plus several other unspecified items			

Figure 17   Gastronom food store no. 1, Moscow 1934. (Source: RGAKFD)

The technical standards expected from these shops were also quite high. Gastronom no. 2 in Moscow was technically well equipped. It had three refrigerators, goods lifts, forty sets of scales, an internal telephone network, an errand boy and so on. It was also active in organizing home deliveries – a service highly appreciated by the authorities and specialists of trade. As a further specialty it regularly delivered lunch boxes to 150 workers of the Moscow Bolshevik Factory.[54]

Judging from the character of the complaints of their directors, Gastronom*s* and Bakaleias were quite well stocked, at least in the early days. During a consultation with forty-six directors of these elite shops in Moscow in April 1935, one of the directors reported that the supply of sausages was perfectly normal, but there was a shortage of confectionery products; pies were also in great demand. At the same meeting, Roshchin, the director of the Bakaleia no. 22, reported that his shop had thirteen kinds of herring but complained that he did not have any anchovy on sale at all. The shops were also well stocked with different kinds of alcoholic drinks.[55] Gastronom had its own trademark and had both wines and other drinks, as well as cigarettes (or *papirosy*), delivered with its own special label on the boxes.

The opening of Gastronom*s* and Bakaleias in the mid-1930s was a typical Soviet gesture to cope with the emerging and increasing problems of food distribution in the country once direct food rationing had been abolished. Instead of effectively organizing the conditions of regular trade all over the country in a less grandiose manner, a few luxurious model shops opened in Moscow and other big cities, serving as hallmarks of the supposed new abundance. Just like the new department stores, they were intended to act as examples or models of the more cultured trade and as showcases of material abundance for the rest of the country, as well as all the thousands and thousands of less fortunate shops all over the country. As Shinkarevskii, a specialist of Soviet trade, wrote in *Sovetskaia torgovlia* in 1936,[56] 'the shops with a purpose to instruct and to act as models to others were allowed to have bank accounts of their own, to make independent deals with the providers and to act as creditors in relation to providers' – all operations forbidden to regular shops.

In these model shops the roles of the customer and the seller would ideally be reversed from the norm in the Soviet Union: 'The buyer will not search for the commodity as earlier but the commodity, the shop will search for the buyer.'[57] These new cultured shops were characterized, as the official instruction said, by a cultivated intercourse with the buyer, provided through a study of their tastes and an individualistic approach to their demands, plus, of course, smart displays of goods.[58] As evidenced by the long queues in front of most Soviet shops, provided they had anything to sell, throughout the 1930s and beyond, such a cultured relationship with customers was a dream that hardly ever materialized. More likely, the Soviet consumer was greeted with the tired faces of overworked salespersons.

7

The Political Struggle over the Development of the Restaurants

Workplace Canteens or First-Class Restaurants

A struggle between the supporters of ordinary workplace canteens and those of more luxurious restaurants and cafés erupted in 1936–37. As was sadly the case in Stalin's USSR, many leading specialists and administrators had to pay for their 'mistakes' with their lives. In addition to the dire political consequences, what makes this struggle especially interesting is that it clearly demonstrates the almost diametrically opposing views held by politicians and technical experts concerning the future development of Soviet mass consumption, commercial markets and central regulation. The case is illuminating in another respect as well. These disputes were never openly articulated in terms of economic policy, weighing different alternatives and their costs and benefits with one another. Instead, both parties claimed that they represented the real interests of the working people and accused others not only of mistakes but also of economic or political crimes with malign intentions.

Prior to 1936, there were very few genuine restaurants in the Soviet Union. Bars and canteens could be 'open' or 'closed'. While everyone had access to 'open' canteens or cafés, 'closed' restaurants were either workingplace canteens open only to the workers of a specific organization or factory, or to a strictly restricted, privileged clientele. In 1931 only about 1 per cent of all the dishes served by the ORS, which was essentially responsible for distributing all the food eaten in the capital at that time, were eaten in what might be termed restaurants.[1]

The whole 'open' chain of Moscow restaurants consisted in 1933 of only thirty-one restaurants, thirty-seven canteens, eighty-five cafés and buffets and thirty tea rooms. The situation had improved only slightly by 1936 when there were forty-six regular 'evening restaurants' in Moscow.[2] But specially subsidized canteens in Moscow were thriving during this period with 21,000 men and women dining in them daily in 1933. In these eating establishments, in which prices were relatively low and the quality was often high, dined staff of the Central Committee, Moscow Party committee members and members of the *nomenklatura* of the state offices.

105

The Society of Old Bolsheviks (which was subsequently forbidden shortly after in 1935) and political prisoners of the old regime (also to be expelled in 1935) enjoyed eating privileges as well.[3]

Even during the more affluent years of the 1930s, a large part of all food deliveries took place either through such closed workplace canteens or through the distribution of food directly to the workers of a factory or other economic organization. In Leningrad in 1935, for instance, 1.6 million people ate ready-made dishes that were cooked by the city's twenty 'kitchen factories' every day in canteens and cafés.[4]

According to the notes from a speech by the Chief of the state organization of social nourishment (Obshchepit), Olskii, to the Trade Minister, Veitser, the Obshchepit was, until October 1935, almost entirely occupied with the delivery of foodstuffs to the population through its system of closed canteens. They constituted up to 90 per cent of all the restaurants under its supervision. Of the 1,484 eating places run by Obshchepit, only 155 were located outside the territory of a firm, a school or some similar institution. In Leningrad, of the total 1,631 canteens, only eighty-six were open to the general public. Olskii strongly supported the idea that new restaurants should be open to everyone and divided into three quality categories, and, in the future, special attention should be paid to the development of the two higher quality classes.[5]

On 1 January 1935 the Main Administration of People's Nourishment (Glavnarpit), a governmental department heading the restaurant branch, announced that its 'closed' sector (places open only to a restricted clientele with special permission but not including workplace or school canteens) consisted of seventy-six working cafés and four tea rooms. The same report included a statistical account of the dynamics of its open sector during the year 1934 (see Table 10).

Table 10 The number of different kinds of 'open' restaurants and cafés in the Soviet Union in 1934 and 1935.[6]

	1.4.34	1.7.34	1.10.34	1.1.35
Restaurants, total	369	754	668	398
– in trains	231	230	230	230
– on ships	–	281	276	15*
Canteens	41	34	83	107
Cafés	76	138	156	184
Buffets	341	715	924	892
Tea rooms	61	58	53	61
Beer bars	40	49	39	43

* The reason for the drastic decline in restaurants on ships is not know. It was probably an administrative transfer into another category or some other governmental agency.

As the report indicates, there were no open restaurants or canteens in many suburbs and industrial sites, no place where a worker could take his wife after a working day or meet an old comrade-in-arms. The report echoed Mikoyan's speech of 1933:

> Let's say a worker wants to meet a comrade from the front. Where could he invite him? One cannot invite him home – the apartment is small, there is no place, and even if the apartment were a bigger one there is no one to prepare the meal since the wife is working and only a few can have home help. . . Therefore we must open workers' cafés and restaurants, in addition to the canteens, which one can visit without any coupons, with anybody, with a wife, with a comrade, to sit and eat. We have to provide our workers and employees with such a possibility of rest, or cultured use of time.[7]

As early as 1933, Comrade Sakharova, the director of a large workplace canteen, had proclaimed the new standards of decent dining:

> We have artificial palms. There should be real life ones instead, and not too tall flowers. Individual paper cups – against bacteria. Every table should be provided with a mustard cup with a cover and a spoon. Salt should not be served in open cups from which everyone takes with his own knife or fingers, but in a sifter. Plates should not be made out of metal, but of porcelain. Spoons should be of white metal. Waitresses should not have to carry plates in their hands but on a metallic tray.'[8]

She concluded by stating that this was, however, but the start: a continuation concerning the 'demands of science' put on furniture and service should follow. That these demands were far from being fulfilled in the places where most of the Soviet citizens in reality ate their food during the workday is illustrated by the following open letter which the *kolkhozniks* of the Artel' Khoroshevo in the Sinelnikov area, Dnepropetrovskii region addressed to Ministers Ordzhonikidze and Mikoyan in 1934:

> No soup plates, forks or spoons are to be found in the regional centre, nor in the local centre. And we need them badly. Our *kolkhoz* members eat out of wooden cups, out of plate cans, every one brings his own dish and spoon with him. This is not right. Our *artel'* has the financial means to provide everyone with a plate, a spoon and a fork. But they are nowhere on sale.[9]

The Promotion of Commercial Restaurants

In the mid-1930s the ORS, which was responsible for supplying food for work-place canteens, was eager to enter the commercial market. Customers were ready to pay for better food and service. And many officials in the central administration supported the gradual commercialization of restaurants and canteens. The process had already started spontaneously at the local level, and rules were urgently needed to control and direct it into legal forms. An ORS canteen in the Petrovskii factory not only opened a restaurant outside the gates of the factory but also advertised it in its own newspaper in order to attract more customers. The very same factory already had one open café at its cultural centre and an open restaurant in the city. The dishes were prepared from centrally delivered raw materials intended only for the factory's own workers and not for just anyone wishing to visit the restaurant. This meant that the workers they were primarily supposed to cater for were getting fewer provisions than they were entitled to. Such a procedure was evidently totally illegal, and local representatives of the Trade Ministry were already waging a struggle against such dangerous and over ambitious tendencies towards the com-mercialization of supplies. The situation was said to be similar in Zaporozh'e. There was not a single official legally 'open' restaurant or café in the town, and therefore the success of such 'wild' illegal restaurants showed the extent of customer demand. Government officials saw that more 'open' restaurants and cafés were needed, along with a well-organized system of their administration.[10]

In 1935 a state committee was charged with the task of developing a plan to improve the standard of restaurants and canteens. The Trade Minister, Veitser, was largely responsible for the new measures which included the establishment of the Central Administration of Restaurants and Cafés, GURK, founded in January 1936. Other measures included such rules as no soups should be served – under any circumstances – under the temperature of 70 degrees Celsius.[11] It was esti-mated that the closed canteens served about half the population of the Soviet Union and up to 90–100 per cent in bigger factories, schools and universities. They could not manage the increasing demands of the workers or nourishment standards. The situation had changed in particular after the final elimination of bread coupons. To answer these demands the factory canteens should, first, be allowed to sell dishes with higher prices, and not only mass-produced dishes with fixed prices. This was supposed to motivate them to improve the general quality of the dishes. Second, closed factory canteens should also be allowed to be turned into open ones under the condition that this would not endanger the catering for the factory's own workers. And finally, to make this possible at all, the Trade Ministry was now allowed to sell up to 10 per cent of its total 'commercial fond' directly to canteens and restaurants.[12] In this way they had access to new and better materials.

Figure 18   The summer café on Red Square, Moscow 1938. (Source: RGAKFD)

In a typical manner, in addition to many principal and structural reforms, the official decrees regulated even the smallest details of managing a restaurant or canteen. For example, the prices of the meat and fish main dishes should be allowed to differ from each other. The purpose was to increase the supply of fish dishes. Without doubt, the main 'innovation' proposed by this state committee was the new categorization of restaurants into three groups according to their quality and price level. The governmental central supervisory agencies were reorganized accordingly.

The first category consisted of 'closed' restaurants at workplaces, educational institutions and so on. 'Open' canteens, cafés, tea rooms and beer bars belonged to the second category. According to the resolution of the Trade Minister from December 1935, the second category was to be expanded with a focus on self-service restaurants, like *amerikanki* (canteens with high small tables to stand by), buffets, cafés and *zakusochnye* (snack bars), as well as specialized vegetarian or dietetic canteens. The planning process for these new eating establishments was rapid, as we have seen in other industries. Standardized sketches of the canteen design were ready for approval by the end of 1935 and twenty-six model canteens opened in densely populated urban areas in 1936. The best cooks, chefs and directors were hired. Restaurants belonging to the second category were allowed to increase their prices bu up to 30 per cent to encourage them to improve the quality of their dishes and service.[13] Meanwhile, the taxes on sandwiches and some other buffet type products were simultaneously reduced by about one third. This was the beginning of a long tradition of serving relatively cheap sandwiches, with caviar, smoked fish, cheese or ham, in all Soviet buffets and summer pavilions.

The third and final category encompassed traditional restaurants with quality design, good service and fine table wear. They were not allowed to serve mass-produced dishes or even work from fixed menus but had to only prepare meals to order. They were encouraged and even obliged to organize home deliveries and party services. They also started selling speciality ready-made dishes, such as sausages and smoked meat prepared on site and sold in shops adjoining the restaurants.

Prior to the formation of GURK, restaurants had belonged to the Administration of Peoples' Nourishment (Obshchepit) under the Food Supply Ministry. According to Olskii, most restaurants now working under GURK were located in big cities, mostly in Moscow or Leningrad. Restaurants in trains and on ships now also belonged under the supervision of GURK. In smaller towns, there were approximately 800 small cooperative restaurants not working under GURK but as part of the Cooperatives' Central Union. The Union had 138 restaurants in bigger cities as well. In the health spa region of the Crimea and the Caucasus, restaurants were part of a separate system of administration, the Supply of Health Spas (Kurortsnab).[14] Therefore, several organizations remained active in the restaurant 'business' in the biggest cities of the Soviet Union beyond the control of GURK.

The new directors of GURK eagerly promoted their own course even at the cost of others. One of the leading figures in promoting fine dining was Bezdezhkii, the newly appointed head of GURK. He claimed that the growth of his own department was faster than that of other parts of Obshchepit, which were concerned with regular canteens. In his opinion, this was a natural consequence of the fact that good restaurants and cafés were becoming much more popular. As evidence, he demonstrated that during the first three quarters of 1936 GURK's turnover had almost doubled from 176.8 million roubles to 289.7 million. In the near future, the Trade Ministry should pay special attention to the development of higher category restaurants and cafés, which operated under his command, and establish the example of how to run a more 'cultured' catering industry.[15]

The improvement of poor quality of food was not the only issue in these, often detailed, reform plans and resolutions. The new finer restaurants and canteens were supposed to cultivate table manners among the workers. Workers were also calling for an improvement in the standards of the canteens and the dishes served in them.

Some canteens started decorating their dining rooms with curtains and tablecloths. Surviving photographs of the more prosperous canteens from this period show an orchestra playing during the lunch break and tables covered with snow-white tablecloths. A photograph of the canteen at the railway wagon factory at Tambov[16] for instance, shows a whole big band playing during dining hours.

People's Enemies in the Central Administration of Restaurants and Cafés

Olskii and several other directors of GURK were publicly denounced and arrested in 1937. The charges against this 'group of fascist bandits' led by Olskii were that they were leading the institutes of social nourishment into a wrong and harmful direction with disastrous consequences. According to GURK's 1937 annual report commissioned by its newly nominated director Zverev, the troublemakers were accused of vigorously promoting a policy geared toward the establishment of quality restaurants, a policy that had previously been adopted officially by the Trade Ministry and its various agencies in 1935. (In fact, the Trade Minister, Veitser, was also arrested and repressed in 1937. It is not, however, clear whether Veitser's arrest was related to Olskii's. Given Veitser's central role in many trade reforms, he probably gained many personal enemies and was likely a natural target for all kinds of political accusations.)

Zverev's report made his predecessors' activities look criminal and conspiratorial. By promoting the opening and renovation of finer restaurants and cafés, so the accusations went, the aim of the traitors was to fulfil the plan not through satisfying mass demand by producing a greater variety of cheaper dishes but through the production of fewer numbers of more expensive products. The report also pointed out that the value of 'mass dishes with fixed price' had diminished by over 50 per cent during the year. But equally incriminating was another alarming tendency, which took up much space: the share of vegetarian dishes had decreased sharply during 1937 at the cost of more expensive meat dishes. The annual statistics bore clear evidence of such a 'criminal tendency' (see Table 11).[17]

Table 11   The share of different types of main courses among all the dishes served by GURK in 1935–37 (per cent).

	1934	1935	1936	1937
Meat	37.7	46.7	52.3	61.5
Fish	14.3	10.3	5.7	6.9
Vegetarian	48.0	43.0	42.0	31.6
Total	100.0	100.0	100.0	100.0

The decreasing share of vegetarian dishes is a particularly curious 'crime' since the downturn in such dishes could easily have been a testament to the increasing standard of living in the Soviet Union where more meat was now available. Nearly two thirds of all dishes had some meat in them in 1937, compared with slightly over one third four years earlier. Zverev went to great lengths, however, to prove the malicious intent in the downturn in vegetarian dishes. He argued that workers preferred vegetarian and fish dishes, and this was proven by the fact that the miners of the Donetsk region – who needed a high caloric intake – were choosing a higher proportion of vegetarian dishes than urbanites in Moscow and Kiev (see Table 12). Zverev further argued that if the workers themselves did not understand the benefits of vegetarian and meat dishes, then that was because GURK had failed to maintain high standards of food preparation.

Table 12 The share of meat, fish and vegetarian (or hulled grain) dishes served in the canteens in Moscow, Kiev and the Donetsk region in 1937 (per cent).[18]

	Meat	Vegetarian (or hulled grain)	Fish	TOTAL
Moscow	67.8	29.1	3.1	100.0
Kiev	74.5	19.8	5.7	100.0
Donetsk region	46.2	44.9	8.9	100.0

Clearly these figures could be interpreted in a very different way. Olskii and others, if given a fair chance to defend themselves, could have argued that the consumption of meat was an indicator of the increasing material well-being of the Soviet Union and resulted in a greater demand for more expensive dishes. It was only natural that the preference for meat was visible first in prosperous cities such as Moscow and Kiev rather than in poorer regions like Donetsk. Instead of accusing Olskii and company of not serving enough cheaper vegetarian dishes in Moscow, one could just as well have blamed them for favouring Moscow with meat dishes and neglecting to develop their trade in Donetsk. As usual, the truth behind such political accusations had little bearing on the judicial process. In order to incriminate others, it was generally sufficient simply to raise suspicion about the sincerity of their intentions.

The hunt for traitors and Trotskists in the Soviet restaurant industry did not limit itself to the central administration in Moscow. Similar accusations were made in other parts of the country as well. In Leningrad the local directors were put on trial and the local administration liquidated shortly after the Moscow proceedings of GURK leaders at the end of 1937 and beginning of 1938. In February 1938, the newly appointed director of the Leningrad City Organization of People's Nourishment, Comrade Abramov, told the members of his local organization that the director of People's nourishment, Olkhovskii (Olskii's name had obviously been misspelled), had been revealed to be a people's enemy and a Polish spy. In Leningrad he had had criminal collaborators too who had closed down 300 canteens under the pretext that they were unprofitable. At this meeting Abramov repeated the same list of accusations that had been presented against the presumed Moscow traitors: they had sold alcoholic drinks, opened shops and beer bars and built expensive open-air pavilions. Also many children's canteens had been closed.[19] Demonstrating the horrible deeds that the traitors were capable of, he described an incident at the canteen of the Technical Institute in Leningrad in which 'an enemy's hand had placed on a student's plate a cooked and skinned rat'.[20] The push for high-end restaurants and cafés was vigorously condemned by 1937. In the political climate of the late 1930s, it could even have dire consequences. After the traitors were arrested, the number of luxury restaurants was somewhat diminished. Zverev then focused on opening new canteens with mass-scale service, but he admitted that the change in restaurant policy was slower to materialize than he would have wished.[21]

In the ongoing accusations against Olskii and his collaborators, they were blamed for a massive closing down of ordinary workplace canteens, which, in fact, had begun in many parts of the country in 1936 and 1937. In order to promote their 'criminal' cause of opening luxurious restaurants, Olskii and company had neglected to take care of the needs of common workers. In reality the closing down of canteens was due to a lack of food available because of the economic crisis and bad harvest of 1936. At least in the Donbass coal mining region 'the quality and quantity of available food supplies deteriorated sharply by the end of 1936, resulting in the closing of 450 of the area's 860 workplace canteens.'[22] If the situation was similar in other regions of the country, as was likely, this could easily explain the greatest part of these 'treacherous' tendencies in the Soviet restaurant industry.

This story is instructive in two ways. First, there were clearly genuine, highly politicized, differences of opinion as to how to develop Soviet restaurants. One opinion was more egalitarian in approach, favouring strong central regulation to guarantee each Soviet worker at least a minimum of daily nourishment. The other opinion was more liberal, supporting, or at least allowing for, some kind of consumer segmentation and favouring more commercial solutions of regulation. Under the prevailing conditions, both lines of action were problematic. Since the real 'enemy' – a bad harvest compounded by poor administration and unrealistic planning – could not be openly discussed, a scapegoat was required. This case also demonstrates the familiar paradox – that in the midst of poverty, Soviet authorities were still planning a luxury economy. The authorities felt considerable pressure to perform: they had to prove that the abundance proclaimed in Party propaganda did indeed exist in some material way, despite all evidence to the contrary. It is difficult to say who lived in a more imaginary world, those who promoted sophisticated restaurants in the middle of a shortage of basic food stuffs or those who found people's enemies and spies everywhere.

Since the authorities often had little chance of solving any practical problems and could not discuss them openly, finding scapegoats became a natural substitute. The continuous publication of vitriolic accusations continued in the restaurant industry. In the July 1938 issue of the trade journal *Voprosy sovetskoi torgovli*, Comrade Rupasov did not mince words in condemning the people's enemies, which had been revealed in the Soviet Administration of Restaurants and Canteens. They were characterized with all the possible insulting epithets that could be thought of: from traitors and enemies of the people to bloody fascist dogs and the helping hands of Trotsky and Piatakov. They were accused of selling the people to the fascists in order to restore capitalism. They were also implicated in such illegal deeds as selling vodka, cigarettes, beer and chocolate in their cafés and canteens instead of providing the population with nourishing dishes.

Despite the liquidation of this 'fascist-trotskyist' group of traitors, the new directors had to admit that the reopening of the closed factory canteens had been extremely slow. Of the 1,250 closed canteens only 600 had been reopened thus far. And even the reopened canteens functioned mostly on paper only. In Moscow alone 522 canteens had been closed and only forty reopened. In Leningrad the situation was similar: 350 closed and fifty-four reopened. The numbers in Kiev were even more alarming: 152 canteens had been closed and only three opened again. The situation in the countryside was even worse.[23]

In the report in which these serious worries and accusations were presented, Rupasov recounted that all the vegetables in Moscow restaurants had been of a very poor quality in July and August. Typical seasonal summer dishes such as beer soup, salads, radish with sour cream and others were absent.[24] In Leningrad, the canteen of the Svoboda factory had received only seventeen cucumbers during the whole summer of 1938. Salad and other vegetables were not even available.[25] Rupasov did not accuse any people's enemies for the lack of cucumbers and other vegetables. Some cases could be admitted to be the fault of bad organization.

Despite the condemnation and arrest of Olskii and others in 1937, the same 'harmful' tendencies continued in 1938 and 1939. The authorities again had to pay special attention to the continuously diminishing share of vegetarian dishes as well as to the equally low share of mass-produced meals with fixed prices.[26] As the annual report for 1938 concludes, there were real social and economic causes on both the supply and demand side that favoured the prolongation of these dangerous tendencies: on the one hand, cheaper meals and dishes were less profitable to restaurants and, on the other, the population had got tired of simple uniform mass-produced dinners served at their canteens. Many also regarded them as too expensive compared to their often poor quality.[27] These were essentially the same arguments that Olskii had presented for his reforms. Once the campaign against the traitors was over their ideas could be used again and the objective reasons for the failures at least partly admitted.[28]

Despite the ongoing political struggle within the restaurant industry, the building and opening of finer restaurants and cafés continued. The highest leadership of the Party recognized that a demand existed for more refined and luxurious forms of consumption in the Soviet Union. Olskii's critics had, in fact, never denied this. The promotion of luxury was criminal only if it came into conflict with other and equally 'sacred' goals of the Party. According to the annual report from 1937 there were only forty-six higher class restaurants and sixty-eight cafés and buffets, over 2,000 'open' canteens of various degrees and 3,500 outdoor buffets, plus 766 snack bars, beer bars or tea rooms.[29] The end of the 1930s saw, however, the opening of some real showpieces of Soviet luxury. It is revealing that their building and functioning was possible only through an almost total concentration of all the financial resources of GURK. In Moscow, a new café with the characteristic name Lux was planned. One million roubles had been reserved for its planning and construction.[30] At the new, large Moskva Hotel, next to the Kremlin, a whole range of restaurants and cafés were built on the decision of the Central Committee of the Party from 15 August 1938. (The fact that the decision was made by the Central Committee meant that this was an object of special importance and attention.) By the end of 1938, 4.1 million roubles had been invested in its construction. In 1940 the hotel had one restaurant, one canteen, one café and several snack bars and buffets (in 1941 a total of thirteen).[31]

The history of the construction of the Moskva Hotel with its several restaurants and cafés is a good example of how such enormous projects could overturn the projections for an entire industry. Stalin and the Central Committee spearheaded the Moskva project, and, under the wings of the Central Committee, it enjoyed total precedence over any other minor projects or plans. Focusing on one large project was often the death knell for other, carefully constructed plans. The Moskva construction project, for instance, ate up all the finances that were originally planned for use in building and opening small cafés in other parts of Moscow and some other cities.[32] Consequently, in 1939 no other new cafés could be opened in the whole of the Soviet Union. The building of the Moskva Hotel is a prime example of the often totally contradictory measures adopted in the Soviet system of economic administration. A project that demanded huge investments could be started on Stalin's initiative at the same time as other more modest projects were condemned as wasteful.

American Ice Cream Bars and Eskimos

Modern snack bars, commonly called *amerikanki* could have been a modern ('American') alternative in the dispute between the supporters of workplace canteens and quality restaurants. They could – or were expected to – sell cheap standardized food portions effectively to a great number of customers. This should, in fact, have made them an ideal solution in the eyes of many Soviet administrators. As the reports already referred to reveal, they were proposed and discussed and some were opened in big cities. Shortly before the war, even some hamburger kiosks were opened in Moscow. They were, in practice, not seen as a primary solution to the problems of catering to the Soviet people. The ideals of good dining in both workplace canteens and restaurants were similar: they strived to offer their customers real three-course lunches and dinners. Regardless, 'American' ice cream bars became quite popular among Soviet customers, children and youth in particular. In contrast to restaurants and canteens, ice cream bars had a more recreational function. Ice cream was certainly a luxury, in the sense that it was not a necessity and was an item out of the ordinary. Ice cream bars offered pleasure and moderately priced food to virtually anyone.

A young worker with his girlfriend could, for instance, celebrate a birthday in the mid-1930s by visiting an American-style ice cream parlour in the middle of Moscow. On 4 February 1936 the Vice Minister of Food Industry, Belenskii, wrote a letter to the secretary of the Moscow Party Committee, Khrushchev, asking for suitable accommodation for special new cake shops and ice cream shops. According to Belenskii, there only existed one ice cream shop in the whole city. Therefore, in his opinion, at least five or six ice cream shops should be opened during the year 1936 in addition to between ten and twelve new well-equipped cake shops.[33]

Industrially mass-produced ice cream was one of the main Soviet novelties of the 1930s. The Minister of Food Industry started to worry about ice cream production in the years 1935 and 1936. At the end of 1935, the Ministry approved of the technical projects of building ice cream factories in Moscow, Kharkov and Odessa. These factories were built in 1936 and 1937. Others were later built in Tashkent and other big cities. The decisive year for Soviet ice cream production was 1936 when four big factories started operating at once. As *Pravda* reported in May 1936 one could now buy ice cream on the railway platforms on many stations of the Soviet Union.[34]

One of the main tasks of Mikoyan's visit to the US in 1936 was to buy ice cream machines from the United States: 'As far as ice cream is concerned we adopted the technology totally from the States, since until then all ice cream production [in the USSR] had been manual.'[35] The building of factories of freezing equipment went on parallel to that of ice cream production. Freezing equipment was also in great demand in other fields of food production and delivery, but it was naturally

Figure 19   Customers at an ice cream kiosk, Moscow 1935. (Source: RGAKFD)

essential to ice cream production and distribution.[36] Many specialists who visited capitalist countries reported of the advanced 'state of the art' in food technology, transport and trade. Mikoyan told an audience in 1933 that while sitting at a table in an American restaurant, one could expect to be served a glass of water with ice cubes before even ordering. He suggested that the Soviet restaurants and canteens should start selling ice to customers at a moderate price of twenty kopecks a kilo. As he argued, one could make good profits in this way since the presumed production costs were estimated to be over ten times smaller than the price.[37]

The production of electric refrigerators and icing or freezing machines as well as the production of artificial ice – both essential to modern food provisioning – first started in the Soviet Union in the middle of the 1930s. In Soviet economic histories, the mid-1930s are often characterized as the years of the 'refrigerator revolution' (in industry, not in private homes). In 1933 the first factory of artificial ice was established in Moscow. In a report about the state of the total Soviet refrigerator capacity from 1935 one can read that there were only two imported electric refrigerators in the whole of Soviet Union, one in Gorky Park in Moscow and the other, for some reason, in Minsk in a newly opened Gastronom food store. In addition, there were thirteen electric 'compressor refrigerators' in all the shops in the Soviet Union and 112 in restaurants and cafés. Different kinds of boxes and storerooms with natural or artificial, 'dry' ice were used in greater quantity instead.[38] At the beginning of the 1937 all the organizations of Food Ministry had a total of 207 refrigerators with machine cooling.[39]

It is characteristic of the times that in 1937 the Petrozavodsk refrigerator manufacturer Glavkhladprom in Karelia made a deal with the Leningrad ice cream factory about the delivery and selling in the town Petrozavodsk of 29 tons of ice cream and 1,480,000 Eskimo ice cream bars. Once this deal came to the notice of the Minister of Food Industry, he expressed serious doubts about it in a worried letter addressed to the administrations of both factories. The dealers were reminded that they had not paid proper attention to the size of the population of the town of Petrozavodsk. It had only 60,000 inhabitants. The climatic conditions of the city should have been taken into consideration too. The summer lasted only about two and a half months there. In addition, there were other producers selling ice cream within the Karelian Autonomous Soviet Republic. As was to be expected, by 20 July, the Petrozavodsk factory had, in fact, been able to sell only 210,000 Eskimos (about four per every inhabitant of the town) and 4 tons of ice cream. In the same note, the ministry asked the factories to correct their plans accordingly: by the end of the year it was realistic to expect that another 200,000–250,000 Eskimos and no more than 16 tons of ice cream could be sold.[40] If these estimates were realistic, they meant that each inhabitant of the small provincial town Petrozavodsk ate between seven and eight Eskimos and almost half a kilogram of other kinds of ice cream during the summer of 1937. This was not a bad achievement considering that 1937 was only the second year of industrially-produced ice cream in the Soviet Union. It was made possible because ice cream enjoyed the undivided support of the central authorities and became one of the most popular small delicacies in the Soviet Union.

8

Soviet Consumption Amidst General Poverty

The Second Five-Year Plan and the Question of the Growth of the Consumer Goods Industry

In his 1946 work *The Great Retreat,* the American-Russian sociologist N.S. Timasheff[1] argued that a major change took place in Communist Party politics and in the principles of the building of socialism in the Soviet Union in the early 1930s. This change meant virtually giving up many of the earlier basic and 'holy' aims of the Bolsheviks. As later observers have also pointed out, a gradual awakening of a spirit of commercialism and even a kind of idolatry of material goods, became noticeable. Timasheff notes in particular the significance of the delayed ratification of the Second Five-Year Plan, which was not approved until a year after the First Five-Year Plan was completed. By the end of the First Five-Year Plan the Party could proudly announce that the programme of 'enforced industrialization' had been successfully completed and the foundations of heavy industry created – as we now know, with heavy human costs. The working masses did not have any share in the fruits of this industrialization. The great famine caused by forceful collectivization of agriculture lead to mass starvation at the same time.

Drawing on published reports concerning the Second Five-Year Plan as discussed at a Party conference, Timasheff reached the conclusion that a major reorientation towards promoting 'light' or consumer goods industry had taken place in the politics of the Party during and immediately preceding the conference. According to Timasheff, the Minister of Heavy Industry, Sergo Ordzhonikidze, supported Piatakov, the head of the Central planning office, Gosplan, who had set new economic policy tasks and aims, promising more investments in consumer goods industries. Ordzhonikidze made even more concessions and promised people some real relief, compared with their lives under the First Five-Year Plan.[2]

Recent work by historians R.W. Davis and O.V. Khlevniuk challenges the interpretation of Timasheff.[3] They argue that the role of the central state planning office, Gosplan, and other government and Party institutions in developing the Second Five-Year Plan in the early 1930s shows no significant systematic changes in the politics of economic planning. What changes might be evident bear witness more to the disorganized and chaotic state of the Party than to any clear, major change in the general Party line. The target figures and the relative shares of investments in different fields of production and construction were altered during the planning process several times. The final targets for investments were slightly more realistic while both Gosplan and the Ministry of Finance regained some of their previous weight in the planning process that they had lost to Party institutions during the 'wild' years of the First Five-Year Plan.

That Ordzhonikidze received public credit – at least in Timasheff's book – for promoting people's interests in increasing consumption and the availability of mass-produced consumer goods was probably due more to his public image than any genuine contribution. There is little evidence that Ordzhonikidze would have acted and promoted the 'people's interests' in any more decisive a manner than others in the Party in emphasizing the importance of the production of consumption goods. If there were differences of opinion, within the Party leadership about economic policies, they were not challenging the overall strategy but merely raising some questions of emphasis. The opinion that the 'light' and food industries needed more attention was shared by many, Stalin included.[4]

According to the economic historian Eugene Zaleski's close examination of the Second Five-Year Plan, the changes were finally approved and realized after a long process of planning but many adjustments were not especially remarkable. The target figures for 'light' industry had been adjusted but they were totally unrealistic:

> This change in economic politics, if there was any, did not promise any major relief as far as the Soviet ordinary consumer was concerned. These target figures of the plan should not be taken too seriously either since the possibility of their full realization was from the very beginning negligible. (If all the planned investments were summed up, the total yearly national product would hardly have been enough to cover them all!)[5]

According to the official Party line, once the fundamentals for heavy industry were in place, it was time to move onto light industry. In 1935, Stalin wrote to Molotov about the importance of paying attention to consumption. In his letter Stalin made some adjustments in the 'control' figures of the Five-Year Plan for 1936:

> 22 billion was not enough, and couldn't be either. An increase on school building (+760 million), light, timber and paper, food and local industries (altogether + over 900 million), on health care, on Moscow canal construction and other state expenditure (over 600 million) determined the physiognomy and the amounts of these control figures.

I do not have regrets since everything that makes the production of mass consumer goods possible should absolutely be increased from year to year. Without such measures there is no chance of advancement now.[6]

There is no indication that the new interest in light industry ever posed a threat to heavy industry. Heavy industry was always of primary importance, and it became increasingly so with the boom in military spending at the end of the 1930s. The threat of aggression from countries hostile to the Soviet Union naturally necessitated the focus on military spending at the end of the decade. Defence of the fatherland became a major rallying force, and the government warned citizens that the Soviet Union was in special danger because other countries were opposed to the world's first socialist country. This argument, repeated endlessly in defence of Stalin even after his death and the years of de-Stalinization, was formulated by Stalin himself in a speech at the inauguration of the officers from the Academy of the Red Army, on 4 May 1935:

Certainly, with billions of roubles of foreign currency which we have earned by the strictest measures of economizing and which we have used to build our own industry, we could have imported raw materials and increased the production of the goods of mass consumption. No doubt, this is also a 'plan' of its kind but such a plan would make us defenceless in front of our enemies. We should end up destroying the foundation of socialism in our country. We should end up as hostages of both the domestic and foreign bourgeoisie.[7]

This book does not attempt to evaluate the full impact of changes in economic policy during this time, but it is clear from production figures that the 1930s witnessed some genuine changes and reorientations in the production of material culture that paralleled similar changes in other fields. From the early 1930s, the USSR saw an increase in the production – if not of all – at least of certain kinds of consumer goods. The overall quantitative increase was often rather modest and its effects short-lived. The ideological changes, which also reflected changes in the production of the different types of consumer goods, were, however, quite clear and noticeable. Soviet culture of consumption was, at the same time, characterized by an acute awareness of shortages and by officially approved and encouraged ideals of material abundance.

Throughout most of the 1930s, the great majority of the population lived in poverty, and, at times, some segments even faced starvation. The lot of the *kolkhoz* peasants and other villagers in many remote parts of the country seems to have been the worst. Even though there were better years in the middle of the 1930s, the 'good times' never lasted long and the situation soon deteriorated again. Amidst general poverty there were short periods of relative well-being which mostly, however, were restricted only to some parts of the population and areas. The majority of the population simply lived at the mercy of alternating good and bad harvests. For instance, the good harvest of 1937 improved the situation on food provisions, but the situation rapidly deteriorated again in the winter of 1939, which saw shortages of bread and long queues in many localities. In the springs of 1937 and 1940, local famines broke out and there was a general lack of basic foodstuffs like potatoes.[8] The Soviet Economy was more or less in a state of a crisis from 1937 until 1940, or until the German occupation in the summer 1941.[9] This crisis was produced both by occasional bad harvests, worsening conditions of foreign trade and the militarization of the economy, but it was made worse by the problems inherent in Soviet economic organization. Industry was suffering from a chronic shortage of many important raw materials and means of transport. The high rates of growth of the first years of the Second Five-Year Plan were never reached again. The reason that the population did not suffer as much as during the great famine of 1932–33 was that now the government 'delved into its now sufficient food reserves . . . to provide famine relief on a massive scale, mainly in the form of food and fodder loans on generous terms to collective farms.'[10]

Nevertheless, people were hungry again. To take just two examples from letters of complaint to the authorities cited by Osokina:

> From the first decade of December 1939 we buy bread in queues in which one has to stay almost 12 hours. The queue starts to gather at 1 or 2 am and sometimes already in the evening. My wife and I both work and we have three children, the oldest is at school. Often for two or three days we cannot buy any bread. (January 1940, Alapaevsk, Sverdlov region)

> I want to tell you about the heavy conditions which have been created in Stalingrad during the last months. No one sleeps here now. At 2 am people start queuing for bread, at 5–6 in the morning there are 600–700–800 people in the queue. . . If you are interested how workers are fed in the canteen, what was earlier given to pigs is now given to us. . . There is a huge stream of people now into the canteens, with families they come but there is nothing to eat. . . During the whole winter in the shops of Stalingrad we have not seen any meat, cabbage, potato, carrots, beetroot, onion and other vegetables, no milk at state prices. . . No butter has arrived in the shops. (Winter 1939–40, Stalingrad)[11]

The Finnish war in the winter of 1939–40, essentially a minor armed conflict at the North-Western frontier, nonetheless had serious economic repercussions and caused disturbances on the railway. Zhuravlev and Sokolov comment:

> As many letters from the provinces show, the country was again in 1939 almost at the verge of food and other consumer goods rationing. But this would have meant that the

leadership had acknowledged that they were not capable of realizing their promises and had to abandon the widely propagated announcements of their increasing care taking of the Soviet people whose life was with every passing year supposed to become better and better. Stalin could not possibly admit this.[12]

Nevertheless, in spring 1939 special 'closed' shops –officially forbidden after the end of rationing but in practice still in service – officially opened again. They served the Soviet army and navy, railway workers and industrial workers based at plants with military objectives; later in 1940 the officers of the secret police, the NKVD, also gained access to these shops. This was both a sign of the increasing importance of the military in times of approaching war but also a sign of the failure to provide a decent standard of living to the population at large. As Zhuravlev and Sokolov[13] argued, such open favouritism for some workers over others naturally led to envy and the charge that the new Soviet society was not living up to its principles of social equality.

As Osokina has demonstrated, many regions and towns faced pressure from below to introduce strict food rationing and coupons again. The average citizen felt that such rationing was fairer since it guaranteed a minimum share of bread and other basic necessities without the need to stand in queues throughout the night. Many citizens shared the opinion of the 1935 report 'Results of the increasing Soviet trade from the VI to the VII meeting of the Soviets' which summarized earlier experiences of food rationing and proudly stated: 'Thanks to this [the coupon system of rationing] it was possible, despite the lack of resources of food products and their rapidly increasing demand, to take full care of the primary needs of the most important parts of the construction of socialism.'[14]

Social Hierarchies of Consumption and Poverty

In order to see better the importance of the reforms in the mid-1930s, it is necessary to draw comparisons with the situation prevailing during the immediately preceding years. During the first half of the 1930s food provisioning was strictly regulated by the central government. In January 1931, the All-Union system of rationing was introduced with coupons for bread and other basic necessities delivered to the population. *Kolkhoz* peasants (80 per cent of the whole population) as well as those without political rights were excluded. The daily or monthly rations were not, however, uniform but depended on person's role and status in industrial production and distribution. All workers, peasants at the state farms and white-collar workers were divided into different classes. The first list consisted of workers in the main industrial enterprises. Although only 40 per cent of the work force was employed in the main industrial enterprises, they received as much as 70–80 per cent of allocated provisions.[15] The second and third lists consisted of small industrial enterprises (such as bakeries, textile and paper manufacturers) and small workshops of artisans. They received rations for bread, sugar, flour, grains and tea only. The norms were lower than for the first group. These workers were otherwise supposed to live on local resources and products of the local industry, which were not centrally allocated and planned.

Further complicating the hierarchical order, individuals were divided within each of these regional or production units into different groups depending on their personal role and status in production. Industrial and transport workers were more privileged than others. State farms belonged to different categories as well depending on the estimated importance of their produce. As a result, industrial workers of the most important factories, mainly in heavy industry, metallurgy and electricity, were the most privileged ones. The relative share of white-collar workers and administrators, even though lower than the workers', varied again in accord with the estimated or presumed social importance of their work task or field of work. This principle of hierarchy – rewards in relation to the imagined input based on the position or the type of work in question – permeated all fields of society: even deported ex-kulaks and prisoners of labour camps were, at least in principle, fed according to the norms of free labourers depending on their field of work and position in the social distribution of labour. In general, the closer to important material production one worked, the better were the provisions and one's living standards.[16] According to Osokina, this was a strictly hierarchical system of poverty.[17]

An individual's personal well-being varied greatly depending on the site of work where he or she was based. In addition to better rations, many big and important factories and mines, as well as some other organizations, had special economic resources which were not centrally allocated and which they could mobilize in order to feed their workers better than the average. From the early 1930s, for instance, many industrial trusts had farms of their own; or the produce of special farming areas were allocated to them exclusively, and they were encouraged to take care of these farms by the authorities. These farms delivered pork, rabbits, eggs, or milk exclusively to them and their workers' canteens. Many workers undoubtedly lived under worse conditions than the official statistics indicate. But, in some cases, they lived considerably better, with such farm supplements for example. Given the lack of skilled labour and rapid turnover in the labour force, factory directors had to try to retain staff in innovative ways.

During the first years of the Second Five-Year Plan, a large portion of all the workers in the Soviet Union ate their daily lunches or dinners at their workplace canteens. In 1935, 60 per cent of workers who had families ate at workplace canteens across the USSR, and the figure for Moscow and Leningrad was much higher at 80 per cent. These canteens were ordered hierarchically, following similar principles as the rest of society: the most important workers of the most important factories ate the best food at lower prices. Most of the factories operated separate dining rooms for different categories of workers. According to Tuominen, the Finnish Communist leader working at Comintern at Moscow,[18] each factory and work place canteen was divided into at least three hierarchical departments.

Both the system of provisioning and of production were highly centralized. In 1933 Moscow and Leningrad, with 3-4 per cent of the total population living in them, received about half the available margarine and meat; one third of all fish products, wines and spirits; a quarter of all flour and grains; one fifth of butter, sugar, tea and salt centrally distributed to all the cities and towns of the USSR.[19] This was partially due to the fact that almost all the higher Party functionaries and civil servants lived in Moscow. The main reason was, however, that the industrial production, in particular the strategically important machine building and electrical industry with more privileged workers, was highly centralized and concentrated in Moscow. According to Colton:

> Moscow produced all of USSR's ballbearings in 1934, two thirds of its machine tools, 42 percent of its automobiles, and one third of its instruments – not to mention aircraft and other military machinery, where the figures were classified. . . . In 1940, before the wartime evacuation scalloped into its share, the city of Moscow put out 98 percent of the country's ballbearings, half of its machine tools and instruments, 49 percent of the autos, and more than 40 percent of the electrical equipment.[20]

It was mainly in mining, metallurgy and electric power plants – such as the Magnitogorsk metallurgical plant – that any other region of the USSR could seriously compete with Moscow in the allocation of rations.

The rationing of bread was officially abandoned on 1 January 1935, but even after that free trade in bread was not generally practised except in Moscow and some larger cities, where it was possible only because of strong centralization of all available resources at hand. In many places bread coupons were taken into use again soon after the official end to rationing and monthly limits of trade introduced due to serious shortages. In October 1935 the coupons for meat, cheese, fish, sugar and potatoes were also officially eliminated and from the 1 January 1936 the coupons for the rest of the regulated food products too. The Party and the government treated the official end of rationing as a sign of great abundance. The liberalization of trade was met with mixed feelings among the population, and many people demanded or expected a rapid return to the system of strict rationing, which they felt to be more just and fair. After the end of rationing, the following menu expressing sceptical feelings was found written on the canteen door at the Kirov factory in Leningrad:

Dinner for workers:
Starter – cabbage soup with kerosene
Main course – fresh moss with sour cream
Desert – a sweet desert of turnips[21]

Relative Abundance in the Middle of Poverty

As Osokina has argued

all workers, including the industrial vanguard, shared a condition of semi-starvation
during the period of food rationing in the early 1930s. In practice, no one, not even the
families of the industrial workers in the capital, received fats, milk products, eggs, fruits
or tea from the state resources or fonds. The provisioning of meat could be regarded as
only symbolic: a worker in the Moscow or Ivanovsk regions ate on average not more than
10 grams per day. Compared to that workers in the capital received more: 35-40 grams
per day, but this was not enough for people engaged in heavy physical work.[22]

This was, however, only part of the truth. There were privileged people in the
Soviet Union as well, the so-called *nomenklatura*, higher Party, army, governmental administrators who mainly lived in Moscow. As Osokina[23] points out,
during the first half of the 1930s the number of people in the list of special provisioning – a good estimate of those belonging to higher *nomenklatura* – increased
to 55,500 families of which 45,000 lived in Moscow. It was not common, at least
not officially, for the local *nomenklatura* of the Republics and the regions to enjoy
these privileges. They nonetheless certainly often knew how to take advantage of
them themselves.

In Osokina's opinion, even those people who belonged to the new Soviet elite
lived if not in straightforward permanent poverty, then under conditions that could
be regarded as extremely modest according to any Western standards. Her main
examples come from the early or mid-1930s.

Here is one example of special provisioning. It was received in the summer 1932 by
persons living in the governmental building at the Bolotnaia Square [in Moscow]. The
monthly rate included 4 kg of meat and 4 kg of sausages and *Wurst*, 1.5 kg of butter and
2 l of oil, 6 kg of fresh fish and 2 kg of herring, 3 kg of sugar and flour (not to count the
800 g of wheaten bread received daily), 3 kg of grains, 8 cans of canned food, 20 eggs,
2 kg of cheese, 1 kg of black caviar, 50 g of tea, 1,200 cigarettes (*papirosy*), two pieces
of soap, and also one litre of milk per day. Plentiful, but with the exception of caviar,
without any extras. Cakes and candies, as well as fruit and vegetables belonged to the
menu too.

Other goods, such as clothes and shoes, were received by order from special shops, tailors' or shoemakers' according to special norms.[24]

The members of the Moscow elite or *nomenklatura* could additionally buy other products from the *kolkhoz* market or second-hand shops. They did not live in poverty or lack any basic necessities. What is peculiar about these descriptions is not so much the amount of any single food stuff or product delivered almost free of charge, but the fact that the variety of the products available was always strictly limited and rather monotonous. As A.G. Mankov wrote in his recently published diary of 'an ordinary man' in 1940,

> together with the poor there are people who are fully supplied and well provided for. But the most important thing to understand is what this could possibly mean under the circumstances: two to three costumes, one of which is imported, an imported bicycle (or motorcycle) and an unlimited opportunity to buy grapes at the price of 11 roubles a kilo (if they happen to be on sale).[25]

If a person living in an elite house in Moscow wanted to change his or her diet it would have been practically impossible. He or she had to eat what was delivered to them or what was available at their workplace canteen. The same was even more the case with the privileged workers of a central, important industrial plant.

Arvo Tuominen, the Finnish communist leader and a close friend of Otto Ville Kuusinen, who worked in the Comintern in the 1930s, told a characteristic story of a Finnish Christmas party in Moscow in the mid-1930s. He and Kuusinen were invited to celebrate a Finnish Christmas at the home of Heikki Kaljunen, the legendary Red commander in Karelia during the Civil War and now a director of an important ski factory in Moscow. What impressed Tuominen, in addition to the colourful personality of his host, was the fact that on the dinner table there were all kinds of traditional, Finnish Christmas dishes: 'rutabaga casserole, herring salad, and rice porridge – only codfish was missing. Caviar and other Russian delicacies completed the meal. Nor was there any shortage of good wines.'[26] Caviar was a self-evident part of a Soviet 'gourmet' meal in the 1930s but obviously it demanded someone with all the social connections and skills of a general director of a big Moscow plant to get the raw materials to make rather simple and modest peasant dishes like herring salad and rice porridge.

Osokina offers another example of abundance among the *nomenklatura* in the early 1930s. In 1933, the year of mass hunger, in the words of an official document,

> the monthly consumption of food products of a official railway wagon of the Central Committee consisted of 200 kg of butter, 250 kg of Swiss cheese, 500 kg of sausages, 500 kg chicken, 550 kg of different kinds of meat, 300 kg of fish (in addition to 350 kg of

canned fish and 100 kg of herring), 100 kg caviar, 300 kg of sugar, 160 kg of chocolate and candies, 100 boxes of fruit and 60,000 exported cigarettes (*papirosy*).[27]

No wonder that the curtains of the restaurant wagons of the trains taking members of the elite to the health spas at Sochi in the South were ordered to be strictly closed during stops at stations. It would not work to have the hungry masses see what was on the tables. As Arvo Tuominen remembered, two armed Red Guards entered the wagon at Rostov and stood guard at both ends all the way to Sochi and the luxurious sanatoriums.

'Many Stakhanovites are Earning a lot of Money'

The 'equal wages' policy (*uravnilovka*) had been officially abandoned at the seventeenth Party Congress in 1934 as anti-Marxist and petit bourgeois. The principles of the new wage policy were expressed in a form comprehensible to every fisherman in the editorial of the monthly journal of the Soviet fish industry: 'Now [after the liquidation of *uravnilovka*] every worker and state administrator should be able, without any restrictions, to buy all the necessaries and things of consumption, in relation to his earnings, and, which is the same thing, in relation to the quality and quantity of his work.'[28] The same author formulated the new principle of economics in a condensed manner: 'A fisherman pulling out to sea must be able to trust that he can buy bread, and that his family has bread.'[29] As Comrade Ishkov wrote in the same journal in 1936: 'A bike, radio, *patéfon* – have ceased being unreachable dreams of a *kolkhoznik*. Now all these are, in fact, available to every *kolkhoznik*, and, they in fact possess these things.'[30]

In 1934 the trade press *Sovetskaia torgovlia* reported that the workers at the Stalin Car Factory in Moscow, undoubtedly one of the model factories of the country, were taken special care of. They had access to special shops and canteens and could order clothes within a special system of quotas: 'The best of all the best workers are served by two special shops and have access to home deliveries. These shops have the best goods. Two times a month the list of these privileged workers is checked.'[31] The *udarniki* had special heavily subsidized meals at the canteen. During the previous year, these shock workers had received a right to 25,000 orders of shoes and clothes. The workers talked about the winter coats, trousers and household utensils that they had earned *po udarnoi*, as a reward for their exceptional industriousness at work. *Udarniki* were rewarded mainly with access to closed shops and other delivery outlets. In 1934 at least a few of the workers of the Stalin Car Factory were said to have their names on a waiting list to be allowed to buy a private car of their own – with their own money.[32] Whether any private cars werc, in fact, ever sold to private persons in the 1930s is not known. But motor-cycles were highly appreciated presents to workers.

Workers in 1934 were almost totally dependent on the catering of their factory, which in the case of such a privileged factory as the Stalin auto plant could be quite satisfactory. This is evident in the testimony of one of the workers:

> I earn on average 220 to 230 roubles a month. I eat at the factory canteen. The lunch consists of two meat dishes and one sweet dish and costs from 90 kopecks to 1 rouble 20 kopecks. Last month I spent 25 roubles on lunch.
>
> From the factory shop this month I received 400 grams of butter, 400 grams of margarine, 2 kg of meat, 1 kg of herring, 2 kg of grains, 2 kg of sugar, 18 kg of potatoes, 25 grams of tea, 2 kg of biscuits, 2 kg of chocolate, 2 kilos of apples. [This family thus consumed as much chocolate as meat!]
>
> In addition, every day I spent 35 kopecks on cigarettes (*papirosy*) and 40 kopecks on bread. On all food products plus cigarettes I spend 91 roubles 40 kopecks a month.
>
> My wife is not employed and she takes care of the household. Despite this we have extra money. During the last three months I have bought boots for 27 roubles, a warm winter coat with a fur collar for 228 roubles, and a couple of sets of underwear, shirts and socks for my wife. We are satisfied and we eat well.[33]

In his memoirs of an 'ordinary worker' Mankov ironically described the new canteen opened at his workplace in 1933:

> In our factory a new canteen was opened for the *udarniki*. It is meant, as they say, to stimulate the productivity of labour. They separated half the area from the general canteen, surrounded it with a glass partition, painted it with oil, hung curtains in front of the windows, brought in small tables covered with white tablecloths. On the window sills and on the tables fresh flowers. Lamps with designer lampshades. Very few people are allowed in, mostly directors. Dishes served are better. In one word: a restaurant. . . While in the general canteen soup with macaroni or pure cabbage is served as the first course, and macaroni with sugar (more seldom with margarine) as the second course, in the 'restaurant' there are dishes with meat, and if with macaroni then always with real butter too.'[34]

The centrally allocated rations could, at times, turn out to be rather favourable even to the politically repressed groups of the population. For example, a peasant called Pietari Simonpoika Jääskeläinen from the Finnish village Keltto near Leningrad, whose entire family was deported to the Northern regions of the river Jenisei, together with other 'kulaks' of the village, wrote in a letter to his relatives a detailed account of the material conditions of life in Siberia.[35] In his opinion, living conditions were fairly decent – especially if compared with the situation a couple of years earlier. His 'extended' family consisted of dozen members, several working adults and children. They received nineteen different kinds of rationed food each month. (As he also mentioned, chocolate could be bought without restrictions.) The rations were rather plentiful:

168 kilograms of flour
25 kilograms of grain
10 kilograms of meat
1.5 kilograms of butter
3.3 kilograms of vegetable oil
32 kilograms of fish
12.4 kilograms of sugar
5.6 kilograms of biscuits
500 grams of tea
2.6 kilograms of dried vegetables
7 kilograms of salt
12 cans of food
2.2 kilograms of tobacco
1,800 papirosy (cigarettes)
3.7 kilograms of soap
9 pieces of perfumed soap
75 boxes of matches
26 meters of cloth

In addition to centrally rationed foodstuffs, which undoubtedly were often of poor quality and available only irregularly, one could also buy many other items in the local shops. The price of a pair of shoes was 5 roubles 50 kopeks, a kilogram of wheat flour was 28 kopeks and rye flour 25 kopeks. These could, however, only be bought with gold. In one sense the local miners and workers were privileged. They had the right to wash gold on the river bank on sites no longer suited to more mechanical methods of gold mining. This, together with the industriousness and Northern farming skills of these Finnish peasants, at least partly explained their relatively decent living conditions in Siberia in particular if one compares them, for instance, with the destinies of a later wave of Finnish deportees who were destined to Tashkent and who lived in a state of semi-starvation for many years.[36]

As these reports show, not only members of the *nomenklatura* but even ordinary workers at important, privileged factories could live relatively well in the Soviet Union in the early 1930s. Furthermore, things were getting better in 1934. But even these relatively well off workers were totally dependent on the outlets of their own factories or workplaces as far as all their daily necessities were concerned. Their

*Figure 20   The Stakhanovite worker N.T. Popov with his wife ordering cakes for a
family party, Sverdlov 1936. (Source: RGAKFD)*

factories delivered provisions to them according to a very complicated and centrally regulated system of rationing.[37] If the workers had any extra money to buy
anything else, they needed coupons to make orders from special 'closed' shops
joined to their factories. In the mid-1930s the situation gradually started to change.
Now many workers could earn more money and they could buy things more freely
in the commercial shops.

   Workers' budgets offer another source of information about the lived reality of
'abundance.' Such budgets were regularly published in both the general and
technical press. The new system of Stakhanovites (introduced in August 1935)
witnessed the first system of direct individual monetary rewards, which helped
give rise to the establishment of more commercial shops. They were meant to
satisfy the newly created demand for commodities sold openly to anyone with
sufficient money. Both the work achievements and the earnings of these new
industrious workers were widely publicized, creating a whole genre of Stak-
hanoviana. For instance, Maria Rovenskaia, 21 years old, a Stakhanovite from a
Stalingrad meat factory made the following, typical vow at a conference of the
Soviet Meat Industry:

I must tell you that I do not work out of fear, but out of conscience and my records were performed only for the love of the Party of Lenin and Stalin, because life has become merrier and better. In such a mood I come to work every day. . . . I was brought up at an orphanage. I was educated by the Party, I'm a pure proletarian. My work norms are high because I work conscientiously and I want to pay back the upbringing which was given to me by the Party and the government.[38]

To those who had expressed doubts about her record performance she made a promise: 'You will see, as soon as I return home I will produce not 3,000 kilos but 4,000 kilos!' The shock worker, Marusia Demina, inspired by Rovenskaia's words made a promise of her own: 'I will not be left behind and I will give a product of even better quality and more.' The general goal adopted collectively by the conference was to make the best sausage in the world.[39]

The Stakhanovite movement was widely reported and hailed as the solution to the problems of work discipline, lack of performance and lack of professional schooling. The very same Moscow factory opened its huge sausage plant in 1935 'with people who came for the first time to sausage industry, and most of them came for the first time not only to sausage, but industry in general.' Their productivity was very low. But as reported by the factory, the local Stakhanovite movement, started in October 1935, helped increase the productivity of labour. For instance, the workers Egorchenko, Leontieva, Melnikov – all without any formal qualifications – started to fulfil their work norms up to 180-200 per cent.[40]

Shock workers and Stakhanovites such as Rovenskaia and Demina could earn a lot of money too. They were people with at least some real 'buying power'; they were, in a sense, becoming their own customers. The report of the same Mikoyan Miasokombinat (meat trust) in Moscow boasted about the earnings of its top workers as early as 1935. According to a study by the local trade union the needs of these Stakhanovites grew in line with their budgets; they needed more food, cultural products, and other items of general consumption. Brigadier Dorodnikov had, for instance, in October 1935 earned 849 roubles and his wife another 112 roubles. They bought a new mattress, a man's suit, shoes for their children and improved their standard of eating in general. Another shock worker in the same factory, Popov, had earned together with his wife 762 roubles. With their extra money they bought a table, a woman's winter coat worth 300 roubles and food. They were planning to get good chrome boots, chairs and a *patéfon* in the near future. Worker Tsyprov bought a bed with a mattress, a man's winter coat made to order (162 roubles), shoes and clothes for his children, bed linen and a table. In addition to their monthly salaries, the factory took care of their cultural needs: every day thirty theatre tickets were available free of charge to the Stakhanovites.[41]

The Moscow meat trust reported in 1936 that among its approximately 6,000 workers there were already 1,110 Stakhanovites who fulfilled their norms up to

120-200 per cent even though the general norm had already been increased by 45 per cent – due to the general growth of productivity.[42] In November many Stakhanovite workers from this factory earned well: Gorelov who was a worker in the butcher's department – 1,247 roubles, Andrianov, a worker from the sausage plant – 1,150 roubles, Golodin – from the same department – 1,129 roubles. A large group of workers received over 500 roubles each. (The price of a kilo of meat was at the time 9 roubles 60 kopecks; which means that a worker earning 1,000 roubles could have bought about 100 kilos of meat with his or her monthly wages. The other side of the coin, which is never referenced in these reports, is that meat was not actually readily available to most workers and farmers.) Now was the first time that many workers and their families could afford to buy their first tables, mattresses, winter clothing and so on, not to speak of such *kulttovary* as *patéfons*. Previously they were simply not available or workers could not afford them with their regular wages.

In these and similar reports the Stakhanovite*s* were thus not only presented as ideal Soviet workers but also as ideal Soviet consumers. They could earn considerable money in the mid-1930s. What was probably as important from the point of view of their material standard of living was that they enjoyed many privileges and received other material rewards from their factories. Such rewards and gifts from the factories or the authorities – often presented at public occasions – were celebrated and publicized both in the All-Union and local press. Overcoats and leather boots were typical gifts. More advanced workers or foremen could also 'earn' a free place of study at a technical school or institute. When a meeting of Stakhanovite workers was held in Moscow in 1936, Ordzhonikidze, the Minister of Heavy Industry, presented the participants with fifty cars, twenty-five motorcycles, 150 gramophones, 200 hunting rifles and 150 pocket watches.[43] As retold by Natalia Lebina,[44] the Moscow filer Ivan Gudov remembered what the participants at an All-Union meeting of Stakhanovite*s* planned to buy with their higher wages. They dreamed of milk-coloured slippers worth 180 roubles, a *crepe de chine* dress worth 200 roubles and an overcoat worth 300 roubles.

As soon as the Stakhanovite movement advanced in many factories and shops, a great proportion of all the workers became Stakhanovite*s*. As the reports demonstrate, their Stakhanovite*s* could increase to well over one third or almost half of all the workers of a factory. In October 1935 a Komsomol member Comrade Saburova started, for instance, the Stakhanovite movement at the Rot Front factory. This was reported to have resulted in a big leap forward. Towards the end of the year there were already 734 Stakhanovite workers at the factory, 32 per cent of the whole labour force.[45] It is understandable that in line with the general increase in productivity of work, partly caused by the very same Stakhanovite*s*, and their increasing numbers and share in the labour force both these earlier often spectacular wage differentials and other privileges diminished. In the end, the whole movement was reduced to a rather unsystematically realized organization of piece rate wages, which allowed for much arbitrariness. The arbitrary rules of work and renumeration were one of the main complaints expressed by the foreign workers at the Moscow Elektrozavod, the electric factory in the early 1930s.[46]

In 1936 the Central Committee of the Komsomol Union published interesting statistics about an 'inventory of goods of culture' among young industrial workers in the major Soviet cities of Moscow, Leningrad, Kharkov, Dnepropetrovsk, Donbas, Ivanov, Orekhov, Gorki and Sverdlovsk. These statistics revealed that many commodities such as radio receivers, musical instruments, bicycles and *patéfons* were fairly common by 1935 among young men and women, many of whom were probably members of the Stakhanovite movement. Also of interest is the fact that these 'goods of culture' were not that much more common among those workers with higher wages than others. What explained the rate of ownership was gender, on the one hand, and education, on the other. All these goods could be found much more often among men than women. The relationship between education and ownership was more intriguing. All these cultural goods were more common among young workers with a medium level of education than among those with little education and those in higher education. To take a few examples, in the group with a medium level of education 32 per cent of men had radio receivers, 14 per cent *patéfons* and 18 per cent bicycles. The respective percentages were as low as 10, 2 and 2 in the group with little education and 18, 4 and 10 among male students of higher education.[47] Students who did not earn money and lived on very low state grants simply could not afford to buy such relatively expensive items, but otherwise the correlation between degree of education and ownership seemed to confirm the authorities' belief that a new Soviet citizen with new and more cultured demands was, in fact, gradually being born.

Raising Living Standards and Dissatisfied Consumers

What was the reality of the much-hyped 'abundance' of the mid-1930s? There is no doubt that compared with the period immediately preceding it many things had improved. The first Five-Year Plan had given a devastating blow to the availability of the most ordinary consumer goods both in the towns and the villages. Accounts of foreign visitors to the Soviet Union offer some interesting insight about the condition of shopping in Moscow in the early 1930s. As retold by Sheila Fitzpatrick, an American engineer returning to Moscow in June 1930 after some months of absence described the dramatic impact of the new economic politics adopted at the beginning of the First Five-Year Plan: 'On the streets all the shops seemed to have disappeared. Gone was the open market. Gone were the Nepmen (private ill-reputed small scale businessmen of the NEP period.) The government stores had showy, empty boxes and other window-dressing. But the interior was devoid of goods.'[48]

The Danish traveller Nielsen reported experiences with a Soviet friend on a shopping tour in Moscow in spring 1932. This was when the First Five-Year Plan had just been completed – a time when there were very few regular shops in Moscow.

A Western European who is used to being able to buy anything that he needs in his daily life if only he has the money cannot even imagine how much it takes in Russia to get hold of a couple of everyday utensils one happens to need. It does not matter what the utensils in question are: a rubber tap for a bathtub, a doorknob, some window sashes, a couple of electric bulbs or a fuse, the most ordinary kitchen tools, an axe, a spoon, or a kettle to boil water in.

The same holds true of the necessary material used to repair the most elementary things: a bit of paint, a couple of window edge protection strips, a wooden list, or a box of nails. The only thing to be done is to go on an expedition through the city and to try to get hold of those things in one way or another. Usually it is best to direct your course to the Sukharevskii market. Here all those gather who have something to offer and here stroll all those who are hunting for some thing or another. Every day up to 50,000 people gather here. . . How anybody can find anything one is looking for is totally incomprehensible.[49]

The First Five-Year Plan unleashed a more or less totally unregulated bazaar economy, rather than implementing an efficient, centrally planned distribution system for goods. But, by the mid-1930s, things had changed again. Compared with the hard years of the First Five-Year Plan, the mid-1930s felt like a definite improvement. Consumer goods were once again available, as this book has shown. Even better, the goods could be bought with money from state shops, not only from the *kolkhoz* or black market. The Soviet Union had entered a second era of, however restricted and modified, 'market economy', the birth of which was extremely painful. As government reports show, by the mid-1930s, there were already some products that were being oversupplied, a situation never to be seen in the years directly prior. In discussing the tasks of the newly created chain of Gastronom food stores, Shinkarevskii declared in 1936 that 'it should always be possible for the customer to buy any type of any commodity.'[50] 'The buyer will not search for the commodity as was the case earlier but the commodity, the shop will search for the buyer.'[51] This principle was new to the Soviet Union in both theory and practice.

After several rounds of price increases instituted in order to absorb the monetary savings of workers who could not find anything to buy with their money toward the end of the 1930s, the Soviet consumers faced new kinds of problems with

which they were totally unaccustomed. For the first time, there were products on
the shelves of the shops to buy, although many were out of the range for ordinary
workers because of their high prices. In a letter to Zhdanov in June 1935, after the
end of rationing, a worker recognized that the shops were now full of goods, but
complained that he and other workers could not buy them, and he appealed to
Zhdanov for prices to be halved.[52] Such workers' complaints were often reported
by the authorities. People were used to getting many basic necessities almost free
of charge, if at all, and were not used to the new situation in which the price – and
not the availability alone – determined whether they could achieve desired goods.
Such relative poverty created by lack of money, typical of economies with market
prices, was of a different kind than the poverty caused by the absolute lack or
shortage of products during the system of rationing.

On the other hand, shortages could also be caused by low prices. If things were
given away for nothing their demand could be endless and, consequently, could
never, not even in principle, be satisfied. The Soviet government and the Party
seemed to be in a hopeless situation with solutions hard to come by. Either shops
were full of goods but people complained that the prices were too high, or shops
were virtually empty but the prices were low. As Daniel Bell, in a totally different
context, formulated it, we can only speak of abundance in a limited sense: the
problems of hunger and disease need no longer exist. No imaginary economic
system could possibly solve the problem of scarcity since in economic terms
'scarcity is a measure of relative differences of preferences at relative costs.'[53] The
Soviet government promised its citizens that they would be living in abundance by
the mid-1930s. There is no doubt that the Soviet Union did not really, however,
even fulfil the promise of abundance according the first definition offered above
until long after the Second World War.

By the end of the 1930s, during the Second and the Third Five-Year Plans, the
general population had great expectations of their government based on their
promises. The earlier hardships could be explained away as temporary. But once
the situation deteriorated again towards the end of the decade, instead of getting
better as it should have done, complaints became louder. In Davies' study *Popular
Opinion in Stalin's Russia* several such complaints addressed to the Moscow Party
leader, Zhdanov, are cited. A Moscow worker wrote in 1936 expressing his serious
doubts cautiously: 'the question whether we have reached a wealthy and cultured
life has not yet been decided completely. I think.'[54] Now there were, at least in
Moscow, more consumption goods, such as pencils, writing paper and ordinary
boots, available, but their prices were too high for ordinary workers. Therefore, as
the writer suggested, it was necessary to produce also cheaper models of these
same products, so that ordinary workers could afford to buy them as well.[55]

The new, much advertised abundance in Moscow and other city centres gave
rise to new kinds of dissatisfaction. Visitors to Moscow could see with their own

eyes that the Muscovites lived better than other Soviet citizens. They were often quite openly envious of these privileges and expressed their concern: 'in what ways were they or their children worse than the Muscovites, why do they see neither sugar nor milk.'[56] As one worker commented during the Finnish War in early 1940: 'Just think, our people are sitting in Moscow and drinking champagne.'[57]

One did not, however, have to travel far from Moscow to observe these huge regional differences. *Pravda* could proudly report on 30 November 1934 that in the no. 1 food store, the newly established flagship of the chain of Gastronom shops, there were well over 200 different types of bread available. Two years later the trade press reported of an inspection in the shops at the outskirts of Moscow, in the Moscow region, which had revealed that 261 trade points did not even have salt on sale. On average, they only had half of the minimum amount of goods demanded by official regulations on their shelves.[58] If the shops in the close vicinity of the capital were so poorly stocked compared with those of the city centre it is easy to imagine the almost total lack of any product variety in the more distant regions of the country.

The eagerness with which all the new achievements in the field of 'light' and food industry and trade were reported in the All-Union press could sometimes lead to problems because the benefits were so often restricted to the major cities. In a letter addressed to the Chairman of the Council of Ministers, Molotov, for example, Tabakov, the director of the Magnesit factory (Ogneupor trust, Cheliabinsk region), asked for help with providing his factory workers with better and more individual consumer goods. They had all read in *Pravda* (15 September 1934) about a fashion atelier that had been opened at *the* Moscow Elektrozavod. They expressed the hope that such high quality consumer goods would soon be also available at their workplace, which had well over 500 workers who 'would like to have good cloth for their overcoats and suits as well as hand made shoes'.[59] If the government and the Party had promised that the Soviet worker would dress in a more cultured way, why should only the workers of the Moscow-based Elektrozavod be able to enjoy this new high standard of living? The propagandistic effect of numerous new luxuries and comforts of everyday life, as well as the promise of a better life, was not necessarily that intended by the authorities. When no general improvement on a longer term could be guaranteed, the promises could all too easily lead to general dissatisfaction, as the authorities realized. This explains the importance and the great attention paid both to new items of consumption and the complaints concerning them both by the public and by the authorities.

Enjoyed by the new industrial, political and artistic vanguard as rewards for their supposedly exemplary work for the common good, the new 'luxuries' carried an ambivalent message. They could just as well act as a stimulus for more effort at work and better accomplishments as targets for the envy of millions and millions of less fortunate or less resourceful fellow citizens of the new Worker's Fatherland.

What separates the latter part of the 1930s from the earlier years is that now people increasingly received their 'rewards' in the form of money. They could now use them to buy whatever they liked – or whatever was available in the state or cooperative shops, restaurants and department stores whereas earlier they had direct access to various supplies through a very complicated system of rationing. The earlier system of rationing was very hierarchic and open to corruption. The new system of monetary wages and higher income differentials was problematic too, in particular, since it co-existed side by side with the system of rationing which was never totally abolished.

The very expression of the intention, however restricted in reality, to start producing and improve the availability of non-essential consumer goods was a significant development. Now the Soviet worker was allowed, and even encouraged, to increase his or her consumption and cultural standards, not only quantitatively but also qualitatively. Under the conditions of developing socialism the increasing cultural and material needs of the workers could be legitimately expected to be satisfied. Stalin had said that 'the character and peculiarity of our revolution is that it did not only give freedom to the people but also opened the possibility of a rich and cultured life. That is why life has become merry.'[60] Obviously at least some concrete steps had to be taken – and were indeed taken – to give some credence to such a slogan.

As we have seen time and again, the plans to increase some particular consumer goods were put into practice, usually at the cost of development in some other sector of the economy. By the end of the 1930s, many new goods that had previously never been available, or only in limited quantities, were on sale once more. Even when, as the annual reports of many food trusts indicate, their goods were produced in greater and rapidly increasing quantities, demand far outstripped supply. There is no doubt that the standard of living of the great majority remained very low throughout the 1930s, but for some sectors of the population in certain areas (Moscow in particular) there was a noticeable change in the consumer economy.

Veitser, the Minister of Trade Planning, made notable progress in promoting market relations between industry, agriculture and trade. He also remembered the consumer. In November 1934 his plans received Stalin's uncritical support. In his speech at the Plenary Session of the Central Committee of the Communist Party, Stalin rather surprisingly took a decisive stance in favour of the market economy in the discussion of the end of food rationing: 'We want to strengthen monetary economy . . . in every place install commodity circulation thus changing the present policy of the distribution of products . . . A fashion of money will then arrive; money moves. Something we have not had for a long time.'[61] Stalin believed that the role of money was crucial in normalizing the relations between town and countryside. Stalin's 'market speech' was not made public at the time,

Figure 21   The perfume shop 'TEZHE' in Vyborg following the annexation of the town after the Finnish war (the 'Winter' war) in 1940. Source: RGAKFD)

thus presumably making it easier for him to distance himself from the negative consequences of the market economy, such as high prices.

Things are Getting Better, Anyway

Accounts recalling the standard of living and its rise in the 1930s vary dramatically. According to historian John Barber, 'in the mid-1930s the atmosphere appears to have improved. Higher living standards, the end of rationing, the three good years of 1934-36 in industry, a series of better harvests, together with a temporarily more relaxed atmosphere, produced a more positive mood.'[62] Fitzpatrick is more sceptical, however: 'In popular memory, indeed, the only really good year of the 1930s in Russia seems to have been 1937 – ironically the first year of the Great Purges – when the harvest was the best in the decade and there was plenty of food in the stores.'[63]

Most sources indicate that the years 1934-36 were, by both objective and subjective standards, the most comfortable ones of the decade. These were the first years after a long period of extremely hard times and they witnessed noticeable improvements, even if restricted to the urban areas. These years saw the end of rationing and the opening of Mikoyan's much-advertised giant meat and sausage factories. In many other fields of food production, from chocolate to canned fish, new production on a large scale was started. But there were other signs of the better times to come too, which became cherished memories among the population. The Moscow Metro was officially opened on 15 May 1935. The general plan of Moscow was adopted with its new housing policy promising new and better apartments and shops for the population. According to this new plan, for instance, the ground floors of all the city buildings higher than three stories were to be reserved for shops. The first Soviet department stores opened their doors to customers. In 1936, the New Year officially gained its status as the Soviet Christmas with typical seasonal products and decorations, the Christmas tree (now known as the New Year's tree) included. These were also the years of the popular Soviet heroes and pilots who explored unknown Northern regions or made new world records of flying among others. Many Soviet citizens must have shared the feeling that now things were definitely and rapidly changing and the final victory approaching. The period culminated in the celebrations of Stalin's new constitution and the numerous carnivals in 1936.

By 1937, however, the economy was facing new challenges and the effects of the bad harvest of the summer of 1936. The huge promises made on consumer goods production simply could not be kept. The unrealistically rapid increase in some areas often meant stoppages in others while almost all the available resources were concentrated in some conspicuous enterprise that happened to be the priority of the moment. At least partly, the purges of 1937 and 1938 could be explained by these sharpening economic conflicts and problems: the Soviet system searched for scapegoats and looked for enemies who could be blamed for all these difficulties.

Those who argue, as Fitzpatrick does, that the year 1937 was the highlight of Soviet material culture before the Second World War could undoubtedly also refer to many new 'victories.' There was the birth of Soviet champagne in 1936. New, more luxurious restaurants, bars and ice cream parlours opened in the big cities – a policy which faced serious resistance from the side of the more egalitarian oriented authorities and Party functionaries. These were also the years that saw the emergence of Soviet advertising on a large scale, in newspapers and journals, on the radio and in the movies. New more luxurious food stores were opened in all the bigger cities. The targets of the new Third Five-Year Plan, which started in 1937, were also quite spectacular in the field of consumer goods production. Such developments were actively publicized by the authorities, as a sign of the new Soviet democracy guaranteed by Stalin's new constitution. These were, however, also the years during which public attention in the Soviet Union was directed towards the Spanish Civil War, where Soviet forces were fighting for the Spanish Republic.

Because such evaluations are subjective and depend on the observer's personal experience it is better to leave the question concerning the 'best years' of the 1930s open. One could argue that there were in fact two major leaps in the construction of a consumer goods society of the 1930s. And these efforts by the authorities bore some fruit at least. Many goods were now, for the first time since the NEP, available in the first place. Of equal importance, they were available – or were meant to be – on the commercial market, meaning that anyone, in principle, who could afford the goods could buy them. Previously they had been available only, if at all, through the system of closed nets of distribution to those who had access to them. This gradual and cautious establishment of some important features of a market economy was in people's minds probably as remarkable a change as any increase in the production figures of consumer goods. By the end of the 1930s it undoubtedly looked, in the eyes of many, as if the advances made in the middle of the decade in promoting the food and consumer goods industry and in creating the fundamentals of a more cultured system of trade had come to nothing. The living conditions of the population were in many ways reminiscent of the worst years of the early 1930s. This is, however, only part of the truth. Facing again severe problems of providing the population even with the most basic necessities of daily life, local officials in many regions reverted to old measures of rationing and regulating the food supply obviously supported by the popular mood. Officially, however, the many reforms of the organization of Soviet trade adopted in the mid-1930s were never abolished before the war. The ideals and the goals did not change remarkably even though many of them might have seemed to be as Utopian now as when they were first invented. It is understandable that people who were desperately fighting to find their daily bread could not afford to buy champagne even if it were available in their local shops. But, on the other hand, the production of champagne and many other similar, under the prevailing conditions, amazing luxuries went on as before and new increased targets were adopted. This was the other side of the planned economy: problems in some sectors of economy certainly spread to others too but these were supposed to follow their original plans as far as possible, and act as if nothing had happened. Utmost poverty could exist side by side with signs of abundance and luxury. Therefore, all through the 1930s, in the middle of poverty there were both many visible symbols and concrete islands of abundance in the Soviet Union. And if people were increasingly dissatisfied at the end of decade it could, at least partly, be explained by their increasing expectations and the unrealistic promises made by officials.

The Soviet Regime and the People

According to the prominent Soviet Union historian Martin Malia,[64] the 'revisionist history writing', represented by scholars such as Sheila Fitzpatrick, has committed a serious mistake by presuming that negotiations between the state power and the common people have been a 'driving force' in Soviet history. In his opinion it is wrong to presume that there was 'a social dynamic driving these events from below'. Instead, he advocates the old thesis of totalitarianism according to which 'the Soviet regime sought to direct all human activity – economic, social and cultural – to one overriding ideological end, and that it used institutional terror to reach it'. In saying so Malia does not deny that the 'mice's resistance' (people's opposition) produced periodic NEP-like concessions. But these are not essential to the understanding of the dynamics of Soviet history.

An examination of the development of the Soviet culture of consumption in the 1930s largely supports the totalitarian thesis. The government and the Party directed and initiated everything from above. Virtually nothing could be done independently or without the knowledge of state authorities except on the periphery or on the outskirts of the system. Such initiatives most often did not leave any permanent traces in the functioning of the system as a whole. There was, however, one serious problem which the Communist regime had to face. Even though it placed great confidence in the plasticity of the human soul and body, it could not totally neglect to monitor the reception and success of its various activities and enterprises among common people.

It was often easier to blame the lack of political vigilance or low cultural standards of the people for any political or economic failures. Dissatisfied or dissident individuals could always be arrested and annihilated. But the system also desperately needed positive examples and models – model citizens, model workers and model consumers. It needed stories of success and happiness. It could not entirely neglect the demands and the wishes of the population at large. Most of the people could be wrong most of the time and the government right, but not all of the people all the time. This was a real challenge in particular since the coming happiness and material well-being of the greatest number had always been the foremost legitimation of the regime. Therefore it had to invent something and offer some gratification to the people – interesting and attractive cultural experiences, material goods and services, possibilities of gratifying social interaction and arenas of mutual sociability. And so it also had to be interested in monitoring the responses and reactions of the workers and peasants, not just in order to foresee and prevent uprisings and mutinies but also to learn something – to do things better and stop attempting things that proved to be totally impossible. The history of the material culture of the Soviet Union therefore offers a modified, more nuanced, understanding of the totalitarian argument.

Terry Martin[65] has, in analyzing the politics of the Soviet Union between the two World Wars, made a useful distinction between hard-line and soft-line policies. The hard-line policies were the core Bolshivik tasks whereas soft-line policies were designed to make those policies palatable to the larger population. The Soviet bureaucracy was also divided between hard-line and soft-line institutions. Soft-line institutions dealt directly with the Soviet public and their job was to present current Soviet policy in as attractive a light as possible. In this sense, the ministries of Food Industry and Trade were typical soft-line institutions, the secret police, the NKVD, and the Politburo of the Communist Party hard-line institutions. In the policies of consumption soft-line and hard-line institutions mostly lived peacefully side by side often paying little attention to the activities of others.

The histories of the founding of Soviet champagne and cosmetics are good examples. The institutions promoting and producing these more luxurious consumer goods could, quite amazingly, go on functioning for a long time as if nothing serious had happened in the middle of mass arrests and repressions, as long as the presented reasons for the arrests did not directly touch the specific goals and methods of these institutions. The people's enemies could be treated just as 'ordinary wreckers or saboteurs', guilty of the same political crime as their colleagues in any other institution or workplace. To the factory directors, the arrests were but one more little nuisance disturbing the normal functioning of their enterprises by depriving them, for instance, of competent labour power. The case of the canteens and the restaurants discussed in Chapter 7 offers another kind of an example. Here the very activity of the Central Administration of Restaurants and Cafés was presented as the main reason for the arrests. The directors had made themselves guilty, not just of 'ordinary' criminal wrecking or sabotage, but had in their institutions promoted a line of activity which was politically dangerous and harmful by opening better, commercial restaurants under the pretext of satisfying a popular demand.

As Martin suggests, the real policy resulted from the dialogue between these two kinds of institutions. The tasks of both were equally important and real to the functioning of the state. The soft-line institutions did not simply bluff by pretending to be promoting the good of the ordinary citizens. On the other hand, the role of the hard-line institutions was more decisive in that they had the last word in many matters. The soft-line institutions could enjoy much autonomy for a long time and more or less effectively pursue their own policy lines as long as they did not violate or threaten the realization of the major Bolshevik core tasks.

The hard-line institutions had an upper hand because they were the ones who had the right to determine what the core tasks and issues really were and – as importantly – how they should be rightly interpreted. Since the policy lines were hardly ever clearly determined in a formal bureaucratic manner and their interpretation could arbitrarily change due to rather abrupt changes in the politics of the leadership of the country, the soft-line institutions could never be certain whether they were really following the correct Party line. Under conditions of great inefficiency, one could go on violating many rules for a long time without being punished. In addition, a competent director almost always had to violate some rules in order to be able to follow others. The purpose of the show trials was to signal to the local and minor authorities or to the representatives of soft-line institutions what the most urgent and prioritized tasks where at the time. And what, at the same time, could be left for the improvisation of the local authorities:

> The most important central signalling device was the terror campaign. Local officials were constantly being asked to fulfil an unrealistic number of often contradictory assignments. They therefore had to read central signals to determine which policies were high priority and must be implemented and which could be deferred or ignored with impunity. Terror was the most important signal marking a policy as hard-line and mandatory.[66]

The question of the limits of the commercialization of the Soviet culture of consumption – the role of the market and monetary relations vs. centrally allocated and regulated provisioning of resources – was one of the main questions in which the soft-line policy and hard-line policy contradicted each other. This issue repeatedly brought the hard- and soft-line policies into conflict, leading to political repressions and show trials. In trying to make the policy more attractive to the people, to provide them with more varied and attractive consumer goods and services, the directors of trade and industry often tried to promote, to use Stalin's own expression, 'the fashion of money.' The hard-line institutions felt obliged to interfere at some points when they thought that the market started to threaten the realization of some basic goals like the equality of its citizens, the state ownership of production or the military safety of the country. Stalinist-Leninism taught that once you gave your little finger to the devil of commercialism, it took your whole hand. Inside every little peasant or a shopkeeper a potential capitalist with dangerous bourgeois inclinations lived. Another tendency which was never fully explicated but obviously had even more far-reaching repercussions lurked behind: if the consumers were let loose there would be no way to stop them. If freedom was given to their demands and wishes, they could no longer be satisfied with the system.

9

Conclusion: Socialist Realism in the Material Culture

The Rise of the Soviet Consumer and the End of Socialism

As I have argued, the overall picture of the Soviet culture of consumption in Stalin's time was not always as grey and dull as is often thought – at least not in Moscow and some other large cities. The creation of a luxury goods economy and its rapid growth bears witness to this. This is not to gloss over the widespread poverty and desperation many in the USSR experienced at this time, but it serves to complicate the picture we have of Soviet society. Many attractive, yet relatively inexpensive, new products were available, at least in principle, to the ordinary consumer. However, Soviet industry and commerce did not strain under a constant pressure to invent and launch new goods on an even larger scale in the same way that the developed capitalist countries of North America and Europe did. One of the merits of the socialist economy was, so the ideology went, that it did not create artificial needs in order to make profit. Neither was there any mechanism of artificial ageing of commodities such as fashion at work in the USSR. The Soviet economy was, after all, a planned economy in which the task of the planning offices and officials was to interpret, predict and try to direct the needs of the population. Despite these acknowledged differences, Soviet factories and shops were made to compete with each other over the rapid introduction of novelties.

In socialism there were no genuine commercial fashion cycles; or at least it is safe to say that fashion did not play as active a role in Soviet society as it did in capitalist societies. Georg Simmel argues that fashion is a phenomenon of modernity par excellence. Since fashion is an ongoing process of social imitation and individual differentiation mutually reinforcing each other, it enables every member of society both to express his or her own style while simultaneously merging with a larger social totality. According to Simmel, fashion provides a provisional solution to one of the most acute problems of our time by mediating between the tendencies of individualization and collectivization, between the one and the whole.[1]

145

In socialist society, the relationship between the individual and the society is organized in another way. The individual was intended to be firmly embedded into the social collective. However, even in this society there were factors that promoted the emergence of a monetary economy and a commodity culture that allowed gradually more room for the development of individual taste and fashion. To improve taste and to create a new socialist way of life, alternatives and mutually competing objects of choice were required. Soviet leaders were convinced that a totally new and more advanced human civilization was on its way. It was only natural that the majority of commodites of material culture had to be created anew as well.

In his article 'Communism – a post mortem'[2] Zygmunt Bauman argues that the development of consumers' demands and needs was a decisive factor in the dissolution process of socialism. As long as needs remained relatively simple and communal, it was largely possible for the state to satisfy them. The more individualized needs became, the more difficult it was, even in principle, to satisfy them. Consequently, in a socialist state consumers were doomed to eternal dissatisfaction. In a capitalist society the consumer could hardly blame the government if they could not find useful or attractive products on the market. In socialism, they could always blame the state and the Party. This was a chronic tension inherent in the socialist economy, and some contemporaries recognized the problem. Comrade Kasimov, the Party secretary of the Kirovskii district, advised workers during his visit to the Krasnyi Treugol'nik factory in Leningrad 'the consumer does not blame Krasnyi Treugol'nik and [its directors] comrades Vasiliev, Konstantinov and Denisov. Instead he says 'Soviet power'! The power has changed but there are no galoshes! That's how good the Soviet power is!'[3] Workers blamed the state for any failures in the system, including a lack of consumer goods. In turn, the Communist Party blamed 'traitors' for such failures.

Bauman's thesis, however, presumes that a continuous process of individualization took place in socialism. Yet there were strong tendencies working against the individualization of demands in the Soviet Union. The norms of socialist decency, of *kulturnost'*, effectively prevented expressions of individuality. It was not considered good manners to 'show off' or to deviate too much from the common norm. Even while promoting more individualized expressions of taste, the Soviet state only did so in small doses in a highly controlled and centrally administered way.

Under the conditions of a permanent shortage of goods, personal relations become more important than money in getting hold of rare commodities. Due to its pricing policy, the Soviet economy was by definition a deficit economy.[4] Under these circumstances, social networks, based either on familial or collegial ties, are crucial to the redistribution of goods.[5] An unofficial network of reciprocal obligations and duties comes into being out of necessity. (For discussion on the use of connections, or *blat* relations, see the work of Alena Ledeneva and Markku Lonkila.)[6] The ethics of such a society are the ethics of a clan. In such a system of social relations, the ethical norms applied to the members within a social group differ from those applied to outsiders. Strong feelings of resentment are typical. Others – outsiders – will have succeeded or done better only because they have used some unfair or criminal means or because they have enjoyed some special favours of those in power. This can effectively prevent the emergence of any individualistic ethics. Rewards and benefits are distributed inside the group according to its own specific norms of justice, which can prevent or interfere with their distribution according to one's personal achievements.

Even in the Soviet Union, however, elements of an individualistic culture of consumption gradually emerged despite the existence of strong counter-tendencies. The emerging culture was still, at the same time, characterized by a great degree of conformity. It was also constantly centrally monitored and regulated. As we have seen, Stalin and other leaders took a strong personal interest in developing the taste and etiquette of the common people. As a consequence, Soviet material culture offered many – smaller and bigger – delights and pleasures to its consumers – but only in strictly controlled ways. As such it was reminiscent of a culture of estates with strictly determined and separate lifestyles and tastes. In this sense, the government liked to compare the situation of the Soviet worker to an aristocrat living under the tsarist times – even though the luxuries available in the socialist society were certainly far less luxurious or even simply cheap imitations and kitsch. The rules of Soviet decency united, however, all the growing masses of more affluent workers and experts.

Soviet Middle-class Decency and the Concept of *Kulturnost*

The new Soviet way of life was characterized by *kulturnost*, a special cultural consciousness.[7] Lynne Attwood has succinctly described *kulturnost:* 'though the concept was never clearly defined, [it] included behaving in a well-mannered way, having appreciation of music, theatre and literature, taking an interest in one's appearance and displaying "good taste" in clothes'.[8] To become 'cultured' was to become cultivated in a similar rather ephemeral way as it was understood in many Western guidebooks of good behaviour and etiquette. It was more a question of an internalized unconscious disposition than any explicit formal rules of good behaviour.

It was good to display and make use of one's prosperity – otherwise material stimuli would have been of no use – but it would have been indecent to 'show off.' In discussing the characteristics of female fashion in post-war Soviet Union, Olga Vainshtein comments on how 'modesty' was encouraged in the framework of an

Figure 22   *'Life has become more joyous, comrades.' I.V. Stalin, A.I. Mikoyan, V.I. Chubar and V.M. Molotov at a reception of Armenian female workers at the Kremlin, December 1935.(Source: RGAKFD)*

ideology of collectivism – discipline demanded that one did not stand out from the masses.[9] On the other hand, as Vainshtein also observes, a 'style of excess' giving an impression of abundant luxury was equally typical of women's dress in the Soviet Union. Ordinary office clerks with their excessive make-up and style of dresses often looked in the eyes of an outsider as if they were going out to a night club. Vainshtein concludes that this style of excess or desire to dress up in the middle of 'puritan modesty' cannot be explained only as some kind of a compensatory mechanism – it was an act of subversion against the prevalent principles of ascetic modesty to show off one's individual taste. The psychological genesis of such a style of excess is more complex: 'these clothes, after all, parade not so much wealth per se as "a condensed image" of wealth'.[10] Such a duality, as hopefully this book demonstrates, was characteristic of the relation of Soviet culture to material goods and wealth: sudden outbursts or occasional expressions of not so much individuality, but images of wealth or a common popular luxury, amongst the general standardization and greyness.

A large part of the privileges and signs of such well-being often came in the form of gifts from the government or the Party and not in cash. *Udarniki* were given the right to order overcoats, cultured dresses, suits and chrome boots from the tailors and shoemakers. When invited to the meetings of the Stakhanovit*es* or other such conferences in Moscow, workers and *kolkhozniks* were expected to be well dressed and therefore such an invitation often almost automatically was accompanied by a coupon allowing the right to make orders from special shops. Holiday trips to health spas, summer houses, private family houses or apartments, cars or motorcycles were signs of belonging to the *nomenklatura*, the Party or industrial elite.

But the intelligentsia, the new Soviet middle class also appreciated cosiness and a homely atmosphere, which it could design and create itself according its own taste. The literary historian Vera Dunham characterized this atmosphere by quoting Gauser's popular novel from 1947: 'tea was served under an orange lampshade in red, polka-dotted cups. In this small, gay and bright paradise, everybody was pleased with life and discussed how good it was that work in the [cultural] club was becoming so well organized. . .'[11] Together with fresh underwear, clean shaven faces and other similar signs of personal hygiene, window curtains, lampshades and snow-white tablecloths became essential symbols of a cultivated household in the Soviet Union.[12] To this list one could add the appreciation of good food, chocolate included, and finer drinks like champagne and cognac.

As the historian Richard Stites has demonstrated[13] these newcomers appreciated privileges. They were also expected to develop decent manners and good taste, to act in a cultured way: 'The newcomers were invested with privilege and expected to develop respectable habits and tastes. . . They thirsted for old high culture as a badge of distinction; for entertainment they enjoyed sentimentalism, fun, uplift, and an affirmation of their values.'[14] Accordingly Stalin bought the loyalty of the new middle class with 'trinkets' but also with real privileges and access to traditional 'high culture' thereby allowing for widening status differences. These newcomers adopted light classical art as their status symbol, together with an eclectic collection of symbols of middle-class normality, such as happy and harmonious family life, and they invested in the future of their children and their education. The personal – even the relations between a man and a woman – was no longer in contradiction with the happiness of the state (see in particular the sentimental and extremely popular wartime songs 'Dark night' and 'In the dugout').

The educated people were at the avant-garde of taste and consumption too. They set the example for others to follow. They served as a model for the uneducated masses to respect and admire until that time came when such culture and material prosperity would be available for everyone.[15] They showed the way to the bright future. In the 1930s, the authorities made many concessions to popular taste and adopted a more permissive attitude toward consumption. At the same time, they actively worked on moulding the popular taste better to fit their ideals. In any case, the new consumerism was more effective and left more permanent, deeper marks in society than the earlier more direct attempts at social engineering and political agitation of the Cultural Revolution.

Socialist Realism as a Soviet Mentality

The problems of decorating and furnishing a family apartment with lampshades or new curtains, buying a nice set of silverware or organizing the work at the cultural club were hardly problems with which most Soviet people, in reality, were struggling daily in the 1930s or the 1950s. Such luxuries were clearly out of reach for most ordinary peasants or workers living with their families in one room in *kommunalki*, sharing a barrack with a dozen other comrades or living in country shacks or dugouts without any modern conveniences. They were only ideals or part of the dream worlds of popular literature or culture. But these dreams were encouraged by the authorities and shared by millions of fellow citizens. They represented ideals of socialist realism in the sphere of material culture.

Socialist realism was not realism of any kind. It was the direct opposite. It presented 'reality' in an idealized and beautified way. It was not meant to be a 'reflection' of reality with all its problems and contradictions. It was, in fact, a highly abstract art form, which 'abstracted' from reality only some selected features, which it then presented with full force. In his study *The End of Utopia* Morozov[16] argued that, contrary to popular belief, the only real challenge to socialist realism in art was not the various artistic vanguard movements that had flourished in the Soviet Union in the early 1920s but, in fact, classical realism.

The task of the Soviet artist following the principles of socialist realism was to reveal the tendencies often barely visible in the present socialist society. This explains also the high esteem accorded to artistic creativity and originality.[17] The task of the Soviet artist – or of the Soviet engineer – was to paint – or design – the picture of the society as it would be in the future once the 'positive' tendencies had all been realized and the negative, contradictory ones swept away. This also explains the quest for novelties in the sphere of material culture. This was to be a picture of a new abundant country and its strong and happily smiling inhabitants. The new society was waiting just around the corner – but it was still difficult to see to many a common eye since the clear vision was hindered or blurred by many remnants of the old class society. Therefore, one could not rely solely on the ability of individual people or individual artists to see the future as it inevitably would turn out to be. Only the Party could interpret future tendencies in a reliable manner and distinguish the genuinely socialist tendencies leading to communism from other, often threatening, ones. Therefore, the principle of *partiinost'*, loyalty to the principles of the Party, was to become the highest principle of socialist realism in art.

The Moscow metro served as one of the most visible symbols of the new spirit of the 1930s. Like the building of the White Sea canal (which is still commemorated daily by thousands of smokers of the *papirosy* Belomorkanal) or the power plant of Dneprostroi, the metro was one of the most ambitious socialist construction projects of the 1930s. As Morozov[18] has shown, the Moscow metro, with its highly decorated underground stations, became a popular part of Soviet myth building. It was a concrete material symbol of the almost unnatural capacity of the working man of New Russia to conquer the earth. It symbolized the almost unlimited possibility of the purposeful transformation of the world, inside the earth.

Timothy Colton, in his history of the city of Moscow, described the meaning of the Moscow metro as follows: 'Finally, glamorous projects made sense as a source of vicarious satisfaction for the population, a first instalment of the good life to come. They would, as Lazar Kaganovich put it, refute the falsehood "that socialism is a barracks" peopled by look-alikes.'[19] Kaganovich, who was the party leader of Moscow at that time, formulated this principle in a condensed manner: 'When our worker takes the subway, he should be cheerful and joyous' feeling as if in 'a palace shining with the light of advancing, all victorious socialism.'[20]

The luxurious palace-like stations of the newly opened metro line in Moscow were thus intended to be palaces for the people, not only in the same way as former palaces of the Tsar or the Russian nobility had been turned either into museums, sanatoriums or clubs open to common people on special occasions.[21] The new palaces of metro stations were to become even more concretely part of everyday socialist life. Every Moscow inhabitant or visitor to the capital would pass through them on his or her way to work or on other daily errands. In doing so, he or she was not only reminded of the glorious future soon to come but could, in fact, enjoy a foretaste of it in practice by admiring the impressive stations.

Many advancements in the fields of material culture, other than architecture or city planning, can equally be understood as concrete tokens in miniature of the rapidly approaching bright socialist future. Whether a new perfume in a crystal bottle, a box of chocolates or a bottle of champagne given as a present on one's birthday or some public celebration or a new 'fashionable' pair of leather shoes or a winter coat, they all can equally be seen as if 'shining with the light of the advancing, all victorious socialism'. Much of the development of the Soviet material culture in the 1930s is evidence of such an attitude, either emphasizing the new cultured standard of Soviet life like champagne and perfumes or bearing witness to the victories of Soviet engineering like gramophones or motorbikes.

As Fitzpatrick has emphasized, 'Socialist realism was a Stalinist mentality, not just an artistic style. Ordinary citizens also developed the ability to see things as they were becoming and ought to be, rather than as they were.'[22] In the Soviet Union, everyone's eyes were turned towards the future. The past served only as a contrast to the new bright new future to come. The press photographs of the Soviet cameramen of the 1920s and the 1930s also bear witness to such an attitude. They often portray young men and women with bright, open, almost naïve-looking faces from an angle below, looking into the distant horizon.[23] The new vanguard was young – most Stakhanovites were in their early twenties. This was a youthful culture idealizing the youth – or a culture living for the sake of the future:

It emphasised the youth, and the country, in fact, felt young and lived in the hopes for the future, in dynamic rhythm full of the powers of a young human being... Part of this worldview was shared by the older and middle aged generations. For the sake of the future people were ready to offer anything, to close their eyes for injustice and to justify any wrongdoing.... In addition, in their heads a thought dominated, a thought that to communism only a short distance remained to be covered. For the sake of this, they endured.'[24]

It is impossible to ignore the obvious contradiction between what was promised and what existed in practice. Immediately after the rationing of the most elementary commodities was abandoned, the authorities declared that a new era of general happiness had arrived. This was promulgated in the press, on the radio and in the movies, and the authorities took substantial measures to realize these promises. Big projects, demanding huge amounts of resources, both human and material, began and were followed up by big publicity campaigns. In a country of well over 150 million inhabitants starting at the production point of zero, one would have needed hundreds of millions of bottles of champagne or perfume or boxes of chocolate or thousands of new fashionable food stores in order to boast, even in principle, of having sufficient supply for the majority of citizens.

The average Soviet citizen certainly noticed the gap between theory and practice. After suffering the deprivations of the 1920s, people were eager to believe the talk about the good life. Yet they also knew from experience not to take such rhetoric at face value. Most Soviets were neither naive communist believers nor cynical citizens who either blindly believed everything that was said or had totally lost their faith in all the promises of the authorities. They willingly enjoyed the delights offered to them in their daily lives and endured the hardships in an expectation of a better future to come – or in the absence of any alternatives.

Notes

1 Introduction: The Birth of the Soviet Consumer

1. Mikoyan, A. (1971a), 'Dva mesiatsa v SshA', SshA. *Ekonomika, politika, ideologiia.* no. 10: 68.

2. Gide, André (1937), *Back from the USSR*. London: Martin Secher and Warburg, 33–4.

3. Ibid., 36.

4. Ibid., 36.

5. Osokina, Elena (1998), *Za fasadom 'Stalinskogo izobiliia'. Raspredelenie i rynok v snabzhenii naseleniia v gody industrializatsii, 1927–1941*. Moskva. Rosspen; Zhuravlev, S.V. and Sokolov, A.K. (1999), *Obshchestvo i vlast.' 1930-e gody.* Moskva: Rosspen.

6. *Reabilitatsiia. Politicheskie protsessy 30-50-kh godov.* Moskva: Izdatel'stvo politicheskoi literatury, 1991, 30.

7. In the following, I refer to People's Comissars systematically as Ministers and People's Comissariats as Ministries.

8. See my earlier discussion of these trends in Gronow, J. (1997): *The Sociology of Taste*. London & New York: Routledge.

9. Timasheff, N.S. (1946), *The Great Retreat. The Growth and Decline of Communism in Russia.* New York: E.P. Dutton.

10. Fitzpatrick, Sheila (1999), *Everyday Stalinism. Ordinary Life in Extraordinary Times. Soviet Russia in the 1930s.* New York & Oxford: Oxford University Press.

11. Hessler, Julie (2000), 'Cultured trade. The Stalinist turn towards consumerism', in Fitzpatrick, Sheila (ed.), *Stalinism. New Directions.* London & New York: Routledge, 182–209.

12. Stites, Richard (1992), *Russian Popular Culture. Entertainment and Society since 1900.* Cambridge: Cambridge University Press, 65.

13. Ibid., 75–7.

14. Timasheff, *The Great Retreat*, 314–15.

15. Kelly, Catriona and Volkov, Vadim (1998), 'Directed desires. Kultur'nost' and consumption', in Kelly, C. and Shepherd, D. (eds), *Constructing Russian Culture in the Age of Revolution: 1881–1940.* Oxford & New York: Oxford University Press, 301–303.

16. *Komsomol'skaia Pravda* 1938, cited in Kelly and Volkov, 'Directed desires'.

17. Dunham, Vera (1976), *In Stalin's Time*. Cambridge: Cambridge University Press.

18. Fitzpatrick, Sheila (1992), *The Cultural Front. Power and Culture in Revolutionary Russia.* Ithaca & London: Cornell University Press, 179.

19. See Kelly and Volkov, 'Directed desires', 291–313.

20. Hoffman, David (1993), 'The Great Terror on the local level. Purges in Moscow factories', in Getty, J. Arch and Manning, Roberta T. (eds), *Stalinist Terror. New Perspectives.* Cambridge: Cambridge University Press, 167.

21. 'Our engineer could serve as a prime example of such a newly educated and young technical specialist. He finished the technical college, belongs to the Party. His salary is 400 roubles, but in addition to this, he receives regular premiums, and who knows what, which means that he earns 1000 roubles a month – and even more. He is satisfied, frighteningly satisfied.' (Mankov, A.G. (1994), `Iz dnevnika riadovogo cheloveka 1933–1934', *Zvezda*, no. 5, 159.) The author of the diary from which these lines are taken, A.G. Mankov, was at the time (1933) an ordinary office worker and earned 130 roubles a month.

22. Papernyi, Vladimir (1985), *Kultura 'Dva'*. Ann Arbor: Ardis. 87–8.

2 Soviet Champagne: Stalin's Great Invention

1. The page with the article was in the Russian State Archive of Economy among other documents about wine cultivation and champagne production (RGAE, F. 8543, Op. 1, D. 416, L. 76). It was preserved in the archive 'as an attached note, page 75' and was originally addressed to the Minister of Food Industry, Anastas Mikoyan, with the following text: 'Anastas Ivanovich, I thought it was necessary to draw your attention to the article in *Izobilie* no. 96.' It was signed on 22 November 1937 by Gerasimov. *Izobilie* was the organ of the 'political part' of the wine trust Abrau-Diurso in the late 1930s.

2. Abrau-Diurso is located near Rostov-na-Donu in Southern Russia. It was wellknown for its sparkling wines even before the Revolution.

3. One of the earliest orders about the cultivation of champagne was issued by Peoples Commissariat [Ministry] of Food Industry on 21 July 1936 (Prikaz NKPP no. 1802, 21.7.1936; RGAE F. 8543, Op. 1, D. 169, L. 82–84). It included, an order 'to organize the selection of the best wine grapes which will give a bigger and stable vintage'. Such an order could, quite reasonably, be interpreted by the local wine growers as an encouragement not to cultivate finer – and less productive – sorts of grapes.

4. It was, for instance, mentioned in all the four editions of the famous best-selling Soviet cook book *Kniga o vkysnoi i zdorovoi pishche* published in 1952, 1953, 1954 and 1955. The book included a special chapter on wines. Millions of copies were sold and it belonged to the kitchen of cultivated Soviet homes.

5. Solzhenitsyn, Alexander (1979), *The Gulag Archipelago 1918–1956*. Vol. 1. Glasgow: Collins, Harvill Press and Fontana, 528.

6. RGAE, F. 8543, Op. 1, D. 415, L. 121–3.

7. RGAE, F. 8543, Op. 1, D. 416, L. 152.

8. In the context of the Soviet Union, a 'trust' functioned similarly to a business conglomerate in that it was a large, multi-branched firm. In the USSR, such trusts were state-owned monopolies.

9. RGAE, F. 8543, Op. 1, D. 415, L. 139.

10. See Thurston, Robert (1993), 'The Stakhanovite Movement. Background to the Great Terror in the factories, 1935–1938', in Getty, J. Arch and Manning, Roberta T. (eds), *Stalinist Terror. New Perspectives.* Cambridge: Cambridge University Press, 153–60.

11. Ibid., 159–60. See also Rittersporn, Gábor T. (1993), 'The omnipresent conspiracy. On Soviet imagery of politics and social relations in the 1930s', in Getty and Manning, *Stalinist Terror*, 99–115.

12. Karpatsenko, P.K. (1939), 'Zadachi sovetskogo vinodeliia i vinogradarstva', *Vino-delenie i vinogradarstvo SSSR*, no. 1: 4–7. In 1940 A.M. Frolov-Bagraev referred to the

Party and government resolution about the production of Soviet champagne, Massandra desert and table wines as the important starting point. (See *Vinodelenie i vinogradarstvo*, (1940) no. 5: 3.)

13. Molotov, V. (1934), 'Zadachi vtoroi piatiletki', *Pravda*, no. 36 (5922); Mikoyan, A. (1934), 'Za sovetskuiu torgovliu, za uluchshenie rabochego snabzheniia', *Pravda*, no. 32 (5918).

14. The abruptness of this change in the production politics is shown by the fact that in the official plan of the Ministry of Food Industry for 1937 no production figures for champagne were given. In 1938 the target was 1 million bottles. There existed no plans concerning the production of wines for 1937 either. Wine was thus not a centrally planned product. For the year 1938 the target for grape wines was set at 8 450 000 decalitres. (See RGAE, F. 8543, Op. 1, D. 305, L. 154.)

15. 'Sovetskaya Shampan', *Izvestiia*, no. 228, 29 September 1937.

16. RGAE, F. 8543, Op. 1, D. 416, L. 110–11; see also RGAE, F. 8543, Op. 12, D. 415, L. 70–74.

17. The new 'reservoir' method made the production process much faster. The wine was not slowly matured in bottles but was preserved in big tanks and was ready to be sold when bottled.

18. RGAE, F. 8543, OP. 1, D. 415.

19. RGAE, F. 8543, Op. 1, D. 416, L. 61.

20. GARF, F. 5446, Op. 1, D. 119, L. 101–03.

21. Resoliutsia SNK SSSR and TsK VKP(b), no. 1369; GARF, F. 5446, Op. 1, D. 119, L. 104–07.

22. Postanovlenie SNK SSSR, no. 213, 5.02.1937; GARF, F. 5446, Op. 1, D. 125, L. 193–202.

23. RGAE, F. 8543, Op. 1, D. 169, L. 270.

24. Ibid., L. 296.

25. RGAE, F. 8543, Op. 1, D. 517, L. 186. Order of the NKPP, no. 1329, 14 December 1938.

26. Ibid., L. 1.

27. See e.g. RGAE, F. 8543, Op. 1, D. 517, L. 219 about Tiflis, 15 December 1938; D. 499, L. 132 about Abrau-Diurso, 2 November 1937; D.499, L.174-6 about the cultivation of grape plants, 19 December 1938.

28. Mikoyan, Anastas (1999), *Tak bylo. Razmyshleniia o minuschem.* Moskva: Vagrius, 315. On his way back from his much advertised trip to the US Mikoyan stopped in Paris where Frolov-Bagraev was waiting for him. Frolov-Bagraev was at the time heading a delegation of Soviet viticulturalists in France and suggested that he could take Mikoyan to see the vineyards at Champagne. In spite of the fact that Mikoyan had already spent quite a long time away from home he agreed and they made a short trip to the homeland of French champagne – one more sign of the top priority of the production of champagne in the mind of the Soviet Minister of Food Industry as well as of the industriousness of professor Frolov-Bagraev in promoting the matter.

29. RGAE, F. 8543, Op. 1, D. 415, L. 124–5.

30. *Vinodelenie i vinogradarstvo.* (1943) no. 3.

31. *Vinodelenie i vinogradarstvo.* (1945) no. 10–11: 2–8.

32. *Leningradskaia Pravda*, 3 November 1940.

33. RGAE, F. 7486, Op. 1, D. 256, L. 56.

34. CMAM, F. 516, Op. 1, D. 24, L. 22.

35. Mikoyan, A.I. (1971a), 'Dva mesiatsa v SshA'. SShA. *Ekonomika, politika, ideologiia,* no. 10: 70.

36. *Pravda*, 30 May 1936.

37. CMAM, F. 520, Op. 1, D. 19, L. 97.

38. Ibid., L. 97ob.

39. CMAM, F. 520, Op. 1, D. 23, L. 94.

40. CMAM, F. 520, Op. 1, D. 27, L. 102–03.

41. Ibid., L. 14–30.

42. Ibid., D. 40, L. 26–32, 37–8.

43. See for instance the documents of the Moscow Wine and Cognac factory. CMAM, F. 516, Op. 1.

44. RGAE, F. 8543, Op. 1, D. 415, L. 39–52.

45. RGAE, F. 8543, Op. 1, D. 416, L. 144.

46. Ibid., L. 48.

47. Ibid., L. 50.

48. Ibid.

49. RGAE, F. 8543, Op. 1, D. 415, L. 16.

50. RGAE, F. 8543, Op. 1, D. 416, L. 144.

51. RGAE, F. 8543, Op. 1, D. 415, L. 2.

52. RGAE, F. 8543, Op. 1, D. 499, L. 124, 132–3.

53. Stepankin, I.A. (1997), 'Pervyi v Rossii. Istoriia pivovarennogo zavoda imeni Sten'ki Razina'. *Istoriia Zavoda v XX veke.* Sankt-Peterburg, 137–9.

54. RGAE, F. 8543, Op. 1, D. 305, L. 79.

55. RGAE, F. 8543, Op. 2, D. 351, L. 32–5.

56. Vodka and other alcoholic drinks were throughout Soviet times important items of taxation, financing a remarkable portion of the State budget. The number of special stores selling alcoholic drinks grew rapidly in the 1930s. In 1940 there were 3750 such shops, more than two times the number of shops selling vegetables, fruit, meat, fish or milk. See Takala, I.R. (2002), *Veselie rusi. Istoria alkogol'noi problemy v Rossii.* Sankt-Peterburg: Neva, 215.

3 Soviet Kitsch and Organized Carnivals

1. RGAE, F. 7971, Op. 1, D. 77, L. 91.

2. Ibid., L. 90.

3. Ibid., L. 17, 35.

4. RGAE, F. 7971, Op. 1, D. 77, L. 139–40.

5. 'Postanovleniia, rasporiazheniia i spravochnye materialy'. *Biulleten Leningradskogo oblastnogo i gorodskogo otdelov snabzheniia Lenoblispolkoma i Lensoveta po sovetskoi torgovle, rabochemu snabzheniiu i pishchevoi promyshlennosti,* no. 4. July 1934: 4. The information concerning the rate of monthly salaries comes from Lebina, Natalia (1999), *Povsednevnaia zhizn' sovetskogo goroda. Normy i anomalii 1920/1930 gody.* Sankt-Peterburg: Neva, 224.

6. Vishnitser, A. (1936), 'Bor'ba za assortiment prodtovarov. (Opyt Gastronoma no. 1)'. *Sovetskaia torgovlia* no. 4–5: 110.

7. Interviews with old inhabitants of Leningrad about their lives in the 1930s conducted as part of Timo Vihavainen's project financed by the Academy of Finland 'Norms, values

and deviation in the Soviet society and culture in the 1920s–1950s'. Some interviews have been published in Vituhnovskaia M. (ed.) (2000), *Na korme vremeni. Interv'iu s lenin-gradtsami 1930-kh godov*. Sankt-Peterburg: Zhurnal Neva.

8. Almost 90 per cent was distributed and consumed in the Soviet Union, see Saffron, Inga (2002), *Caviar. The Strange History and Uncertain Future of the World's Most Loved Delicacy*. New York: Broadway Books, 115.

9. See my previous analysis in Gronow, J. (1997), *The Sociology of Taste*. London & New York: Routledge, 51–3.

10. CMAM, F. 1953, Op. 1, D. 18, L. 62.

11. German, M. Iu. (1997), *Slozhnoe proshedshee. Glavy knigi vospominanii. Nevskii Arkhiv. Istoriko-kraevedcheskii sbornik III*. Sankt-Peterburg: Atheneum-Feniks.

12. Beriia, S. (1994), *Moi otets – Lavrentii Beriia*. Moskva: Sovremennik, 5–6.

13. Fitzpatrick, Sheila (1999), *Everyday Stalinism. Ordinary Life in Extraordinary Times: Soviet Russia in the 1930s*. New York & Oxford: Oxford University Press, 102.

14. *Istoriia sotsialisticheskoi ekonomiki SSSR*, T. 4, (Moskva: 1978), 475.

15. For a detailed history of the rehabilitation of the New Year and the fir tree, see Petrone, Karen (2000), *Life Has Become More Joyous, Comrades. Celebrations in the Time of Stalin*. Bloomington & Indianapolis: Indiana University Press, 84–100.

16. Agoneva, S.B. (1999), 'Istoriia sovremennoi novogodnei traditsii.' *Mifologiia i povsednevnost*. Vyp. 2. Materialy nauchnoi konferentsii 24–26 fevralia 1999 goda. Sankt-Peterburg: Institut russkoi literatury RAN, 368–88.

17. Biulleten' oblastnogo otdela vnutrennei torgovli Lenispolkoma, no. 125. Leningrad, 1936: 2; Biulleten' oblastnogo i gorodskogo otdelov vnutrennei torgovli, no. 59 (431). Leningrad, 22 December 1938.

18. CMAM, F. 485, Op. 1, D. 14, L. 8.

19. See e.g. CMAM, F. 32, Op. 1, D. 8, L. 30 about a Gormostorg report concerning the advertisement of New Year's decorations not only through local press and radio broadcastings but also through letters to individual persons.

20. *Pishchevaia industriia*, no. 158 (2472), 11 June 1936.

21. 'Parks of Culture and Rest' became an essential part of Soviet popular culture at the same time, see Lunts, L.B. (1934), *Parki Kul'tury i otdykha*. Leningrad: Gostroiizdatelstvo.

22. *Pishchevaia industriia*, no. 161 (2475), 15 June 1936.

23. Sartorti, Rosalinda (1990), 'Stalinism and Carnival: Organisation and Aesthetics of Political Holidays', in Günther, H. (ed.), *The Culture of Stalin the Period*. London: Macmillan, 41.

24. Ibid., 42.

25. Ibid., 66–71.

26. 'Soviet jazz', a parallel phenomenon to continental or 'German Jazz', was often played by big dance bands which often had, in addition to saxophones, trombones, drums and guitars, more traditional 'folk' instruments like accordions and violins. The music they played was often closer to waltzes, polkas and marches than jazz.

27. See Petrone, *Life Has Become More Joyous, Comrades*, 100–09.

28. Stites, Richard (1992), *Russian Popular Culture. Entertainment and Society since 1900*. Cambridge: Cambridge University Press, 75. As Stites has pointed out, with the tightening of the cultural atmosphere in 1937, jazz in the Soviet Union shared the fate of its German counterpart. 'As a whole, Stalin's clean-up of jazz resembled that in Hitler's Germany where dance had to be slow and smooth, with strings and "folk" instruments added to the "jazz" complement'. (ibid., 76).

29. Henry Scott was a black American student of the International Lenin University at Moscow who had been expelled from the university because of bad results and political inalertness. See Zhuravlev, S.V. (2000), *'Malenkie Liudi' i Bolshaia istoria. Inostrantsi moskovskogo Elektrozavoda v sovetskom obstshestve 1920-kh-1930-kh gg.* Moskva: Rosspen, 106.

30. Lebina, Natalia (1999), *Povsednevnaia zhizn' sovetskogo goroda. Normy i anomalii 1920/1930 gody.* Sankt-Peterburg: Neva, 260–1.

31. Glebkin, V.V. (1998), *Ritual v sovetskoi kulture.* Moskva: Janus-K.

32. Zdravomyslova, Elena and Temkina, Anna (1997), 'October demonstrations in Russia. From official holiday to a protest manifestation', in Temkina, A., *Russia in Transition. The Cases of New Collective Actors and New Collective Action.* Aleksanteri instituutti: Kikimora, 143.

33. Papernyi, Vladimir (1985), *Kultura 'Dva'.* Ann Arbor: Ardis, 101.

34. Zdravomyslova and Temkina, 'October demonstrations in Russia', 144.

35. Ibid., 141.

4 Increasing Variety

1. CMAM, F. 864, Op. 1, D. 10-13, L. 32.

2. *Pravda*, 30 January 1934.

3. CMAM, F. 864, Op. 1, D. 9, L. 1–6.

4. Mikoyan, A. (1934), 'Za sovetskuiu torgovliu,za uluchshenie rabochego snabzheniia', *Pravda*, no. 32 (5918).

5. CMAM, F. 485, Op. 1, D. 9, L. 5–5ob.

6. CMAM, F. 485, Op. 1, D. 10, L. 1, 5, 24, 30ob, 31, 32.

7. Ibid., L. 36ob.

8. Ibid., L. 41ob, 43–43ob.

9. Ibid., L. 22 and CMAM, F. 485, Op. 1, D. 11, L. 1, 18–18ob.

10. CMAM, F. 485, Op. 1, D. 11, L. 22–3.

11. The figures on novelties differed slightly from one report to another. Even within the same report there often appear seemingly contradictory figures. This is at least partly explained by the fact that on some occasions the same product packed in packages of different sizes is counted as so many different products, while on other occasions only product types are counted. Whatever the case, the increase and the great attention paid to the development of novelties is evident.

12. CMAM, F. 864, Op. 1, D. 11, L. 18ob.

13. Ibid., L. 24.

14. *Sovetskaia torgovlia. Statistitseski sbornik.* Gosudarstvennoie statistitsheskoie izdatelstvo. Moskva, 1956, 60–69.

15. CMAM, F. 864, Op. 1, D. 11, L. 33.

16. CMAM, F. 864, Op. 1, D. 12, L. 16, 28, 32ob.

17. Ibid., L. 32ob.

18. CMAM, F. 864, Op. 1, D. 13, L. 13.

19. Ibid., L. 13.

20. Ibid., L. 28ob.

21. CMAM, F. 864, Op. 1, D. 14, L. 7–8.

22. CMAM, F. 485, Op. 1, D. 1, L. 1.

23. CMAM, F. 485, Op. 1, D. 6, L. 1–1ob.

24. *Golos konfetchika*, no. 3, 21 January 1934.

25. *Golos konfetchika*, no. 28 (126), 19 August 1934.

26. RGAE, F. 8543, Op. 1, D. 266, L. 25.

27. Ibid., L. 86.

28. Ibid., L. 95.

29. RGAE, F. 8543, Op. 1, D. 266, L. 38 and 42.

30. RGAE, F. 8543, Op. 1, D. 264, L. 5.

31. Ibid., L. 37.

32. Ibid., L. 11.

33. Ibid., L. 163.

34. *Vneshnaia torgovlia SSSR za 20 let 1918–1937gg. Statisticheski spravochnik.* Moskva: Mezhdunarodnaia kniga, 1939, 60–69.

35. CMAM, F. 864, Op. 1, D. 10, L. 41ob, 43–43ob.

36. CMAM, F. 864, Op. 1, D. 11, L. 22–3.

37. CMAM, F. 864, Op. 1, D. 12, L. 7. In the same report two other sets of figures are mentioned: 1) 103 novelties plus 158 different special seasonal or celebratory sweets (the novelties included nineteen types of oriental sweets) and 2) 261 novelties out of which eighty-one were based on new recipes (including twenty oriental sweets). The other novelties consisted of newly designed packages or boxes with different, smaller weights. (Ibid., L. 67–57ob.)

38. CMAM, F. 864, Op. 1, D. 13, L. 32.

39. RGAE, F. 8543, Op. 1, D. 266, L. 38.

40. CMAM, F. 485, Op. 1, D. 4, L. 16.

41. Biulleten' oblastnogo i gorodskogo otdelov vnutrennei torgovli, no. 7. Leningrad, 1935: 3–12.

42. Biulleten' oblastnogo otdela vnutrennei torgovli Lenispolkoma, no. 87. Leningrad, 1936: 14–15.

43. RGAE, F. 8543, Op. 1, D. 264, L. 201.

44. RGAE, F. 8543, Op.1, D. 265, L.14.

45. Ibid., L. 41–3: D. 256, L. 53, 56, 95. Cf. also the reports of the Moscow organisation of food supply, Mosselprom, ibid. L. 30.

46. CMAM, F. 485, Op. 1, D. 6, L. 1–1ob.

47. RGAE, F. 8543, Op. 1, D. 265, L. 101, 103.

48. RGAE, F. 8297, Op. 2, D. 60, L. 2.

49. Ibid., L. 4.

50. Ibid., D. 61, L. 18. The order of the NKPP from April 1936 about the minimum selection in sausage departments in food stores.

51. RGAE, F. 8297, Op. 2, D. 60, L. 129.

52. *Miasnaia industriia SSSR,* no. 1, 1934: 1–3.

53. RGAE, F. 8543, Op. 1, D. 91, L. 3.

54. Ibid., D. 90, L. 4.

55. RGAE, F. 8297, Op. 4, D. 208, L. 11–12.

56. RGAE, F. 8297, Op. 4, D. 411, L.44.

57. RGAE, F. 8297, Op. 1, D. 62, L. 19–20.

58. RGAE, F. 8543, Op. 1, D. 110, L. 149.

59. RGAE, F. 8543, Op. 1, D. 379, L. 47.

60. RGAE, F. 8297, Op. 1, D. 62, L. 122.

61. RGAE, F. 8543, Op. 1, D. 305, L. 154.

62. RGAE, F. 8543, Op. 1, D. 305, L. 131–2. Prikaz NKPP no. 1826, 26 July 1936.

63. Dikhtiar, G.A. (1961), *Sovetskaia torgovlia v periode postroeniia sotsializma.* Moskva: Izdatelstvo Akademii nauk SSSR, 412.

64. Rybakov, Anatolii (1998), *Deti Arbata. Trilogiia. Kniga vtoraia. Strakh.* Moskva: Terra, 52. See also Azhgikhina, Nadezhda and Goscilo, Helena, (1996) 'Getting under their skin. The beauty salon in Russian women's lives', in Goscilo, H. and Holmgren, B. (eds), *Russia, Women, Culture.* Bloomington & Indianapolis: Indiana University Press, 98.

65. Iurina, M. (1936), 'Kultura i krasota'. *Rabotnitsa,* no. 3: 17

66. For a more detailed discussion see Saari, Kirsikka (2001), *Täytyy pukeutua puhtaasti ja hyvin, siististi ja kauniisti. Keskustelu pukeutumisesta ja normeista Neuvostoliitossa 1923–1928.* Master of Arts thesis at the Department of History, University of Helsinki: unpublished.

67. RGAE, F. 8551, Op. 2, D. 88, L. 3, 7a–8.

68. RGAE, F. 8551, Op. 1, D. 9.

69. RGAE, F. 8551, Op. 1, D. 10, L. 14ob.

70. Ibid., L. 16.

71. Ibid., L. 16, 18, 22ob, 32ob.

72. RGAE, F. 8551, Op. 1, D. 18, L. 6.

73. Ibid., L. 18–18ob.

74. Ibid., L. 32–4.

75. Ibid., L. 38.

76. On 4 April 1934 *Pravda* announced that Comrade Volfson, senior worker of the Leningrad perfume factory of TEZHE had performed successfully at a competition with his French colleagues organized at the factory by making 'one hundred per cent Soviet odours'.

77. *Vneshnaia torgovlia SSSR za 20 let 1918–1937gg. Statisticheski spravochnik.* Moskva: Mezhdunarodnaia kniga, 1939, 60–69.

78. CMAM, F. 488, Op. 1, D. 1., L. 20.

79. CMAM, F. 488, Op. 1, D. 3, D. 4, L. 24, D. 9, L. 6, 10, 16, 121. In some product groups 'speculative demand' was reported. This was, however, rather exceptional in these reports. It belonged under the jurisdiction of other state agencies, like the state police. Osokina, Elena (1999), 'Predprinimatel'stvo i rynok v povsednevnoi zhizni pervykh piatiletok. Na primere rynka potrebitel'nykh tovarov', *Sotsialnaia istoriia. Ezhegodnik 1998/99.* Moskva: Rosspen, 350.

80. A manuscript collection of interviews with old inhabitants of Leningrad about their lives in the 1930s conducted as part of Timo Vihavainen's project financed by the Academy of Finland 'Norms, values and deviation in the Soviet society and culture in the 1920s–1950s'. Some interviews have been published in Vitukhnovskaia M. (ed.) (2000), *Na korme vremeni. Interv'iu s leningradtsami 1930-kh godov.* Sankt-Peterburg: Zhurnal Neva.

81. *Molodezh SSSR. Statisticheski sbornik TsUNH Gosplane SSSR i TsKVLKSM.* Moskva: Soiuz orguchet, 1936, 336–7.

82. *Sovetskaia torgovlia. Statisticheskii sbornik,* 57–8.

83. 150 million gramophone records were sold in the US in 1929. This pre-war record was first overcome a long time after the Second World War. See Gronow, P. and Saunio, I. (1998), *An International History of Recording Industry.* London & New York: Cassell, 57.

84. RGAE, F. 7971, Op. 1, D. 1803, L. 83.

85. RGAE, F. 7925, Op. 2, D. 1, L. 64–7.

86. Ibid., L. 64.

87. 'O merakh po uluchsheniiu proizvodstva grammofonov, grammofonykh plastinok i muzykal'nykh instrumentov'. *Postanovlenie Soveta Narodnykh Komissarov*, no. 372. In *Sobranie zakonov i rasporiazhenii raboche-krest'ianskogo pravitel'stva SSSR*, no. 62, Otdel pervyi. 15 October 1933.

88. Ibid.

89. *Sovetskii patefon*, no. 16 (169), 3 April 1937.

90. Likhov, S. (1934), 'Shkola bor'by za kachestvo tovarov'. *Sovetskaia torgovlia*, no. 4: 67.

91. RGAE, F. 7971, Op. 3, D. 30, L. 51–8.

92. RGAE, F. 7971, Op. 3, D. 88, L. 48.

93. Lebedev, G. (1934), 'Rabota legkoi promyshlennosti v 1933 g'. *Sovetskaia torgovlia*, no. 1: 96.

5 Soviet Novelties and their Advertising

1. *Golos konfetchika*, no. 1 (141), 3 January 1935.

2. Perepeletskii (1936), 'Novoe v assortimente i oformlenii'. *Organizatsiia i tekhnika sovetskoi torgovli,* no. 6. *Moskva*, 44–7.

3. Ibid., 47.

4. Mikulina, E. (1936), 'Tvortsy sovetskoi mody'. *Organizatsiia i tekhnika sovetskoi torgovlim*, no. 5. Moskva: 46–51.

5. Ibid., 50.

6. Ibid., 51.

7. RGAE, F. 7971, Op. 1, D. 80, L. 19.

8. Ibid., L. 49.

9. *Ogoniek*, no. 20/21 (30 July 1937).

10. Gide, André (1937), *Back from the USSR*. London: Martin Secher and Warburg, 32.

11. *Pravda*, 1 April 1936.

12. See Zhuravlev, S.V. (2000), '*Malenkie liudi' i Bolshaia istoria. Inostrantsi moskovskogo Elektrozavoda v sovetskom obstshestve 1920-kh–1930-kh gg*. Moskva: Rosspen, 70–78.

13. Zhuravlev, S.V. (1999), 'Inostrannaia koloniia moskovskogo Elektrozavoda v nachale 1930-kh godov: opyt mikroissledovaniia'. *Sotsialnaia istoriia*. Ezhegodnik 1998/99. Moskva: Rosspen.

14. Mikoyan, A.I. (1971b), 'Dva mesiatsa v SShA'. Part 2. SShA. *Ekonomika, politika, ideologiia*, no. 11: 74–6.

15. Ibid., 77.

16. Narkom miasnoi i molochnoi promyshlennosti SSSR. *Miasnaia industriia SSSR. Kratkii ekonomicheskii ocherk*. Moskva & Leningrad: Pishchepromizdat, 1941, 41.

17. *Pravda*, 16 May 1937.

18. RGAE, F. 7971, Op. 1, D. 371 'A'.

19. Ibid., L. 6.

20. Narkom Vnutorg SSSR. *Sovetskaia torgovlia*. Moskva & Leningrad: Gostorgizdat, 1936, 13.

21. RGAE, F. 7971, Op. 1, D. 371 'A', L. 5.

22. Ibid., L. 7.
23. Ibid., L. 8.
24. RGAE, F. 7971, Op. 1, D. 246, L. 1–51.
25. Ibid., L. 19–20/21.
26. Ibid., L. 27.
27. Ibid., L. 2–6.
28. Ibid., L. 7.
29. Ibid., L. 12, 19.
30. Ibid., L. 36.
31. *Pravda*, 27 April 1937.
32. Hessler, Julie (2000), 'Cultured trade. The Stalinist turn towards consumerism', in Fitzpatrick, Sheila (ed.), *Stalinism. New Directions*. London & New York: Routledge, 191.
33. RGAE, F. 7971, Op. 1, D. 246, L. 51.
34. *Pravda*, 2 November 1936.
35. Stenogramma soveshchaniia u zam. narkoma tov. M.I. Khlopliankina s rabotnikami pechati i isskustva po voprosu o reklame. 25 February 1936. RGAE, F. 7971, Op. 1, D. 247, L. 1–15; Soveshchanie v Narkom vnutorge SSSR po voprosu organizatsii reklamnogo dela. 11 March 1936. RGAE, F. 7971, Op. 1, D. 247, L. 16–74.
36. RGAE, F. 7971, Op. 1, D. 247, L. 61.
37. *Pravda*, 6 April 1936.
38. *Pravda*, 21 April 1936.
39. See *Ogoniek*, no. 4 (20 February 1934); 15 (5 August 1934).
40. *Ogoniek*, no. 23 (20 August 1937).
41. *Ogoniek*, no. 20–21 (30 July 1937).
42. About the historical stages of advertising, see Falk, Pasi (1994), *Consuming Bodies*. London: Sage.
43. RGAE, F. 7971, Op. 1, D. 247, L. 9.
44. Narkom vnutorg SSSR. *Sovetskaia torgovlia*. Moskva & Leningrad: Gostorgizdat, 1936, 15.
45. Kiritsenko, V. (1936), 'Voprosy sovetskoi torgovoi reklamy'. *Sovetskaia torgovlia*, no. 11–12: 69, 72.
46. CMAM, F. 1864, Op. 1, L. 1–10.
47. RGAE, F. 7971, Op. 1, D. 247, L. 17.
48. Ibid., L. 22.
49. Ibid., L. 24.
50. Ibid., L. 21.
51. Ibid., L. 20.
52. Ibid., L. 60.
53. 'Kak reklamiruet Torgreklama' 5 February 1938. A newspaper clip, the original source of which is unknown, probably from some trade press, the so-called multitirazhni, found in the archives of NKVT, RGAE, F. 7971, Op. 3, D. 92, L. 38.
54. CMAM, F. 1953, Op. 1, D. 18, L. 81.
55. CMAM, F. 1953, Op. 1, D. 14, L. 15–16.

6 The Emergence of the Soviet System of Retail Trade

1. CMAM, F. 1953, Op. 1, D. 9, L. 1–3.
2. Dikhtiar, G.A. (1961), *Sovetskaia torgovlia v period postroeniia sotsializma.* Moskva: Izdatelstvo Akademii nauk SSSR, 387.
3. *Itogi razvitiia sovetskoi torgovli ot VI k VII S'ezdu Sovetov SSSR.* Moskva: Izd.tsentralnogo instituta ekonomicheskikh issledovanii Narkom vnutorga SSSR, 1935, 57.
4. Narkom vnutorg SSSR. *Sovetskaia torgovlia.* Moskva & Leningrad: Gostorgizdat, 1936, 27.
5. CMAM, F. 1953, Op. 1, D. 18, L. 58.
6. 'Izuchenie potrebitel'skogo sprosa tovarov shirpotreba'. *Organizatsiia i tekhnika sovetskoi torgovli*, no. 1. Moskva, 1934: 11–13.
7. Narkom vnutorg SSSR. *Sovetskaia torgovlia*, 15.
8. Khaidenov, F. (1936), 'O rasshirenii assortimenta i kultura obsluzhivaniia. Opyt Kharkovskogo univermaga, NKVT. *Sovetskaia torgovlia*, no. 9: 54.
9. RGAE, F. 7971, Op. 1, D. 80, L. 32.
10. Ibid., L. 2/16.
11. Ibid., L. 42.
12. L'vovich, Gr. (1934), 'Zametki ob odnom magazine'. *Sovetskaia torgovlia*, no. 2: 111–17.
13. Stenogramma predvaritel'nogo zasedaniia komissii Politbiuro po voprosu o pere-dache selskokhoziaistvennykh detsentralizovannykh zagotovok v vedenie narkomata vnutrennei torgovli. 21 November 1934. Dokument no. 34. *Stalinskoe Politbiuro v 30-e gody. Sbornik dokumentov.* (Sost. O.V. Khlevniuk, A.V. Kvashonkin, L.P. Kosheleva, L.A. Rogovaia.) Seriia 'Dokumenty sovetskoi istorii' Moskva: AIRO-XX, 1995, 50–55.
14. See Srubar, Ilja (1991), 'War der reale Sozialismus modern? Versuch einer struktu-rellen Bestimmung'. *Kölner Zeitschrift für Soziologie und Sozialpsychologie.* vol. 43, no. 3: 415–32.
15. RGAE, F. 7971 (NKVT), Op. 1, D. 80, L. 8–9.
16. Ibid., L. 6.
17. Ibid., L. 17–19.
18. Ibid., L. 24.
19. Ibid., L. 30.
20. Ibid., L. 30–35.
21. Ibid., L. 13.
22. CMAM, F. 1953, Op. 1, D. 18, L. 62.
23. *Nashi dostizhenia*, no. 6. June 1936. See Kettering, Karen (1997), 'Ever more cosy and comfortable. Stalinism and the Soviet Domestic Interior, 1928–1938'. *Journal of Design History.* Special Issue: Design, Stalin and the Thaw. (Guest editor: Susan E. Reid.) vol. 10, no. 2: 127.
24. RGAE, F. 7971, Op. 1, D. 80, L. 37.
25. RGAE, F. 7971, Op. 1, D. 119, L. 17, 18.
26. In *Pravda* (30 November 1934) the amount was said to be 220.
27. CMAM, F. 1953, Op. 1, D. 11, L. 14.
28. CMAM, F. 1953, Op. 1, D. 14, L. 18.
29. CMAM, F. 1953, Op. 1, D. 18, L. 70, 80.
30. Lebina, Natalia (1999), *Povsednevnaia zhizn' sovetskogo goroda. Normy i anomalii. 1920/1930 gody.* Sankt-Peterburg: Neva, 222.

31. *Pravda*, 18 September 1934.

32. RGAE, F. 7971, Op. 1, D. 80, L. 32.

33. CMAM, F. 1953, Op. 1, D. 9, L. 3.

34. Cf. Horowitz, T. (1975), 'From elite fashion to mass fashion'. *Archives Europeénnes Sociologie*, vol. 16, no. 2: 283–95.

35. *Modeli plat'ia*, no. 2 (Leningrad, 1938).

36. Lebina, Natalie, *Povsednevnaia zhizn' sovetskogo goroda*, 223–4.

37. *Za obraztsovyi univermag*, no. 9 (21), 11 May 1936.

38. *Pravda*, 31 October 36.

39. *Za obraztsovyi univermag*, no. 10 (22), 25 May 1936.

40. RGAE, F. 7971, Op. 1, D. 15, L. 104.

41. The whole planning process can be followed in detail in the following archival sources: RGAE, F. 7971, Op. 1, D. 654 'B', L. 3–5, 8, 12, 14–15, 24, 32, 51.

42. RGAE, F. 7971, Op. 1, D. 6546, L. 2.

43. *Fabrika na vzmor'e. Stranitsy biografii kollektiva Leningradskoi Ordena Oktiabr'skoi Revoliutsii i Ordena Trudovogo Krasnogo Znameni sitzenabivnoi fabriki imeni Very Slutskoi.* Leningrad: Lenizdat, 1973, 111.

44. Nove, Alec (1992), *An Economic History of the USSR 1917–1991.* Harmondsworth: Penguin Books, 101.

45. Osokina, Elena (1998), *Za fasadom 'Stalinskogo izobiliia'. Raspredelenie i rynok v snabzhenii naseleniia v gody industrializatsii, 1927–1941.* Moskva: Rosspen, 160–9.

46. CMAM, F. 32, Op. 1, D. 2, L. 8.

47. Ibid., L. 40.

48. Hessler, Julie (2000), 'Cultured trade. The Stalinist turn towards consumerism', in Fitzpatrick, Sheila (ed.), *Stalinism. New Directions.* London & New York: Routledge, 520.

49. RGAE, F. 7971, Op. 1, D. 77, L. 65.

50. Narkom vnutorg SSSR. *Sovetskaia torgovlia*, 19.

51. RGAE, F. 7971, Op. 1, D. 77, L. 68–9.

52. Ibid., L. 66.

53. RGAE, F. 7971, Op. 2, D. 384.

54. Narkom vnutorg SSSR. *Sovetskaia torgovlia*, 21, 24.

55. RGAE, F. 7971, Op. 1, D. 77, L. 30–33.

56. Shinkarevskii, N. (1936), 'Sostoianie i zadachi spetsializirovannoi seti "Gastronom i Bakaleia". *Sovetskaia torgovlia*. no. 3: 50.

57. Ibid., 45.

58. Narkom vnutorg SSSR. *Sovetskaia torgovlia*, 10.

7 The Political Struggle over the Development of the Restaurants

1. Moskovskoe obschestvennoie pitanie. Biulleten' telegrafnogo agenstva SSSR (TASS). Organ Moskovskogo ob'edineniia narodnogo pitaniia 'Mosnarpit', no. 3 (5), 25 November 1931, 13.

2. CMAM, F. 453, Op. 1, D. 2, L. 3 and D. 3, L. 4.

3. In these 'stolovye' meals were highly subsidized: whereas the normal price of a portion of borsch soup was, for instance, 2 roubles 82 kopecks, in 'liternye' the price was only 86 kopecks. Ice cream appeared as a recommended desert on the model menus of these restaurants in 1935. The number of their customers could be used as quite a reliable estimate

of the number of 'privileged' people, or the state elite, in Moscow in 1935. According to the same source, another 37,000 had access to special food stores and deliveries. (See RGAE, F. 7971, Op. 1, D. 201, L. 57.)

4. CGA SPb, F. 1000, Op. 71, D. 3, L. 80.

5. RGAE, F. 7971, Op. 1, D. 326, L. 66–83.

6. RGAE, F. 7971, Op. 1, D. 1, L. 15.

7. Mikoyan, A. (1933), 'Obshchestvennoie pitanie – na novuiu stupen'. *Obshchestvennoie pitanie*, no. 1: 13.

8. Sakharova, P. (1933), 'Mebel' i servirovka'. *Obshchestvennoie pitanie*, no. 8: 24.

9. *Obshchestvennoie pitanie*. (1934). no. 1–2: 30.

10. RGAE, F. 7971, Op. 1, D. 210a, L. 29–34.

11. Ibid., L. 12–13, 18, 24.

12. RGAE, F. 7971, Op. 1, D. 210a, L. 45.

13. Postanovlenie NKVT (December 1935) about the reorganization of the system of 'obshchepit'. RGAE, F. 7971, Op. 1, D. 326, L. 6–19.

14. RGAE, F. 7971, Op. 1, D. 326, L. 84–5.

15. Ibid., L. 62–3.

16. RGAKFD, photo no. 0–14208. Similar photographs of model canteens were regularly published in the journal *Obshchestvennoie pitanie* in the 1930s.

17. RGAE, F. 7971, Op. 3, D. 15, L. 25.

18. Ibid., L. 26.

19. CGA SPb, F. 7384, Op. 11, D. 287, L. 1–2.

20. Ibid., L. 4.

21. RGAE, F. 7971, Op. 3, D. 15, L. 65–8.

22. Manning, Roberta, T. (1993), 'The Soviet cconomic crises 1936–40 and the Great Purges', in Getty, J. Arch and Manning, Roberta T. (eds), *Stalinist Terror. New Perspectives*. Cambridge. Cambridge University Press, 123.

23. Rupasov, A. (1938), 'Osnovnye voprosy obshchestvennogo pitaniia'. *Voprosy sovetskoi torgovli*, no. 7: 32–42.

24. Ibid., 39.

25. CGA SPb, F. 1000, Op. 71, D. 757, L. 38–42a.

26. RGAE, F. 7971, Op. 3, D. 74, L. 46.

27. Ibid., L. 63–64.

28. Such accusations and condemnations which could abruptly and unexpectedly destroy many people and change almost the whole staff of any big administrative unit did not necessarily have to lead to any real changes in the economic line of development. For instance, the director and 8 per cent of the whole staff of the newly founded Moscow-based Institute for Cosmetics were arrested in 1939. It is not known whether any disputes over the development of Soviet cosmetics were used as pretences in the processes to follow. The annual report of the institute only laconically commented that, unfortunately, the work of the institute had suffered from the arrests of its workers as people's enemies. (see RGAE, F. 8551, Op. 1, D. 103, L. 19.) Politics and economy, even though tightly intermingled, also to a large extent lived lives of their own in the Soviet Union.

29. RGAE, F. 7971, Op. 3, D. 15, L. 8.

30. RGAE, F. 7971, Op. 3, D. 74, L. 110.

31. CMAM, F. 453, Op. 1, D. 35, L. 1.

32. RGAE, F. 7971, Op. 3, D. 74, L. 108. This is also a good example the concentration of almost all the resources of mass consumption in Moscow.

33. RGAE, F. 8543, Op. 1, D. 403, L. 91–2.

34. *Pravda*, 28 May 1936.

35. Mikoyan, A. (1971a), 'Dva mesiatsa v SShA'. SShA. *Ekonomika, politika, ideologiia*, no. 10: 11, 76.

36. RGAE, F. 8543, Op. 1, D. 499, L. 122–3.

37. Mikoyan, 'Obshchestvennoe pitanie', 14.

38. RGAE, F. 7971, Op. 1, D. 210a, L. 110.

39. *Istoriia sotsialisticheskoi ekonomiki SSSR*, T. 4. Moskva, 1978, 233.

40. See RGAE, F. 8543, Op. 1, D. 382, L. 141.

8 Soviet Consumption Amidst General Poverty

1. Timasheff, N.S. (1946), *The Great Retreat. The Growth and Decline of Communism in Russia.* New York: E.P. Dutton.

2. According to Aleksandr Bastrykin's and Ol'ga Gromtseva's recent study, *Teni istshezaiut v Smol'nom. Ubistvo Kirova.* (St. Peterburg: Evropeiski Dom 2001, 173–4), Ordzhonikidze was in the mid-1930s until his death in 1937 together with Kirov, Kuibishev, Kosior, Postyshev, and, at times even, Kalinin a representative of a more moderate group among Stalin's close allies. They opposed the escalation of political repressions, demanded a normalization of inner-party life, were against the export of grain and criticized the unrealistic tempo of industrialization during the First Five-Year Plan. They also demanded the end of food rationing.

3. Davis, R.W. and Khlevniuk, O.V. (1993), 'Vtoraia piatiletka, "Mekhanizm smeny ekonomicheskoi politiki"'. *Otechestvennaia istoriia*, no. 3: 93–6.

4. Ibid., 94.

5. Zaleski, E. (1989), *Stalinist Planning for Economic Growth 1933–1952*. London: Macmillan, 129–30.

6. *Pis'ma I.V. Stalina K.M. Molotovu 1925–1936 gg. Sbornik dokumentov*. Moskva: Rossiia molodaia, 1995, 251.

7. *Rybnoe khoziaistvo*, no. 5 (1935): 2.

8. Osokina, Elena (1998), *Za fasadom 'stalinskogo izobiliia'*. Raspredelenie i rynok v snabzhenii naseleniia v gody industrializatsii, 1927–1941. Moskva: Rosspen, 208–10.

9. On 16 February 1940, during the Finnish War, A.G. Mankov wrote in his diary: 'Our Government has gone bankrupt. It has proven incapable of satisfying the most basic needs of its population, of offering them even the most minimal comforts of subsistence.' (Mankov, A.G. (1994), `Iz dnevnika riadovogo cheloveka 1938–1941'. *Zvezda*, no. 11: 184.

10. Manning, Roberta T. (1993), 'The Soviet economic crises 1936–1940 and the Great Purges', in Getty, J. Arch and Manning, R.T. (eds), *Stalinist Terror. New Perspectives*. Cambridge: Cambridge University Press, 123.

11. Osokina, *Za fasadom 'stalinskogo izobiliia'*, 209–10.

12. Zhuravlev, S.V. and Sokolov, A.K. (1999), *Obshchestvo i vlast'. 1930-e gody,* Moskva: Rosspen, 204.

13. Zhuravlev and Sokolov, *Obshchestvo i vlast'*, 206.

14. *Itogi razvitiia sovetskoi torgovli ot VI k VII S'ezdu Sovetov SSSR*. Moskva: Izd.tsentralnogo instituta ekonomicheskikh issledovanii Narkom vnutorg SSSR, 1935, 46.

15. Osokina, *Za fasadom 'stalinskogo izobiliia'*, 90.

16. Ibid., 93, 95.

17. Ibid., 121.

18. Tuominen, Arvo (1983), *The Bells of the Kremlin. An Experience in Communism.* Hanover & London: University Press of New England, 205.

19. Osokina, *Za fasadom 'stalinskogo izobiliia'*, 109.

20. Colton, Timothy (1995), *Moscow. Governing a Socialist Metropolis.* Cambridge, MA & London: The Bellknapp Press of the Harvard University Press, 283.

21. CGA IPD, F. 24, Op. 2v, D. 1373, L. 5.

22. Osokina, *Za fasadom 'stalinskogo izobilia`*, 124.

23. Ibid., 134.

24. Ibid., 128.

25. Mankov, A.G. (1994), 'Iz dnevnika riadovogo cheloveka 1938–1941'. *Zvezda.* no. 11: 190.

26. Tuominen, *The Bells of the Kremlin*, 267.

27. Osokina, *Za fasadom 'stalinskogo izobiliia'*, 131.

28. *Rybnoe khoziaistvo SSSR*, no. 1–2 (1935).

29. Ibid., 4.

30. Ishkov, A. (1936), 'Na pod'eme'. *Rybnoe khoziaistvo SSSR*, no. 2: 29.

31. Smirnov, F. (1934), 'Rabochee snabzhenie na avtozavode im. Stalina'. *Sovetskaia torgovlia.* no. 2: 110.

32. 'Pokupaiu avtomibil". *Obshchestvennoie pitanie.* (1934) no. 4: 19.

33. Ibid., 19.

34. Mankov, A.G. (1994), 'Iz dnevnika riadovogo cheloveka *1933–1934 gg'. Zvezda*, no. 5: 163.

35. A letter written by Pietari Simonpoika Jääskeläinen on 18 October 1934 to his brothers' families, other relatives and villagers of Keltto. Private collection. Relatives who had been left behind in the old home village Keltto had obviously inquired whether it would be wise for them to move voluntarily over to Siberia too since conditions were getting worse at home. Even though the general impression of living conditions in Siberia given in the letter is rather positive its writer did not encourage his fellow villagers to take this step. The travel itself was long, difficult and very expensive. And the winters were very cold.

36. Jääskeläinen, Anni (2001), *Karkotetut. Stalinin ajan karkotuksien merkitykset ja myyttinen historia inkerinsuomalaisen suvun kertomana.* A master's thesis at the Department of Sociology, University of Helsinki: unpublished.

37. In his diary A.G. Mankov gives a good description of the complicated bureaucratic structure, the ORS, which was responsible for delivering the food coupons to the workers according to their performance as it functioned at the shop floor level at his factory in 1933. Mankov worked as an ordinary office worker, whose task was to deliver these coupons to the workers. (See Mankov, 'Iz dnevnika riadovogo cheloveka 1933–1934', 147–8.)

38. RGAE, F. 8297, Op. 2, D. 60, L. 141–2, 348.

39. Ibid., L. 348–9.

40. RGAE, F. 8297, Op. 4, D. 226, L. 13–14.

41. RGAE, F. 8297, Op. 4, D. 208, L. 36–8.

42. RGAE, F. 8297, Op. 4, D. 411, L. 46.

43. Siegelbaum, L.H. (1988), *Stakhanovism and the Politics of Productivity in the USSR, 1935–1941.* Cambridge: Cambridge University Press, 228.

44. Lebina, Natalia (1999), *Povsednevnaia zhizn' sovetskogo goroda. Normy i anomalii. 1920/1930 gody.* Sankt-Peterburg: Neva, 224.

45. CMAM, F. 485, Op. 1, D. 3, L. 2.

46. Zhuravlev, S.V. (1999), 'Inostrannaia koloniia moskovskogo Elektrozavoda v nachale 1930-kh godov. opyt mikroissledovaniia', *Sotsialnaia istoriia, Ezhegodnik 1998/99*. Moskva: Rosspen, 395–401.

47. *Molodezh SSSR. Statisticheski sbornik*. TsUNHY Gosplane SSSR i TsKVLKSM. Moskva: Soiuz orguchet, 1936, 338–41.

48. Fitzpatrick, Sheila (1999), *Everyday Stalinism. Ordinary Life in Extraordinary Times. Soviet Russia in the 1930s*. New York & Oxford: Oxford University Press, 41.

49. Nielsen, Aage K. (1932), *Fra Moskva til Persepolis. Rejserids fra Sovjetrusland og Persien*. Copenhagen: C.A. Reitzels forlag, 37.

50. Shinkarevski, N. (1936), 'Sostoianie i zadachi spetsializirovannoi seti "Gastronom i Bakaleia"'. *Sovetskaia torgovlia, no. 3: 45.

51. Ibid., 45.

52. Davies, Sarah (1997), *Popular Opinion in Stalin's Russia. Terror, Propaganda and Dissent, 1934–1941*. Cambridge: Cambridge University Press, 31.

53. Bell, Daniel (1974), *The Coming of Post-industrial Society*. London: Heinemann, 466.

54. Davies, *Popular Opinion in Stalin's Russia*, 36.

55. Higher wages would have been another natural demand to combat the effects of inflation on the living standards. Such demands could not be publicly made.

56. Zhuravlev, Sokolov, *Obshchestvo i vlast'*, 207.

57. Davies, *Popular Opinion in Stalin's Russia*, 95.

58. Kotik, V. (1936), 'Assortment minimum v Moskovskoi oblasti'. *Sovetskaia torgovlia*, no. 4–6: 111.

59. RGAE, F. 7971, Op. 1, D. 16, L. 54–54ob.

60. I.V. Stalin's speech at the First All-Union Meeting of Stakhanovites, cited in 'Pokupaiu avtomobil", *Obshchestvennoie pitanie*. (1934) no. 4: 19.

61. *Ekonomitsheskaia istoria Rossii XIX–XX vv. Sovremennyi vzgliad*. Moskva: Rosspen, 2000, 112, cited in Bastrykin, Aleksandr and Gromtseva, O'lga (2001), *Teni istshezaiut v Smol'nom. Ubistvo Kirova*. Sankt-Peterburg: Evropeiski Dom, 2001, 182–3.

62. Barber, J. (1990), 'The working-class culture and political culture in the 1930s', in Günther, H. (ed.), *The Culture of the Stalin Period*. London: Macmillan, 9.

63. Fitzpatrick, *Everyday Stalinism*, 7.

64. Malia, Martin (2001), 'Revolution fulfilled. How the revisionists are still trying to take the ideology out of Stalinism'. Times Literary Supplement, no. 5124.

65. Martin, Terry (2001), *The Affirmative Action Empire. Nations and Nationalism in the Soviet Union, 1923–1939*. Ithaca and London: Cornell University Press, 21–3.

66. Ibid., 23.

9 Conclusion: Socialist Realism in the Material Culture

1. Simmel, G. (1981), 'Fashion', in Sproles G.B. (ed.), *Perspectives on fashion*. Minneapolis: Burges. (Originally published in English in *International Quaterly*. no. 10 (1904): 130–55.) See also Gronow, J. (1997), *The Sociology of Taste*. London & New York: Routledge.

2. Bauman, Zygmunt (1990/91), 'Communism: a post mortem', *Praxis International*, vol. 10, no. 3–4: 185–92.

Notes

Notes

3. Cited in Davies, Sarah (1997), *Popular Opinion in Stalin's Russia. Terror, Propaganda and Dissent, 1934–1941*. Cambridge: Cambridge University Press, 30.

4. Kornai, J. (1982), *Growth, Shortage and Efficiency*. Oxford: Basil Blackwell.

5. Srubar, Ilja (1991). 'War der reale Sozialismus modern? Versuch einer strukturellen Bestimmung'. *Kölner Zeitschrift für Soziologie und Sozialpsychologie*, vol. 43, no. 3: 415–32.

6. Ledeneva, A. (1998), *Russia's Economy of Favours. Blat, Networking and Informal Exchange*. Cambridge and New York: Cambridge University Press; Lonkila, Markku (1999), *Social Networks in Post-Soviet Russia. Continuity and Change in the Everyday Life of St. Petersburg Teachers*. Helsinki: Kikimora Publications. Series A:4.

7. Boym, S. (1994), *Common places. Mythologies of Everyday Life in Russia*. Cambridge, MA.: Harvard University Press; Kelly, C., Pilkington, H., Shepherd, D., and Volkov, V. (1998) 'Introduction: Why cultural Studies?', in Kelly, C. and Shepherd, D. (eds), *Russian Cultural Studies. An Introduction*. Oxford and New York: Oxford University Press, 1–20.

8. Attwood, Lynne (1999), *Women's Magazines as Engineers of Female Identity, 1922–53*. Basingstoke: Macmillan, 132. As Catriona Kelly and Vadim Volkov have pointed out, the contents of the concept went through interesting changes during the 1930s, from a consumer oriented to a more spiritual idea of 'being cultivated'. See Kelly, Catriona and Volkov, Vadim (1998), 'Directed desires: Kultur`nost' and consumption', in Kelly, C. and Shepherd, D. (eds), *Constructing Russian Culture in the Age of Revolution: 1881–1940*. Oxford: Oxford University Press, 293–313.

9. Vainshtein, Olga (1996), 'Female fashion, Soviet style. Bodies of ideology', in Goscilo, H. and Holmgren, B. (eds), *Russia, Women and Culture*. Bloomington: Indiana University Press, 70–71.

10. Ibid., 71–2.

11. Dunham, Vera (1976), *In Stalin's Time*. Cambridge: Cambridge University Press, 43.

12. See Kelly and Volkov 'Directed desires', 299.

13. Stites, Richard (1992), *Russian Popular Culture. Entertainment and Society since 1900*. Cambridge: Cambridge University Press, 65.

14. Ibid.

15. Fitzpatrick, Sheila (1992), *The Cultural Front. Power and Culture in Revolutionary Russia*. Ithaca & London: Cornell University Press, 178.

16. Morozov, A.I. (1995), *Konets utopii. Iz istorii iskusstva v SSSR 1930-kh godov*. Moskva: Izdatel'stvo 'Galart'.

17. See Cooke, Cathrine (1997), 'Beauty as a route to "the radiant future": Responses of Soviet architecture'. *Journal of Design History*. Special Issue: Design, Stalin and the Thaw. (Guest editor: Susan E. Reid.) vol. 10, no. 2: 143.

18. Morozov, *Konets utopii*, 88.

19. Colton, Timothy (1995), *Moscow. Governing a Socialist Metropolis*. Cambridge, MA & London: The Bellknapp Press of Harvard University Press, 327.

20. *Pravda*, 20 May 1935, 3. Cited in Colton, *Moscow*, 328.

21. See Kettering, Karen (2000), 'Sverdlov Square metro station: The friendship of the people's and the Stalin constitution', *Decorative Arts*, vol. 3, no. 2: 31.

22. Fitzpatrick, Sheila (1999), *Everyday Stalinism. Ordinary Life in Extraordinary Times: Soviet Russia in the 1930s*. New York & Oxford: Oxford University Press, 9.

23. Palmér, T., Myrdal, J. and Stenholm, O. (1988), *Stalins fotografer: pressbilden som vapen under den första femårsplanen 1929–1932*. Stockholm: Sveriges radio.

24. Zhuravlev, S.V. and Sokolov, A.K. (1999), *Obshchestvo i vlast'. 1930-e gody*. Moskva: Rosspen, 133.

169

Bibliography

Archival Materials

1 Rossiskii Gosudarstvennyi Arkhiv Ekonomiki (RGAE). Moscow.

F. 7925 Narodnyi komissariat mashinostroeniia SSSR.

F. 7971 Narodnyi komissariat vnutrennei torgovli SSSR (NKVT SSSR).

F. 7486 Ministerstvo sel'skogo hoziaistva SSSR.

F. 8297 Glavnoe upravlenie miasnoi promyshlennosti Narodnogo komissariata pishchevoi promyshlennosti SSSR (Glavmiaso NKPP SSSR).

F. 8543 Narodnyi komissariat pishchevoi promyshlennosti SSSR (NKPP SSSR).

F. 8551 Glavnoe upravlenie parfiumernoi promyshlennosti Narkomata pishchevoi promyshlennosti SSSR (Glavparfiumerprom SSSR).

2 Gosudarstvennyi Arkhiv Rossiskoi Federatsii (GARF). Moscow.

F. 3316 Central'nyi ispolnitel'nyi komitet SSSR (CIK SSSR).

F. 5446 Sovet narodnyh komissarov – Sovet ministrov SSSR (SNK – Sovmin SSSR).

3 Central'nyi Municipal'nyi Arkhiv Goroda Moskvy (CMAM). Moscow.

F. 32 Moskovskoe obedinenie predpriiatii torgovli (*Mosgortorg*).

F. 453 Moskovskoe obedinenie predpriiatii narodnogo obshchestvennogo pitaniia (*Mosnarpit*).

F. 485 Konditerskaia fabrika *Rot Front*, Moskva.

F. 488 Moskovskii hrustal'nyi zavod.

F. 516 Moskovskii vinno-kon'iachnyi zavod.

F. 520 Moskovskii spirto-vodochnyi zavod.

F. 864 Konditerskaja fabrika *Krasnyi Oktiabr'*, Moskva.

F. 1864 Fabrika svetohudozhestvennyh rabot tresta *Mosgorsvet* (pozdnee Mosgoroformlenie).

F. 1953 Moskovskii Central'nyi Universam (CUM).

4 Central'nyi Gosudarstvennyi Arkhiv Moskovskoi Oblasti (CGAMO). Moscow.

F. 1033 Mossel'prom.
F. 3836 Dulevskii farforovyi zavod.

5 Central'nyi Gosudarstvennyi Arkhiv Sankt-Peterburga (CGA SPb). St. Peterburg.

F. 1000 Fond Ispolnitel'nogo Komiteta Leningradskogo Gubernskogo Soveta pabochih i krest'ianskih deputatov (1918–1927).
F. 7384 Fond Ispolnitel'nogo Komiteta Leningradskogo Gorodskogo Soveta.

6 Central'nyi Gosudarstvennyi Arkhiv Istoriko-politicheskih Dokumentov (CGA IPD). St. Peterburg.

F. 24 Fond Leningradskogo oblastnogo komiteta VKP(b).

7 Rossijskii Gosudarstvennyii Arkhiv Kinofotodokumentov (RGAKFD). Krasnodar.

Journals and Newspapers

Golos konfetchika
Izobilie
Izvestiia
Komsomol'skaia Pravda
Leningradskaia Pravda
Miasnaia industriia SSSR
Modeli plat'ia
Modeli sezona
Moskovskie novosti
Nashi dostizhenia
Obshchestvennoie pitanie
Ogoniek
Organizatsiia i tekhnika sovetskoi torgovli
Pionerskaia Pravda
Pishchevaia industriia
Pravda
Problemy ekonomiki
Rabotnitsa

Rybnoe khoziaistvo SSSR
Sovetskaia torgovlia
Sovetskii patefon
Trud
Vecherniaia Moskva
Vinodelenie i vinogradarstvo
Voprosy sovetskoi torgovli
Za obraztsovyi univermag
Zvezda

Other Primary Sources

Biulleten' oblastnogo i gorodskogo otdelov vnutrennei torgovli, no. 7. Leningrad, 1935.

Biulleten' oblastnogo i gorodskogo otdelov vnutrennei torgovli, no. 59 (431). Leningrad, 22 December 1938.

Biulleten' oblastnogo otdela vnutrennei torgovli Lenispolkoma, no. 87. Leningrad, 1936.

Biulleten' oblastnogo otdela vnutrennei torgovli Lenispolkoma, no. 125. Leningrad, 1936.

German, M. Iu. (1997), *Slozhnoe proshedshee. Glavy knigi vospominanii. Nevskii Arkhiv. Istoriko-kraevedcheskii sbornik III.* Sankt-Peterburg: Atheneum-Feniks.

Gide, André (1937), *Back from the USSR.* London: Martin Secher and Warburg.

Heyman, S. (1938), 'O roste urovnia zhizni rabochego klassa SSSR'. *Problemy ekonomiki*, no. 3.

Ishkov, A. (1936), 'Na pod'eme'. *Rybnoe khoziaistvo SSSR*, no. 2.

Itogi razvitiia sovetskoi torgovli ot VI k VII S'ezdu Sovetov SSSR. Moskva: Izd.tsentralnogo instituta ekonomicheskikh issledovanii Narkom vnutorga SSSR, 1935.

Iurina, M. (1936), 'Kultura i krasota'. *Rabotnitsa*, no. 3: 17.

'Izuchenie potrebitel'skogo sprosa tovarov shirpotreba'. *Organizatsiia i tekhnika sovetskoi torgovli*, no. 1. Moskva, 1934.

Jääskeläinen, Pietari Simonpoika. Letter, Siberia 18 October 1934. Private collection.

Kaganov, I. (1934), 'Rekonstruktsia material'no-tekhnicheskoi bazy torgovly'. *Sovetskaia torgovlia*, no. 1.

Karpatsenko, P.K. (1939), 'Zadachi sovetskogo vinodeliia i vinogradarstva'. *Vinodelenie i vinogradarstvo SSSR*, no. 1.

Khaidenov, F. (1936), 'O rasshirenii assortimenta i kultura obsluzhivaniia'. Opyt Kharkovskogo univermaga; NKVT. *Sovetskaia torgovlia*, no. 9.

Kiritsenko, V. (1936), 'Voprosy sovetskoi torgovoi reklamy'. *Sovetskaia torgovlia*, no. 11–12.

Kniga o vkysnoi i zdorovoi pishche. Moskva 1952, 1953, 1954 and 1955.

Kotik, V. (1936), 'Assortment minimum v Moskovskoi oblasti'. *Sovetskaia torgovlia*, no. 4–6.

Lebedev, G. (1934), 'Rabota legkoi promyshlennosti v 1933 g'. *Sovetskaia torgovlia*, no. 1.

Likhov, S. (1934), 'Shkola bor'by za kachestvo tovarov'. *Sovetskaia torgovlia*, no. 4.

Lunts, L.B. (1934), *Parki Kul'tury i otdykha*. Leningrad: Gostroiizdatelstvo.

L'vovich, Gr. (1934), 'Zametki ob odnom magazine'. *Sovetskaia torgovlia*, no. 2.

Mankov, A.G. (1994), 'Iz dnevnika riadovogo cheloveka 1933–1934'. *Zvezda*, no. 5.

—— (1995), 'Iz dnevnika riadovogo cheloveka 1938–1941'. *Zvezda*, no. 11.

Mikoyan, A. (1933), 'Obshchestvennoe pitanie – na novuiu stupen'. *Obshchestvennoie pitanie*, no. 1.

—— (1934), 'Za sovetskuiu torgovliu, za uluchshenie rabochego snabzheniia'. *Pravda*, no. 32 (5918).

—— (1971a), 'Dva mesiatsa v SShA', SShA. *Ekonomika, politika, ideologiia*, no. 10.

—— (1971b), 'Dva mesiatsa v SShA'. Part 2. SShA. *Ekonomika, politika, ideologiia*, no. 11.

—— (1999), *Tak bylo. Razmyshleniia o minuschem*. Moskva: Vagrius, 1999.

Mikulina, E. (1936), 'Tvortsy sovetskoi mody'. *Organizatsiia i tekhnika sovetskoi torgovli*, no. 5.

Molodezh SSSR. Statisticheski sbornik. TsUNHY Gosplane SSSR i TsKVLKSM. Moskva: Soiuz orguchet, 1936.

Molotov, V. (1934), 'Zadachi vtoroi piatiletki'. *Pravda*, no. 36 (5922).

Moskovskoe obschestvennoie pitanie. Biulleten' telegrafnogo agenstva SSSR (TASS). Organ Moskovskogo ob'edineniia narodnogo pitania 'Mosnarpit', no. 3 (5), 25 November 1931.

Narkom miasnoi i molochnoi promyshlennosti SSSR. *Miasnaia industriia SSSR. Kratkii ekonomicheskii ocherk*. Moskva & Leningrad: Pishchepromizdat, 1941.

Narkom vnutorg SSSR. *Sovetskaia torgovlia*. Moskva & Leningrad: Gostorgizdat, 1936.

Nielsen, Aage K. (1932), *Fra Moskva til Persepolis. Rejserids fra Sovjetrusland og Persien*. Copenhagen: C.A. Reitzels forlag.

'O merakh po uluchsheniiu proizvodstva grammofonov, grammofonykh plastinok i muzykal'nykh instrumentov'. *Postanovlenie Soveta Narodnykh Komissarov*, no. 372. In *Sobranie zakonov i rasporiazhenii raboche-krest'ianskogo pravitel'stva SSSR*, Otdel pervyi, no. 62. 15 October 1933.

Perepeletskii (1936). 'Novoe v assortimente i oformlenii'. *Organizatsiia i tekhnika sovetskoi torgovli*, no. 6. Moskva.

Pis'ma I.V. Stalina K.M. Molotovu 1925–1936 gg. Sbornik dokumentov. Moskva: Rossiia molodaia, 1995.

'Postanovleniia, rasporiazheniia i spravochnye materialy'. *Biulleten Leningradskogo oblastnogo i gorodskogo otdelov snabzheniia Lenoblispolkoma i Lensoveta po sovetskoi torgovle, rabochemu snabzheniiu i pishchevoi promyshlennosti,* no. 4. July 1934.

Rupasov, A. (1938), 'Osnovnye voprosy obshchestvennogo pitaniia'. *Voprosy sovetskoi torgovli*, no. 7: 32–42.

Rybakov, A. (1998), *Deti Arbata. Trilogiia. Kniga vtoraia. Strakh.* Moskva: Terra.

Sakharova, P. (1933), 'Mebel' i servirovka'. *Obshchestvennoie pitanie*, no. 8: 24.

Shinkarevski, N. (1936), 'Sostoianie i zadachi spetsializirovannoi seti "Gastronoma i Bakaleia"'. *Sovetskaia torgovlia,* no. 3.

Smirnov, F. (1934), 'Rabochee snabzhenie na avtozavode im. Stalina'. *Sovetskaia torgovlia,* no. 2: 110.

Sovetskaia torgovlia. Statisticheskii sbornik. Moskva, 1956.

Stenogramma predvaritel'nogo zasedaniia komissii Politbiuro po voprosu o peredache selskokhoziaistvennykh detsentralizovannykh zagotovok v vedenie narkomata vnutrennei torgovli. 21 November 1934. Dokument no. 34. *Stalinskoe Politbiuro v 30-e gody. Sbornik dokumentov.* Sost. O.V. Khlevniuk, A.V. Kvashonkin, L.P. Kosheleva, L.A. Rogovaia (1995). Seriia 'Dokumenty sovetskoi istorii'. Moskva: AIRO-XX.

Tuominen, Arvo (1983), *The Bells of the Kremlin. An Experience in Communism.* Hanover & London: University Press of New England.

Vishnitser, A. (1936), 'Bor'ba za assortiment prodtovarov. (Opyt Gastronoma no. 1)'. *Sovetskaia torgovlia*, no. 4–5.

Vneshnaia torgovlia SSSR za 20 let 1918–1937gg. Statisticheski spravochnik. Moskva: Mezhdunarodnaia kniga, 1939.

Secondary Sources

Agoneva, S.B. (1999), 'Istoriia sovremennoi novogodnei traditsii'. *Mifologiia i povsednevnost.* Vyp. 2. Materialy nauchnoi konferentsii 24–26 fevralia 1999 goda. Sankt-Peterburg: Institut russkoi literatury RAN.

Attwood, Lynne (1999), *Women's Magazines as Engineers of Female Identity, 1922–53.* London: Macmillan.

Azhgikhina, Nadezhda and Goscilo, Helena (1996), 'Getting under their skin. The beauty salon in Russian women's lives', in Goscilo, H. and Holmgren, B. (eds), *Russia, Women, Culture.* Bloomington & Indianapolis: Indiana University Press.

Barber, J. (1990), 'The working class culture and political culture in the 1930s, in Günther, H. (ed.), *The Culture of The Stalin Period.* London: Macmillan.

Bastrykin, Aleksandr and Gromtseva, Ol'ga (2001), *Teni istshezaiut v Smol'nom. Ubistvo Kirova.* Sankt-Peterburg: Evropeiski dom.

Bauman, Zygmunt (1990/91), 'Communism: a post mortem'. *Praxis International,* vol. 10, no. 3–4: 185–92.

Bell, Daniel (1974), *The Coming of Post-industrial Society.* London: Heinemann.

Beriia, S. (1994), *Moi otets – Lavrentii Beriia.* Moskva: Sovremennik.

Boym, S. (1994), *Common Places. Mythologies of Everyday Life in Russia*. Cambridge, MA: Harvard University Press.

Colton, Timothy (1995), *Moscow. Governing a Socialist Metropolis*. Cambridge, MA & London: The Bellknapp Press of Harvard University Press.

Cooke, Cathrine (1997), 'Beauty as a route to "the radiant future". Responses of Soviet architecture'. *Journal of Design History*. Special Issue: Design, Stalin and the Thaw. (Guest editor: Susan E. Reid.) vol. 10, no. 2.

Davies, Sarah (1997), *Popular Opinion in Stalin's Russia. Terror, Propaganda and Dissent, 1934–1941*. Cambridge: Cambridge University Press.

Davis, R. and Khlevniuk, O.V. (1993), 'Vtoraia piatiletka. "Mekhanizm smeny ekonomicheskoi politiki"'. *Otechestvennaia istoriia*, no. 3.

Dikhtiar, G.A. (1961), *Sovetskaia torgovlia v periode postroeniia sotsializma*. Moskva: Izdatelstvo Akademii nauk SSSR.

Dunham, Vera (1976), *In Stalin's Time*. Cambridge: Cambridge University Press.

Ekonomitsheskaia istoria Rossii XIX–XX vv. Sovremennyi vzgliad. Moskva: Rosspen, 2000.

Fabrika na vzmor'e. Stranitsy biografii kollektiva Leningradskoi Ordena Oktiabr'skoi Revoliutsii i Ordena Trudovogo Krasnogo Znameni sitzenabivnoi fabriki imeni Very Slutskoi. Leningrad: Lenizdat, 1973.

Falk, Pasi (1994), *Consuming Bodies*. London: Sage.

Fitzpatrick, Sheila (1979), *Education and Social Mobility in the Soviet Union 1921–1934*. Cambridge: Cambridge University Press.

—— (1992), *The Cultural Front. Power and Culture in Revolutionary Russia*. Ithaca & London: Cornell University Press.

—— (1999), *Everyday Stalinism. Ordinary Life in Extraordinary Times. Soviet Russia in the 1930s*. New York & Oxford: Oxford University Press.

Glebkin, V.V. (1998), *Ritual v sovetskoi kulture*. Moskva: Janus-K.

Gronow, Jukka (1997), *The Sociology of Taste*. London & New York: Routledge.

Gronow, P. and Saunio, I. (1998), *An International History of Recording Industry*. London & New York: Cassell.

Hessler, Julie (2000), 'Cultured trade. The Stalinist turn towards consumerism', in Fitzpatrick, Sheila (ed.), *Stalinism. New Directions*. London & New York: Routledge.

Hoffman, David (1993), 'The Great Terror on the local level. Purges in Moscow factories', in Getty, J. Arch and Manning, Roberta T. (eds), *Stalinist Terror. New Perspectives*. Cambridge: Cambridge University Press.

Horowitz, T. (1975), 'From elite fashion to mass fashion'. *Archives Europeénnes Sociologie,* vol. 16, no. 2: 283–95.

Istoriia sotsialisticheskoi ekonomiki SSSR, T. 4. Moskva, 1978.

Jääskeläinen, Anni (2001), *Karkotetut. Stalinin ajan karkotuksien merkitykset ja myyttinen historia inkerinsuomalaisen suvun kertomana*. A master's thesis presented in the Department of sociology, University of Helsinki: unpublished.

Kelly, Catriona and Volkov, Vadim (1998), 'Directed Desires. Kultur`nost' and consumption', in Kelly, C. and Shepherd, D. (eds), *Constructing Russian*

Culture in the Age of Revolution: 1881–1940. Oxford & New York: Oxford University Press.

Kelly, C., Pilkington, H., Shepherd, D. and Volkov, V. (1998), 'Introduction. Why cultural studies?', in Kelly, C. and Shepherd, D. (eds), *Russian Cultural Studies. An Introduction*. Oxford and New York: Oxford University Press.

Kettering, Karen (1997), 'Ever more cosy and comfortable. Stalinism and the Soviet domestic interior, 1928–1938'. *Journal of Design History*. Special Issue: Design, Stalin and the Thaw. (Guest editor: Susan E. Reid.) vol. 10, no. 2.

– (2000), 'Sverdlov Square metro station: The friendship of the people's and the Stalin constitution', *Decorative Arts*, vol. 3, no. 2.

Kornai, J. (1982), *Growth, Shortage and Efficiency*. Oxford: Basil Blackwell.

Lavrentiev, Alexander and Nassarow, Juri (1995), *Russisches Design. Tradition und Experiment 1920–1990*. Berlin: Ernst & Sohn.

Lebina, Natalia (1999), *Povsednevnaia zhizn' sovetskogo goroda. Normy i anomalii. 1920/1930 gody*. Sankt-Peterburg: Neva.

Ledeneva, A. (1998), *Russia's Economy of Favours. Blat, Networking and Informal Exchange*. Cambridge: Cambridge University Press.

Lonkila, Markku (1999), *Social Networks in Post-Soviet Russia. Continuity and Change in the Everyday Life of St. Petersburg Teachers*. Helsinki: Kikimora Publications. Series A:4.

Malia, Martin (2001), 'Revolution fulfilled, How the revisionists are still trying to take the ideology out of Stalinism'. Times Literary Supplement, no.5124: 3–4.

Manning, Roberta T. (1993), 'The Soviet cconomic crises 1936–1940 and the Great Purges', in Getty, J. Arch and Manning, R. T. (eds), *Stalinist Terror. New Perspectives*. Cambridge: Cambridge University Press.

Martin, Terry (2001), *The Affirmative Action Empire. Nations and Nationalism in the Soviet Union, 1923–1939*. Ithaca & London: Cornell University Press.

Morozov, A.I. (1995), *Konets utopii. Iz istorii iskusstva v SSSR 1930-kh godov*. Moskva: Izdatel'stvo 'Galart'.

Nove, Alec (1992), *An Economic History of the USSR 1917–1991*. Harmondsworth: Penguin Books.

Osokina, Elena (1998), *Za fasadom 'stalinskogo izobiliia'. Raspredelenie i rynok v snabzhenii naseleniia v gody industrializatsii, 1927–1941*. Moskva: Rosspen.

—— (1999), 'Predprinimatel'stvo i rynok v povsednevnoi zhizni pervykh piatiletok. Na primere rynka potrebitel'nykh tovarov', *Sotsialnaia istoriia. Ezhegodnik 1998/99*. Moskva: Rosspen.

Palmér, T., Myrdal, J. and Stenholm, O. (1988), *Stalins fotografer: pressbilden som vapen under den första femårsplanen 1929–1932*. Stockholm: Sveriges radio.

Papernyi, Vladimir (1985), *Kultura 'Dva'*. Ann Arbor: Ardis.

Petrone, Karen (2000), *Life Has Become More Joyous, Comrades. Celebrations in the Time of Stalin*. Bloomington & Indianapolis: Indiana University Press.

Reabilitatsia. Politicheskie protsessy 30–50-kh godov. Moskva: Izdatel'stvo politicheskoi literatury, 1991.

Rittersporn, Gábor T. (1993), 'The omnipresent conspiracy. On Soviet imagery of politics and social relations in the 1930s', in Getty, J. Arch and Manning, Roberta T. (eds), *Stalinist Terror. New Perspectives*. Cambridge: Cambridge University Press.

Saari, Kirsikka (2001), *Täytyy pukeutua puhtaasti ja hyvin, siististi ja kauniisti. Keskustelu pukeutumisesta ja normeista Neuvostoliitossa 1923–1928*. Master of Arts thesis at the Department of History, University of Helsinki: unpublished.

Saffron, Inga (2002), *Caviar. The Strange History and Uncertain Future of the World's Most Loved Delicacy*. New York: Broadway Books.

Sartorti, Rosalinda (1990), 'Stalinism and carnival. Organisation and aesthetics of political holidays', in Günther, H. (ed.), *The Culture of the Stalin Period*. London: Macmillan.

Siegelbaum, L.H. (1988), *Stakhanovism and the Politics of Productivity in the USSR, 1935–1941*. Cambridge: Cambridge University Press.

Simmel, G. (1981), 'Fashion', in Sproles, G.B. (ed.), *Perspectives on Fashion*. Minneapolis: Burges. (Originally published in English in *International Quaterly*, no. 10 (1904): 130–55.)

Solzhenitsyn, Alexander (1979), *The Gulag Archipelago 1918–1956*. Vol. 1. Glasgow: Collins, Harvill Press and Fontana.

Srubar, Ilja (1991), 'War der reale Sozialismus modern? Versuch einer strukturellen Bestimmung'. *Kölner Zeitschrift für Soziologie und Sozialpsychologie*, vol. 43, no. 3: 415–32.

Stepankin, I.A. (1997), 'Pervyi v Rossii. Istoriia pivovarennogo zavoda imeni Sten'ki Razina', *Istoriia Zavoda v XX veke*. Sankt-Peterburg.

Stites, Richard. (1992), *Russian Popular Culture. Entertainment and Society since 1900*. Cambridge: Cambridge University Press.

Takala, I.R. (2002), *Veselie rusi. Istoria alkogol'noi problemy v Rossii*. Sankt-Peterburg: Neva.

Thurston, Robert. (1993), 'The Stakhanovite movement. Background to the Great Terror in the factories, 1935–1938', in Getty, J. Arch and Manning, Roberta T. (eds), *Stalinist Terror. New Perspectives*. Cambridge: Cambridge University Press.

Timasheff, N.S. (1946), *The Great Retreat. The Growth and Decline of Communism in Russia*. New York: E.P. Dutton.

Vainshtein, Olga (1996), 'Female fashion, Soviet style. Bodies of ideology', in Goscilo, H. and Holmgren, B. (eds), *Russia, Women and Culture*. Bloomington & Indianapolis: Indiana University Press.

Vituhnovskaia M. (ed.) (2000), *Na korme vremeni. Interv'iu s leningradtsami 1930-kh godov*. Sankt-Peterburg: Zhurnal Neva.

Zaleski, E. (1989), *Stalinist Planning for Economic Growth 1933–1952*. London: Macmillan.

Zdravomyslova, Elena and Temkina, Anna. (1997). 'October demonstrations in Russia. From official holiday to a protest manifestation', in Temkina, A., *Russia in Transition: The Cases of New Collective Actors and New Collective Action*. Aleksanteri instituutti: Kikimora.

Zhuravlev, S.V. (1999), 'Inostrannaia koloniia moskovskogo Elektrozavoda v nachale 1930-kh godov. Opyt mikroissledovaniia', *Sotsialnaia istoriia, Ezhegodnik 1998/99*. Moskva: Rosspen.

—— 2000, *'Malenkie liudi' i Bolshaia istoria. Inostrantsi moskovskogo Elektrozavoda v sovetskom obstshestve 1920-kh – 1930-kh gg.* Moskva: Rosspen.

Zhuravlev, S.V. and Sokolov, A.K. (1999), *Obshchestvo i vlast'. 1930-e gody.* Moskva: Rosspen.

Name Index

Subject Index

Black market, 34, 135
  Commodities, 34
  Trade, 34
  See also Speculation
Blood sausage, 55
  see also sausages
Bolshevik
  Non-Party Bolshevik, 12, 65
Bolshevik revolution, 9
Bourgeois
  Deviation, 9
  Luxury, 17
  Nobility and, 33
Bourgeois specialist
  Industry and education, 5
Bracelet, 6
Bread, 8, 33, 124
  Card, 98
  Coupon, 123, 125
  Elimination, 108
  Rationing, 2
  Rye bread, 4
Brewery, 30, 68
  See also Beer
Buffet, 105, 109, 115
  Soviet buffet, 110
Bureaucracy
  Soviet bureaucracy, 142
Butter, 31, 125

Cabbage, 4, 8, 33
Car
  Private, 34, 128
  See also Motorcar
Café, 50, 105, 109, 114, 115
Camera, 6, 61, 91
  See also Photo-optical equipment
Campaign, 4, 15, 58, 115, 152
Candle, 57
Canned maize, 81
Canned vegetable, 6
Canteen, 7, 105, 110–115, 143
  Factory canteen, 98
  Cafés and, 105, 107, 109

Special canteen, 12
Subsidized canteen, 105
Workplace, 105, 107, 113, 116, 124, 125, 127
  See also Restaurant
Capitalism, 6, 114
Capitalist exploitation, 70
Capitalist societiy, 6, 35, 145, 146
Capitalist worker, 35
Carnival, 33, 37, 38
  Constitution Day, 38
Carpet, 91
Catering industry, 110
Caviar, 33, 53, 70, 110, 127
  Quality 31
Celebration
  Official and personal, 14
Celebratory product, 6
Central Administration of Breweries, 30
  See also Glavpivo
Central Administration of perfume production, 56
Central Committee of the Communist Party (CPSU), 5, 6, 14, 20, 22, 24, 55, 105, 115, 138
Central Department Store (TsUM), 33, 68, 78, 85, 87–95, 99
  See also Department store
Centrally allocated ration, 129
  Planned economy, 90
Central provisioning, 4
Central regulation, 105
Central state planning office, 119
Champagne, 3, 6, 15, 17, 26, 30–36, 42, 49, 70, 141, 149, 151, 152
  Bottle of champagne 35, 50
  Mass production, 6, 22, 43
  Industrial method, 22
  Non-industrial champagne, 20
  Production, 19, 22, 25
  Production target, 24
  Raw material base, 18, 19
  Soviet Champagne, 5, 14, 18, 140, 143
Chauffeur, 33, 34